# TRANS STUDIES

# TRANS STUDIES

## The Challenge to Hetero/Homo Normativities

EDITED BY
YOLANDA MARTÍNEZ-SAN MIGUEL
AND SARAH TOBIAS

RUTGERS UNIVERSITY PRESS
New Brunswick, New Jersey, and London

Library of Congress Cataloging-in-Publication Data
Trans studies : the challenge to hetero/homo normativities / edited by Yolanda
Martínez-San Miguel and Sarah Tobias.
pages cm
Includes bibliographical references and index.
ISBN 978–0–8135–7641–1 (hardcover : alk. paper)—ISBN 978–0–8135–7640–4
(pbk. : alk. paper)—ISBN 978–0–8135–7642–8 (e-book (epub))—ISBN
978–0–8135–7643–5 (e-book (web pdf))
1. Transgender people. 2. Transgenderism—Study and teaching. 3. Gender identity. I. Martínez-San Miguel, Yolanda. II. Tobias, Sarah, 1963–
HQ77.9.T71534 2016
306.76'8—dc23      2015021888

A British Cataloging-in-Publication record for this book is available from the British
Library.

Visit our website: http://rutgerspress.rutgers.edu

Manufactured in the United States of America

This book is dedicated to the memory of Sylvia Rivera and Marsha P. Johnson, and to all those trans activists who work to imagine and create a more just world.

# CONTENTS

# ACKNOWLEDGMENTS

Honoring our commitment to academic work that is linked to action, this anthology emerged in conjunction with the annual programming of the Institute for Research on Women (IRW), a research center that advances cutting-edge feminist scholarship on women, gender, and sexuality at Rutgers, the State University of New Jersey. During the 2012–2013 academic year, the IRW organized an annual program on "Trans Studies: Beyond Hetero/Homonormativities," which included a distinguished lecture series, a weekly seminar for graduate students and faculty, and an undergraduate learning community. We also organized a spring colloquium entitled "Trans Politics: Scholarship and Strategies for Social Change," which brought twenty-five scholars and activists to Rutgers to reflect on the productive intersections and collaborations taking place around issues relevant to Trans Studies. Our year-long programming was widely supported by many colleagues and units at the university; thanks to them we had the opportunity to devote an entire year to reflect on the ways in which Trans Studies is and has been transforming Feminist and Gender Studies over the last three decades.

We would therefore like to begin by expressing our gratitude to the sponsors of all our regular programming that year: the School of Arts and Sciences, the Office of the Executive Vice President for Academic Affairs, the Associate Vice President for Academic and Public Partnerships in the Arts and Humanities, Critical Caribbean Studies, the Center for Latino Arts and Cultures, and the Office for the Promotion of Women in Science, Engineering, and Mathematics. We would also like to thank the sponsors of our spring colloquium: the Tyler Clementi Center, the Office of the Executive Dean of the School of Arts and Sciences, Undergraduate Academic Affairs, the Associate Campus Dean of Douglass, the Committee to Advance Our Common Purposes, the Center for Social Justice Education and LGBT Communities, the Douglass Campus Dean, the Department of American Studies, the Department of History, the Institute for Women's Leadership Consortium, the Program in Comparative Literature, the School of Communication and Information, the Department of Latino and Hispanic Caribbean Studies, the Center for Latino Arts and Culture, and the Department of Anthropology.

We also want to thank all the participants in the distinguished lecture series that year: Natasha Omise'eke Tinsley, Aren Aizura, Jin Haritaworn, Leah DeVun, A. Finn Enke, and Myra J. Hird. The twenty participants in our weekly seminar and the guests who visited us during the spring colloquium as well as the twenty-four undergraduate participants in our learning community led by our wonderful coordinator, Yomaira Figueroa, were also part of the vibrant intellectual community that enabled us to define the project of this anthology as a truly multi- and interdisciplinary conversation. We would like to thank all of these colleagues whose ideas, suggestions, and questions undoubtedly inform the rationale and structure of this anthology. We would particularly like to thank the panelists in our spring colloquium "Trans Politics: Scholarship and Strategies for Social Change" for their inspiring contributions to trans scholarship and activism.

Special thanks are owed to Aren Aizura, our 2010–2012 Mellon Postdoctoral Associate at the IRW and in Women's and Gender Studies. Aren generously designed the first course on Trans Studies ever offered at our institution. Dr. Aizura was also instrumental in sharing his erudition and knowledge of the field of Trans Studies by suggesting both readings for the weekly seminar and guests for the distinguished lecture series and the spring colloquium and by mentoring our undergraduate and graduate students, as well as several faculty members who were interested in learning about Trans Studies as a field. Aren is not only a contributor to this anthology but also a constant interlocutor in the work we have done in Trans Studies, and we are extremely grateful for his leadership, intellectual generosity, and personal encouragement to undertake this project.

We want to express our gratitude to the contributors to this volume, who have been willing to work closely with both of us to revise individual chapters in order to enrich the debates and conversations we wanted to showcase in this volume. At Rutgers University Press, we would like to express our thanks to editors Katie Keeran, Kimberly Guinta, and Leslie Mitchner who enthusiastically adopted this project and were willing to work patiently with us to see this anthology become a book. Very special thanks are also owed to the anonymous reviewers of this anthology. Their careful and detailed reading of the manuscript as well as their generous suggestions on how to improve the chapters were very useful for all of us in the final review of this volume. Finally, we would like to thank Heather Love for encouraging the editors to consider the complexity of the relationship between normativity and Trans Studies, which we address in the conclusion. Editing this compilation has been an enriching learning experience and we have been able to complete this project thanks to the consistent encouragement of our many collaborators through this entire process.

Finally, we extend our deepest gratitude to Marlene Importico, program coordinator at the IRW until her retirement in 2013. Marlene took care of the minute details of the day-to-day operations of the IRW, from coordinating the logistics of all our programming and helping us host international visitors to supporting all the fellows in our weekly seminar and prompting us to reschedule programming on snow days. She made sure that all our imaginary plans became concrete reality. Nothing at the IRW could have happened without Marlene, so this volume is profoundly indebted to her.

Yolanda Martínez-San Miguel wants to thank former IRW director Dorothy Hodgson and former executive dean Douglass Greenberg for inviting her to become the director of the IRW and also for supporting her work during her three years as director. She wants to thank Sarah Tobias for her assistance as IRW associate director and for taking the lead in organizing the spring 2013 colloquium on Trans Politics. All the co-directors of the other centers and units that are part of the Institute for Women's Leadership consortium were particularly encouraging of the IRW's work on Trans Studies. We extend special thanks to Radhika Balakrishnan (Center for Women's Global Leadership), Abena Busia (chair, Department of Women's and Gender Studies), and Jacqueline Litt (dean, Douglass Residential College), for their enthusiasm about our initiative to create and expand spaces for Trans Studies at Rutgers. Jenny Kurtz and Zaneta Rago from the Center for Social Justice and LGBT Communities were also instrumental in connecting our programming with undergraduate students and in fighting for the creation of nurturing, supportive spaces for trans students at the university. Yolanda wants to thank Ben. Sifuentes-Jáuregui for being a consistent interlocutor of all her work. Finally, Yolanda wants to thank Eugenio Frías-Pardo for all the free graphic design work he did during the IRW's yearlong programming on Trans Studies, as well as the personal support offered throughout her entire tenure as director of the IRW.

Sarah Tobias thanks former IRW directors Dorothy Hodgson and Yolanda Martínez-San Miguel and current IRW director, Nicole R. Fleetwood, for their generous support, collegiality, and intellectual inspiration; IRW administrative assistant Colleen Martin for always being welcoming and kind; and the wonderful, warm, engaging feminist/queer community at Rutgers who have helped make the IRW such a unique place to think and grow. She thanks those trans and queer activists who work beyond the academy and strive tirelessly for social justice. Finally, she thanks all those friends and family members who sustain her, especially Beth and Talila, for filling her life with laughter, lightness, and love.

# TRANS STUDIES

# INTRODUCTION

## Thinking beyond Hetero/Homo Normativities

YOLANDA MARTÍNEZ-SAN MIGUEL
AND SARAH TOBIAS

Recent events reveal the fundamental redefinition of gender that is taking place in many mainstream media and cultural venues in the United States. For example, on February 13, 2014, social media giant Facebook announced a new menu of gender identities as one of several initiatives related to its tenth-anniversary celebration. The list includes around fifty-one possible options, explicitly contesting binary notions of gender, and recognizing instead that gender identity is much more fluid and complex (Evans 2014). Also in February 2014, Janet Mock published *Redefining Realness: My Path to Womanhood, Identity, Love & So Much More*, a narration of her experiences as an African American male-to-female trans person, which rapidly earned a place on the *New York Times* Bestsellers list.[1] Finally, in June 2014, HBO released its second season of *Orange Is the New Black*, featuring as one of its central characters an African American transgender woman played by Laverne Cox, an African American transgender actress.

In the academic world, many of us enthusiastically followed the cluster hire in Transgender Studies announced by the University of Arizona in fall 2013. Both the 2013 *Transgender Studies Reader 2* (edited by Susan Stryker and Aren Aizura) and the first issue of *TSQ: Transgender Studies Quarterly* (edited by Paisley Currah and Susan Stryker), which was released in May 2014, discuss the institutionalization of the field of Trans Studies in academia, although acknowledging some of the limitations faced by students and scholars researching and teaching in this field. At Rutgers we have yet to hire a Trans Studies scholar, but we have made good progress in making our campuses welcoming to trans students.

It might seem, based on these recent occurrences, that the increased visibility of trans people in cultural, academic, social, and mass media has displaced the violence, pathologization, incarceration, and exclusion regularly confronted by members of trans and gender nonconforming communities. Unfortunately, however, the marginalization and abuse of trans and gender nonconforming people is still prevalent in the United States, as well as in many other countries in the world. Trans and gender nonconforming people encounter severe discrimination and intense, sometimes fatal, violence in their daily lives. For example, the Trans Murder Monitoring Project reveals a total of 1,509 reported murders of trans and gender variant people between January 2008 and March 2014. The project's website notes that "throughout all six world regions, the highest absolute numbers have been found in countries with strong trans movements and trans and gender variant people's strong visibility, and/or trans or LGBT organizations that do a professional monitoring."[2] Violence against trans and gender nonconforming people in the United States occurs against a backdrop marked by the erosion of women's reproductive rights through controversial Supreme Court decisions limiting access to contraception and vaunting religious freedom for corporations.[3] The attainment of personhood for women and for trans and gender nonconforming people is a common area of struggle, reflected in academic discourse as well as in social justice activism.

*Trans Studies: The Challenge to Hetero/Homo Normativities* emerges from this productive intersection and collaboration between knowledge production, social justice, and activism. Some of the central questions we explore in this anthology were addressed during the 2012–2013 academic year at the Institute for Research on Women (IRW) at Rutgers University—a year devoted to intensive programming on Trans Studies. The IRW recognized Trans Studies as a significant new field of study and theoretical prism for approaching feminist scholarship on gender and sexuality. In the call for proposals for our annual seminar, we stated:

> Currently at the cutting edge of interdisciplinary scholarship, Trans Studies have undermined preexisting, oppositional sex/gender binaries by focusing on the fluidity and malleability of gender identity and expression. Trans Studies therefore destabilize and complicate many of the debates about the social, biological, and cultural constructions of gender and sexuality. There has also been a heated debate among scholars and activists—especially in the United States and Latin America—on the distinctions between transgender, transsexual, and transvestite, and the ways in which each one of these terms interrogates scientific, artistic,

popular, cultural, and ethnic definitions of gender and sexuality based on the idea of a set spectrum, or conceived as a result of a particular performance or practice. Scholars and activists who work on trans issues are currently analyzing the social, psychological, and legal impact of surgical gender reassignment, as well as promoting the protection of legal rights for trans people in public spaces. The IRW proposes this topic as an exploration of the new frontiers that are open when the relationships between gender, sexuality, and the body are not conceived within heteronormative or homonormative frameworks, but from the perspective of psychoanalysis and desire, philosophy and subject theory, law and civil rights, cultural and social studies.

The IRW's 2012–2013 programming encompassed a weekly seminar with faculty and graduate students engaging in projects that used Trans Studies as a theoretical lens, a weekly undergraduate learning community that exposed our students to trans feminist theory and mentored them in the design of their first research project, a distinguished lecture series comprised of speakers whose focus was Trans Studies, and a spring colloquium entitled "Trans Politics: Scholarship and Strategies for Social Change."[4] This volume includes contributions from scholars and activists who presented their work at the IRW during the 2012–2013 academic year—either as part of the distinguished lecture series or the spring colloquium—as well as other interventions from colleagues with significant expertise in this field.

While this volume begins from the explicitly feminist work undertaken during the IRW's 2012–2013 programming and traces some of the key relationships between trans and feminist theory within this chapter, many of the essays in this volume do not directly address feminist thought or present themselves as feminist analyses. As we make clear in this introduction, however, the relationship between feminism and Trans Studies is a complex one. The first intimations of Trans Studies emerged in the 1970s in response to hostility from feminists such as Janice Raymond (1979). Although both Trans Studies and feminism challenge oppressive assumptions associated with gender, sexuality, and bodies, their methods do not always overlap. Jay Prosser, for instance, offers a trenchant critique of feminist Judith Butler's work on performativity, arguing that "In its representation of sex as a figurative effect of straight gender's constative performance, *Gender Trouble* cannot account for a transsexual desire for sexed embodiment as *telos*" (Prosser 1998, 33).

Building upon Susan Stryker's insight that "Transgender phenomena challenge the unifying potential of the category 'woman,' and call for new analyses, new strategies and practices, for combating discrimination and injustice based on gender inequality" (Stryker 2006, 7), we conceive this anthology to be a multivocal continuation of the problematization of gender. It constitutes a critical intervention in a conversation that has gone beyond the "autoethnographic and self-representational work by trans subjects" (Stryker and Aizura 2013, 3) to explore how the key concepts and methodologies of Trans Studies can enrich debates and conversations on an interdisciplinary range of subjects. This anthology presents a range of transformative approaches to scholarship, policy, and pedagogy. To allow for a richer exchange and dialogue, we invited authors to submit academic essays or shorter critical reflections and interventions. Although the balance of academic versus non-academic chapters is tilted toward the former, we are pleased to have offered an alternative format that respects the different ways in which knowledge is produced and shared outside academia and that provokes engagement between academics and activists.

This anthology is divided into five sections. The first section, entitled "Gender Boundaries within Educational Spaces," revisits the creation of trans-inclusive learning spaces in institutions of higher education. Three well-known experts in this area (Beemyn, Rankin, and Park) with a long track record of critical interventions in U.S. universities discuss strategies to assess campus climate. They also make concrete recommendations to bridge the divide between academics and activists and build effective coalitions to advocate for more trans-inclusive social and learning spaces.

The second section of this anthology explores the creation of trans-inclusive imaginaries in theater, narrative, and cinema. In these three essays the notion of trans serves as a category to interrogate notions of name and identity in Samuel Beckett's *The Unnamable* (Crawford), femininity and the aporetic postcolonial Caribbean identity (Valens), and the new transnational and trans digital identities produced in *Blade Runner* and Cheang Shu Lea's digital cinema (Chen). One of the main contributions of this section is that it proposes a rereading of canonical and new cultural productions in which subjects experiment on an identitarian journey that is illuminated and complicated by implicit or explicit references to the trans-ing experience.

The third section is devoted to biometrics and the regulation of bodies through migration and airport securitization (Beauchamp, Butler Burke, and Aizura). Yet the focus of this section is not a debate about identity or post-identity, since this is a debate that has already been engaged fully in Queer and Trans Studies. Rather, the three essays in this section address the slippery boundaries of bodies that resist national and international securitization after 9/11. This section combines contributions from activists and scholars and includes thought-provoking insights about some of the white middle-class agendas that often dominate conversations about how nonconforming bodies confront and cross (or are unable to cross) national borders.

The fourth section explores the contributions, productive collaborations, and challenges of trans activism and policy work. The essays address the dynamic relationship between trans and LGBTQ movements in Canada (Enriquez), a study of sexual orientation and discrimination experienced by trans people derived from the National Transgender Discrimination Survey (Herman), and the creation of an inclusive space for trans Latina women in San Francisco (Rodríguez de Ruíz and Ochoa). While the first two essays in this section are academic in character, the third is an engaging conversation between Alexandra Rodríguez de Ruíz and Marcia Ochoa, collaborators and founders of El/La Para Translatinas, a social justice and HIV prevention program.

The last section of this anthology explores how the trans lens can inflect the disciplinary and pedagogical work we do. Hwahng explores the distinct research practices utilized by public health researchers, on the one hand, and critical humanities and social science researchers, on the other, and proposes ways in which a closer collaboration could enrich both academic fields. Enke shares pedagogical strategies to produce gender-inclusive learning spaces that enhance the educational experience for both gender conforming and gender nonconforming students.

## FEMINIST, QUEER, AND TRANS STUDIES

Trans Studies have completely transformed and enriched debates in Feminist and Queer Studies. Notions such as cis- and transgender as well as the whole array of options made possible by gender expression, gender presentation, gender identity, gender variance, genderqueer, and gender (self-)determination have totally revitalized the debates about the cultural, social, and political constructions of gender in past and contemporary historical contexts. If we review the entries for "Cisgender," "Cisgenderism," "Feminism," "LGBT," "Queer," and "Transgender" in the first issue of *TSQ: Transgender Studies Quarterly*, we witness some of the exciting and constructive collaborations currently enriching Feminist, Queer, and Trans Studies.

As the work of Trans Studies luminaries Susan Stryker, A. Finn Enke, and Paisley Currah makes clear, Trans Studies expands, complicates, and enriches scholarship previously done in Feminist and Queer Studies around the constructed character of gender. For example, in the first issue of *TSQ: Transgender Studies Quarterly* (May 2014), Stryker and Currah ask the following questions that are akin to some of the queries explored in this anthology: "The term *transgender*, then, carries its own antinomies: Does it help make or undermine gender identities and expressions? Is it a way of being gendered or a way of doing gender? Is it an identification or a method? A promise or a threat?" (1). By the same token, Enke explores the tense, complex, and rich interactions and collaborations between feminist and trans activists and scholars in *Transfeminist Perspectives in and beyond Transgender and Gender Studies.*

> Real conflict continues to separate transgender studies and feminist studies as arenas of inquiry. Our interests, vocabularies, and epistemological foundations can seem—and at times are—opposed. What do we variously mean by "gender" or "sex"? How is the body made to matter? Critically for us here, how do transgender studies and women's studies each make the body matter such that *each* field suspects the other of essentialized beliefs about which parts matter most? . . . Given these tensions, we might characterize gender studies at the beginning of the second decade of the new millennium to be composed of disparate bodies differently freighting gender and sex while quizzically looking sideways—and occasionally winking—at each other. The sideways glance might be cautious, but it is surely born of a sense that, alone, neither feminist nor trans is living up to its most expansive vision and also that at times, they fail us. (2012, 2–3)

One of the shared areas of interest between Women's and Gender Studies and Trans Studies is the analysis of the complex issue of embodiments in historical, social, and political contexts. As Judith Butler has amply demonstrated in her foundational work, gender has been a crucial category of analysis that inflects how bodies have become culturally intelligible or not (1990, 1993). By the same token, gendered identities are now conceived beyond the masculine and the feminine to include a whole array of "identities and representations that are not fixed to biological sex" (Hines 2014, 85). Feminists and transfeminists have been able to build alliances based on their common interests and to further problematize how gender is defined within a system of power relations that privileges normative expressions at the expense of what are considered nonnormative gender expressions. Notions like cisgender and transgender explore further how embodiment, perceived identification, and lived experience take gender beyond the confines of the binary oppositions of feminine/masculine and butch/femme. "Cisgenderism," on the other hand, enriches and adds precision to terms such as *sexism, homophobia,* and *heterosexism,* by referring specifically to the denial, pathologization, and denigration of nonnormative gender identities and by questioning the dichotomous category of sex assigned at birth (Lennon and Mistler 2014).

The relationship between Queer and Trans Studies has been and is still complicated. On the one hand, these two fields share an interest in interrogating the coherence of a notion such as LGBT. Although originally born out of a desire to establish important alliances between gender and sexually nonconforming communities, it has become evident that the real alliance between Queer and

Trans Studies is their common questioning of normativity, although the focus of Queer Studies is "nonnormative desires and sexual practices" while Trans Studies focuses on "nonnormative gender identifications and embodiments" (Love 2014, 172). Some critics suggest, however, that desire can also be theorized through a Trans Studies lens, if the focus is how that desire is inflected by normative definitions of gender (Murib 2014, 119). On the other hand, if the focus of LGBT movements is sexual orientation, the focus of Trans Studies is the complex disarticulations between the definition of biological sex, culturally constructed gender, and normative or nonnormative sexual desires. Queer theory, on the other hand, shares with Trans Studies a consistent questioning of the notion of identity that is conceived through the theorization of the normative versus the nonnormative. In their constant interrogation of what is conceived as "normal," "natural," and "socially acceptable," both Trans and Queer Studies have been at the forefront of important questions about forms of social and political visibility, co-optation and marginalization. Yet, as Heather Love notes, Queer theory has proved less useful in the exploration of concrete issues of embodiment, perhaps as a result of its "capacious nonnormativity" (2014, 175). By taking the epistemic perspective of the dissidents, both fields have resisted more easily the white middle-class perspectives that were and are sometimes still dominant in some feminist and LGB circles.[5]

Although there are still some spaces of tension and resistance informing the institutional and epistemic relationship between Feminist and Trans Studies (Goldberg 2014; Greer 1999; Jeffreys 1997; Raymond 1979), it is evident that areas of intellectual and institutional growth are still more significant.[6] One of the consistent areas of tension focuses precisely on the definition of womanhood. On the one hand, some radical feminists still insist on the specificity of experience for biological cisgender women, while Trans scholars question the naturalness of the definition of biological womanhood in the construction of gender identities. Further developments of these two fields will provide more room to continue the exploration of the very specific identity formations that are made possible when womanhood is denaturalized while cis- and transgender identities gain complexity and depth as social and embodied experiences.

There are also some areas in which these tensions could be channeled into productive moments of epistemic transformation for the three fields involved. For example, it would be interesting for Feminist, Queer, and Trans Studies to explore further how the inclusion of gender identity in law still reinforces gender binarism by forcing individuals to choose one of two normative genders (Fiol-Matta 2016). By the same token, each of these three fields could have thought-provoking critical interventions around issues of personal and state violence that are motivated by gender identity and gender expression. Finally, all three could make many significant contributions on issues related to how particular embodiments of gender expression and desire are intersected by relationships of power still informed by race, class, relationship with the state, and degree of political self-determination.

Most of the essays in this anthology explore how Trans Studies have and continue to transform scholarship in Women's and Gender Studies, as well as queer theory. For example, Pauline Park's essay uses the history of Women's and Gender Studies programs to advocate for the inclusion of Trans Studies and trans-identified scholars in institutions of higher education. Park notes that the current underrepresentation of trans-identified scholars is deeply problematic and that outrage would likely occur if male professors were the dominant group in Women's Studies departments or white professors dominated African American or Latino Studies departments. In a different vein, Crawford uses Trans Studies to explore new areas of inquiry for the study of canonical authors such as Samuel Beckett, and Valens reexamines the productive intersections between the gendered subject and colonialism in the case of Patricia Powell's novel *The Pagoda*. Meanwhile, Chen probes the intersections between Critical Race Studies, transnational and queer theories to explore alternative forms of sexual and gender identification in the digital films produced by Taiwanese artist Cheang Shu Lea. Feminist and Queer Studies are also central in Enriquez's study of alliances between LGBT and Queer activist movements in Canada as well as Herman's study of how the sexual orientation of transgender subjects becomes relevant to public policy for a particular sector of the trans population. Therefore, the essays collected in this anthology offer encouraging examples of the many productive intersections between these three fields. Our contributors also revisit the relationship between academic research and activism to propose strategic alliances.

## TRANS-ACTIVIST MOBILIZATIONS

The chapters in this volume reflect several of the important ways in which scholarship in the field of Trans Studies relates to trans activism. Trans activism is a growing global grassroots phenomenon, which is often under-resourced and marginalized within larger LGBTI (lesbian, gay, bisexual, transgender, and intersex) movements. A recent report examining the context of trans organizing based on a survey of 340 trans and intersex groups throughout the world reveals that, while the number of activist organizations devoted to work on trans and intersex issues has grown rapidly over the last three years, these groups often struggle to survive financially (Eisfeld, Gunther, and Shlasko 2013). The report notes that the majority of these organizations have an annual budget of under $10,000, and 95 percent of them have annual budgets under $250,000. Groups led by trans and intersex activists suffer acutely, with a median annual budget for intersex-led organizations of under $5,000 and for trans-led organizations of between

$5,000 and 10,000 (16). The scarcity of funding is particularly dire in human rights work. The report notes: "In 2010, 6% of all funding for human rights work went to promote LGBTI rights globally ($72.6 million out of $1.2 billion in total). Of that funding, only $1.6 million addressed trans* issues and just over $40,000 addressed intersex issues—in total, 0.14% of all human rights funding and just 2.3% of all LGBTI funding" (9). This scarcity of resources has occurred despite the fact that the last decade has seen marked increases in the funding allocated by foundations to LGBTI organizations. The report's authors maintain that this discrepancy can be explained because of the ongoing failure of movement organizations to attend to trans and intersex issues: "The 'T' and the 'I' are often included in LGBTI organizations in name only, with little impact on the organizations' programs, priorities, or leadership" (9).

Within the United States and Canada, the fact that trans activists are largely funded to pursue policy change through national LGBT organizations—and that trans-specific organizations are themselves poorly funded—has a discernable effect on activists' policy priorities. As Rickke Mananzala and Dean Spade (2008) note, one consequence of this is that the models and strategies of organizing to advance lesbian and gay issues, steeped in the rhetoric of equal opportunity and individual rights, are frequently repurposed by LGBT organizations to pursue change for trans communities. These policy choices also partly reflect the co-optation of LGBT organizations by neoliberalism. To placate affluent philanthropists who provide their funding, these organizations have adopted more conservative strategies "to better fit those funders' capitalism maintenance and reformist goals than the base-building, visionary organizing goals that might emerge more directly from communities facing oppression" (Mananzala and Spade 2008, 57).

Yet this is only part of the story of trans activism. Alongside the efforts of national LGBT organizations, recent years have also seen the development of a myriad of trans-led activist organizations. Many of these groups are locally based, but some—such as the National Center for Transgender Equality, Trans* Gate, and the Sylvia Rivera Law Project—are national or international in scope. Often these organizations combine the provision of direct services with policy advocacy. Some display a close affinity with feminist intersectional approaches to activist work. Thus the Sylvia Rivera Law Project (SRLP), an organization whose mandate incorporates issue areas from prison organizing to homeless services, stipulates in its core values that it is "committed to taking concrete actions around naming and dismantling white supremacy, patriarchy, ableism, heterosexism."[7] In so doing, SRLP reflects a coalitional politics that is grounded in third-wave feminist intersectional activism.

Indeed, it is noteworthy that transfeminism constitutes an important aspect of contemporary trans activism. "Transfeminism" writes Emi Koyama, "is primarily a movement by and for trans women who view their liberation to be intrinsically linked to the liberation of all women and beyond. . . . Transfeminism embodies feminist coalition politics" (2001). Many transfeminist activists, like their feminist forebears, theorize from outside the academy. Just as early second-wave feminists were often excluded from the academy because of its hierarchical structures of knowledge, trans feminists also make theory and practice activism from the borderlands. Our own organization, the Institute for Research on Women, was founded in 1977 by faculty and administrators seeking to expand feminist scholarship beyond the university's fledgling Women's Studies program and forge links between second-wave feminist activists and academics. In line with that tradition we share Enke's view that "the regulatory mechanisms of academia are part of what makes it necessary for transfeminist studies to continue to fuel the vital connections between academics and the larger world of justice activism" (2012, 9). This collection of essays is an attempt to reinforce these connections.

Several of the chapters in this volume directly address issues confronted by trans activists. Enriquez addresses the complexities of creating alliances between trans activists and those involved in the wider movements for lesbian, gay, bisexual, and queer rights in Québec. Drawing on a set of semi-structured interviews with trans activists, Enriquez observes that alliance making within wider movements is difficult; the persistence of transphobia often results in trans issues being relegated to the backburner (and lesbian, gay, and queer issues assuming dominance), while trans activists rarely occupy leadership roles. In order to create broadly based alliances to precipitate social change, Enriquez suggests the need for consciousness-raising by members of LGBQ groups combined with concerted efforts to incorporate heterosexual trans people within movements. Enabling trans organizations to assume leadership roles within wider movement politics also has the potential to shift the dynamics of alliance building, equalizing power dynamics between LGBQ and T groups.

The challenges confronting trans people are eminently palpable in Herman's chapter, which examines the role of sexual orientation in discrimination against trans people. Herman's data-driven chapter draws upon the National Transgender Discrimination Survey, the largest existing survey of trans and gender nonconforming people, conducted by the National Gay and Lesbian Taskforce and the National Center for Transgender Equality in 2008 and 2009. Herman shows that trans people who identify as sexual minorities (as lesbian, gay, or bisexual) experience a greater likelihood of encountering discrimination, especially when compared to those trans people who identify as straight. Herman's argument implies that activists should take a nuanced approach to organizing on the basis of sexual orientation and gender identity and recognize that these categories may overlap and require specific policy remedies.

Butler Burke reiterates the importance for trans activists of taking a richly intersectional and complex approach to political work. This entails an avoidance of transnormativity, or assuming that the politics and perspectives of white middle-class trans people are the norm. Butler Burke's critique is particularly pertinent as the majority of trans activist organizations are situated at the grassroots. Rodríguez de Ruíz and Ochoa's chapter exemplifies this reality. Marcia Ochoa and Alexandra Rodríguez de Ruíz, founding director and program coordinator of El/La Para TransLatinas, an HIV-prevention and social justice organization, discuss their experiences during the initial stages of the formation of this community organization in the Bay Area. Their conversation captures some of the challenges of doing community work for Trans Latinas and immigrants in San Francisco. They also discuss in detail strategies they have developed to access the community they want to serve and the financial struggles they face to fund their organization.

## TRANS-INCLUSIVE POLICY, PEDAGOGICAL, AND DISCIPLINARY INTERVENTIONS

The third area of inquiry explored by these essays is how trans activism and Trans Studies can transform existing norms and structures as well as the disciplines and pedagogical work of many of us in academia. The issue of transformation hinges on the vision of social change proposed by activists and scholars. In a probing ethnographic analysis, Megan Davidson (2007) argues that there are many different articulations of social change by trans activists. For some, the goal of social change is either "mainstreaming" or "assimilation." These activists aspire to a future where trans identity is "no longer an issue" or "stop[s] being a problem," either because trans people can better "blend in" to their surroundings or because society changes to accommodate trans people, and to recognize their fundamental "sameness" with those who do not identify as gender variant. Under such circumstances, *trans* would ultimately "become a meaningless category of difference." This understanding of social change is tied to the pursuit of formal equality and equal rights (74). Davidson notes that the activists prioritizing mainstreaming or assimilation share a similar profile—as white, middle-class, aged 40–60, and designated as male at birth (75). Davidson's study therefore indicates the necessity of considering race, class, and gender in any analysis of activists' visions and goals.

While a segment of Davidson's interviewees pursued an assimilationist or mainstreaming vision of change, the vast majority were motivated by a different goal—a more broadly based vision of social justice that would simultaneously enable individual self-determination and the fulfillment of individual needs, including those related to health care, housing, employment, and sustenance.

This vision of change applies not only to trans communities but to everyone and entails a process of working in alliance with other oppressed groups to fight structural racism as well as capitalism and colonialism. These activists do not aspire to eradicate the categories of sex and gender and render them meaningless. Rather, they seek "to remove them from a naturalized binary and bring cultural awareness to the social construction of sexed bodies, gender identities, and the understandings of personhood current conceptualizations structure. They envision denaturalized and unmoored understandings of sex, gender, and sexuality that recognize the infinite variability of bodies, identities, desires, and practices" (77). Thus Davidson's ethnographic study reveals that while some trans activists seek equality as a goal, many more are motivated by a complex, justice-based vision of social change.

There are interesting parallels between the aspirations of contemporary trans activists and those of early gay liberationists. Building on feminist critiques of formal equality, gay liberationists in the 1970s and 1980s advocated for justice, calling for a fundamental transformation of society's power structures (Cahill and Tobias 2007, 85–86). The pursuit of rights was seen as inimical to this goal. Thus arguing against the goal of same-sex marriage, lesbian feminist Paula Ettelbrick argued that "obtaining a right does not always result in justice" (1989, 14). Trans scholar and activist Dean Spade also rejects legal reforms in the name of "rights" for failing to provide trans people—and especially trans people of color—with what they need. Spade argues that antidiscrimination protections do not apply to incarcerated people or to low-wage workers unable to afford legal help in order to pursue antidiscrimination lawsuits. Furthermore, these protections do nothing to combat poverty or the material conditions of inequality that have intensified over the last fifty years, the time period during which most laws promoting equality have been passed. Rather, Spade maintains that antidiscrimination laws and the rhetorical use of "rights" enables governments to rebrand themselves as the protectors of marginalized people and promoters of democracy, covering the violent realities of life confronted by trans people and many others on a daily basis. In this sense, law and policy serve as the vehicles of settler colonialism—a type of pink-washing that belies the militarism and exclusion pervading the state. Spade argues for the necessity of stopping new jails from being built, decriminalizing sex-work, ending deportation and the current system of immigration enforcement, and building alternative systems of support from a framework of mutual aid. Spade's approach rejects structural racism, capitalism, and the carceral state and builds on a variety of critical approaches—from feminist approaches to intersectionality to queer and decolonial theory—in order to invoke a wide-ranging vision of change. Spade's politics therefore aims to challenge the norms that currently constrain so many trans people, low-income people, and people of color.[8]

The essays in this anthology advance critiques that promote this much needed vision of change. For example, Aizura's essay addresses the debilitating impact of normativity and the limitations of pursuing a rights-based approach to social change. Aizura proposes a close reading of Daniel Rotman's documentary *Transgression* (2011), about Norma Ureiro's experience with the U.S. immigration system as a trans immigrant from Mexico. Although the film is about the unfair immigration process to which trans immigrants are submitted, Aizura analyzes the many ways in which women of color are still trapped in a script that objectifies and victimizes them at the expense of their own agency to gain the sympathy and solidarity of a white liberal viewer. These particular kinds of narratives also displace the complicity between white nonprofit experts and advocates who help some trans subjects to obtain asylum and/or refugee status at the expense of other trans and nonconforming bodies who are detained and deported as criminal.

Beauchamp's essay suggests a need to extend the critique of normativity to biometric surveillance practices commonly use in airports and to regulate international immigration. Through the lens of Trans Studies, Beauchamp argues that bodies are still opaque to attempts to objectively classify identities. The resistance posed by nonconforming bodies reiterates the insufficiency of existing forms of scrutiny and identification and unsettles the same categories—gender, race, sex, citizenship, and so on—that are used to establish knowable identities.

Much of the focus on transformation within this volume occurs within the context of the academy—both administratively and in the classroom. Trans and gender nonconforming students, faculty, and staff often confront massive obstacles at the institutional level; the pervasiveness of binary gender norms limits their opportunities in and beyond the classroom. Thus in order to create a trans-inclusive academy, careful attention needs to be paid to the construction of institutional and intellectual spaces. Beemyn and Rankin describe best practices for creating a gender-inclusive campus. Their chapter incorporates recommendations for creating trans-friendly classrooms (by not assuming that everyone is traditionally gendered and using students' preferred pronouns and names) and athletics (by creating policies for trans students to participate in intramural competitions). In addition, their chapter emphasizes the need to create trans-supportive health services, gender-neutral housing and bathrooms, and private changing spaces in locker rooms.

Like Beemyn and Rankin, Park also emphasizes the importance of developing a trans-friendly infrastructure and policies. However, Park additionally stresses that colleges and universities should ensure that trans scholars are incorporated into the academy at all levels. Park emphasizes that the intellectual space currently occupied by Trans Studies should be broadened to advance international and intersectional scholarship.

Hwahng and Enke explore disciplinary and pedagogical engagements in which Trans Studies functions as a productive theoretical prism. Hwahng takes advantage of an interdisciplinary training to compare the methods and policy implications of research on trans populations—especially regarding access to social services and citizenship, representation, and visibility—produced in public health, on the one hand, and in the critical humanities and humanistic social sciences, on the other. Beyond the methodological differences of these disciplines, Hwahng notices the lack of collaboration and cross-pollination of the work done in each of these fields, as well as the lack of a common language. Finn Enke takes the concept of language to the classroom in an attempt to create strategies that undermine existing gender dichotomies and produce critically inclusive spaces. Enke's classes engage in exercises that interrogate the notion of gender altogether and open inclusive spaces of academic debate that enrich, rather than limit, dialogue and exchange between gender nonconforming and gender conforming students.

This anthology is born from our conviction that the collaboration and productive intersections between Feminist, Queer, and Trans Studies creates, produces, and makes possible new forms of knowledge and action. As Heather Love reminds us, "Etymologically, both trans and queer refer to crossing, and in that sense both terms invoke mobility as well as its limits" (2014, 175). In this compilation of essays, this idea is taken as fundamental. On the one hand, we firmly believe in the need for independent fields of study that focus on very specific and different *subjects*. Therefore, we firmly support the need of each one of these theoretical lenses—and institutional formations—as crucial for the constitution of solid departments, programs, and research centers focusing on genders and sexualities. On the other hand, it is only through the productive, sometimes tense and difficult but always enriching intersections that new forms of knowledge become possible. Our collaborators' essays illustrate some of the most delicate tensions between academic and theoretical knowledge productions, embodied and political ways of knowing, and the disciplinary, policy, and legal implications of the questions that are posed by the "bodies that don't," to rephrase Teresa De Lauretis's thought-provoking title (1984). In that sense, the group of essays collected here offers many different answers to a simple provocation: how can one find a space beyond the heteronormative and the homonormative? Most likely what is important about the space beyond the normative that is invoked here is not its particular location but the traversing and mobilization through which that space can become possible for all of us.

## NOTES

**1.** A note on terminology: In this introduction, we often use the term *trans*, a shortened version of the umbrella term *transgender*, to refer to people whose gender identity or expression differs from their sex assigned at birth. In addition, following the lead of global activists, we sometimes use the term *trans\**, where the asterisk constitutes "a placeholder for the entire range of possible gender identities that fall under the broad definition of trans\*" (Eisfeld, Gunther, and Shlasko 3). *Gender identity* refers to an individual's deeply felt sense of identification with a particular gender, as male, female, or something other than or in between these binaries. *Gender expression* refers to the external manifestation of a person's gendered self (for example, through dress, speech patterns, and mannerisms). We also regularly deploy the acronym *LGBT* to stand for lesbian, gay, bisexual, and transgender. When referring to work that also includes intersex populations, as is sometimes the case in international human rights discourses and movements, we use the acronym *LGBTI*. Many glossaries of trans-related terminology already exist. In addition to the first volume of *TSQ: Transgender Studies Quarterly*, which is referenced in this introduction, the University of Wisconsin provides a useful and accessible list of key terms at https://lgbt.wisc.edu/documents/Trans_and_queer_glossary.pdf.
**2.** Brazil (602), Mexico (160), Venezuela (81), Colombia (80), Honduras (65), Guatemala (36), and the Dominican Republic (31) in Central and South America; the USA (94) in North America; Turkey (35) and Italy (27) in Europe; and India (35) and the Philippines (29) in Asia. http://www.transrespect-transphobia.org/en_US/tvt-project/tmm-results/idahot-2014.htm.
**3.** We are referring to the 2014 Supreme Court ruling in the *Burwell v. Hobby Lobby* case, which allowed for-profit organizations to be exempt from the contraceptive mandate in the Affordable Care Act. This ruling explicitly recognizes a for-profit corporation's claim for religious belief at the expense of the rights of its female employees for covered contraception through their health insurance.
**4.** For a detailed discussion of the rationale behind the IRW's annual programming in Trans Studies, see Martínez–San Miguel and Tobias 2014.
**5.** This has also been one of the main criticisms against recent depictions of gay activism during the AIDS pandemic as depicted in film renditions of *The Normal Heart* (2014) and *The Dallas Buyers Club* (2013).
**6.** Responses challenging antitransgender feminism can be found in Stone 1996, Feinberg 1996, Namaste 2009, and Serano 2007.
**7.** See the Sylvia Rivera Law Project, *Liberation Is a Collective Process: Sylvia Rivera Law Project Collective Member Handbook*, http://srlp.org/files/collective%20handbook%202009.pdf.
**8.** These specific claims were made during Spade's keynote address at the IRW's 2013 spring colloquium, "Trans Politics: Scholarship and Strategies for Social Change." Many are also outlined in Spade's 2011 book, *Normal Life*.

## REFERENCES

Butler, Judith. 1990. *Gender Trouble: Feminism and the Subversion of Identity*. New York: Routledge.
———. 1993. *Bodies That Matter: On the Discursive Limits of "Sex."* New York: Routledge.
Cahill, Sean, and Sarah Tobias. 2007. *Policy Issues Affecting Lesbian, Gay, Bisexual, and Transgender Families*. Ann Arbor: University of Michigan Press.

Currah, Paisley, and Susan Stryker. 2014. "Introduction." Special Issue. "Postposttranssexual: Key Concepts for a Twenty-First-Century Transgender Studies." *Transgender Studies Quarterly* 1.1–2 (May): 1–18.

Davidson, Megan. 2007. "Seeking Refuge under the Umbrella: Inclusion, Exclusion, and Organizing within the Category *Transgender.*" *Sexuality Research and Social Policy: Journal of NSRC* 4.4 (December): 60–80.

De Lauretis, Teresa. 1984. *Alice Doesn't: Feminism, Semiotics, and Cinema.* Bloomington: Indiana University Press.

Eisfeld, Justus, Sarah Gunther, and Davey Shlasko. 2013. *The State of Trans\* and Intersex Organizing: A Case for Increased Support for Growing but Under-funded Movements for Human Rights.* New York: Global Action for Trans\* Equality and American Jewish World Service, http://globaltransaction.files.wordpress.com/2014/01/trans-intersex-funding-report.pdf.

Enke, A. Finn. 2012. *Transfeminist Perspectives in and beyond Transgender and Gender Studies.* Philadelphia: Temple University Press.

Ettelbrick, Paula L. 1989. "Since When Is Marriage a Path to Liberation?" *OUT/LOOK* (Fall): 9, 14–17.

Evans, Zenon. 2014. "Facebook's 56 New Gender Options Make Science Fiction a Reality." *Hit & Run Blog.* February 18. http://reason.com/blog/2014/02/18/facebooks-56-new -gender-options-makes-sc.

Feinberg, Leslie. 1996. *Transgender Warriors: Making History from Joan of Arc to Dennis Rodman.* Boston: Beacon Press.

Fiol-Matta, Licia. 2016. "Queer/Sexualities." In *Critical Terms in Caribbean and Latin American Thought: Historical and Institutional Trajectories,* 217–230. New York: Palgrave Macmillan.

Goldberg, Michelle. 2014. "What Is a Woman: The Dispute between Feminism and Transgenderism." *New Yorker.* August 4.

Greer, Germaine 1999. *The Whole Woman.* New York: Alfred A. Knopf.

Hines, Sally. 2014. "Feminism." *Transgender Studies Quarterly* 1.1–2 (May): 84–86.

Jeffreys, Sheila. 1997. "Transgender Activism: A Lesbian Feminist Perspective." *Journal of Lesbian Studies* 1:3–4, 55–74.

King, Rosamond. 2014. *Island Bodies: Transgressive Sexualities in the Caribbean Imagination.* Gainesville: University Press of Florida.

Koyama, Emi. 2001. *The Transfeminist Manifesto.* http://www.eminism.org/readings/pdf -rdg/tfmanifesto.pdf.

Lennon, Erica, and Brian J. Mistler. 2014. "Cisgenderism." *Transgender Studies Quarterly* 1.1–2 (May): 63–64.

Love, Heather. 2014. "Queer." *Transgender Studies Quarterly* 1.1–2 (May): 172–176.

Mananzala, Rickke, and Dean Spade. 2008. "The Nonprofit Industrial Complex and Trans Resistance." *Sexuality Research and Social Policy: Journal of NSRC* 5.1 (March): 53–71.

Martínez-San Miguel, Yolanda, and Sarah Tobias. 2014. "Safe Feminist Spaces: Reflections about the Institute for Research on Women at Rutgers–New Brunswick." In *The Entrepreneurial University: Engaging Publics, Intersecting Impacts,* edited by Yvette Taylor, 261–278. London: Palgrave.

Mock, Janet. 2014. *Redefining Realness: My Path to Womanhood, Identity, Love & So Much More.* New York: Atria Books.

Murib, Zein. 2014. "LGBT." *Transgender Studies Quarterly* 1.1–2 (May): 118–120.

Murphy, Ryan, dir. 2014. *The Normal Heart.* New York: Home Box Office.

Namaste, Viviane K. 2009. "Undoing Theory: The 'Transgender Question' and the Epistemic Violence of Anglo-American Feminist Theory." *Hypatia* 23.3: 11–32.

Ochoa, Marcia. 2014. *Queen for a Day: Transformistas, Beauty Queens, and the Performance of Feminity in Venezuela.* Durham, NC: Duke University Press.

Prosser, Jay. 1998. *Second Skins: The Body Narratives of Transsexuality.* New York: Columbia University Press.

Raymond, Janice. 1979. *The Transsexual Empire: The Making of the She-Male.* Boston: Beacon Press.

*Transgression.* Directed by TJ Barber, Toni Marzal, Morgan Hargrave, and Daniel Rotman. 2011. A10 Films, Harvard Law Documentary Studio, 2011. http://transgressionfilm.tumblr .com.

Serano, Julia. 2007. *Whipping Girl: A Transsexual Woman on Sexism and the Scapegoating of Femininity.* Berkeley, CA: Seal Press.

Spade, Dean. 2011. *Normal Life: Administrative Violence, Critical Trans Politics, and the Limits of Law.* New York: South End Press.

Stone, Sandy. 1996. "The 'Empire' Strikes Back: A Posttranssexual Manifesto." In *Body Guards: The Cultural Politics of Sexual Ambiguity*, edited by K. Straub and J. Epstein, 280–304. New York: Routledge.

Stryker, Susan. 2006. "(De) Subjugated Knowledges: An Introduction to Transgender Studies." In *The Transgender Studies Reader*, edited by Susan Stryker and Stephen Whittle, 1–17. New York: Routledge.

Stryker, Susan, and Aren Z. Aizura. 2013. "Introduction: Transgender Studies 2.0." In *The Transgender Studies Reader 2*, edited by Susan Stryker and Aren Aizura, 1–12. New York: Routledge.

Sylvia Rivera Law Project. *Liberation Is a Collective Process: Sylvia Rivera Law Project Collective Member Handbook.* http://srlp.org/files/collective%20handbook%202009.pdf.

Trans Murder Monitoring Project. http://www.transrespect-transphobia.org/en_US/tvt -project/tmm-results/idahot-2014.htm.

Trim, Michael, Piper Kerman, Taylor Schilling, Jason Biggs, and Laura Prepon. 2014. *Orange Is the New Black.* Santa Monica, CA: Lions Gate Entertainment.

University of Wisconsin. Trans, Genderqueer, and Queer Terms Glossary. https://lgbt.wisc .edu/documents/Trans_and_queer_glossary.pdf.

Vallée, Jean Marc. 2013. *The Dallas Buyers Club.* Universal City, CA: Focus Features.

# PART I  GENDER BOUNDARIES WITHIN EDUCATIONAL SPACES

# 1 · CREATING A GENDER-INCLUSIVE CAMPUS

GENNY BEEMYN AND SUSAN R. RANKIN

Although some trans-spectrum students today have a generally positive campus experience, many others attend colleges and universities that continue to force them to run a gender gantlet daily.[1] They wake in their residence hall to a roommate not of their choosing, as they cannot be housed in keeping with their gender identity, or they are in a single room, having paid more to avoid such a situation. Unless they have a shower in their rooms, they are forced to use a group facility that does not reflect their gender identity, making them vulnerable to being "outed" and subsequently harassed. If they decide to work out at a campus recreational center, they are similarly relegated to the "wrong" locker room. When they go to classes, they may be called by a name they no longer use and by pronouns that do not fit how they see themselves. They almost certainly will find no mention of gender-nonconforming people in their courses, as the curriculum, except for Women's and Gender Studies, typically treats gender as a binary. If they need to use a bathroom between classes, they must decide which gender-specific option is less likely to lead to harassment and violence, find a gender-inclusive bathroom, which may be far away, or simply refuse to go until they can "pee in peace." Assuming that they persist until graduation (and many do not), they will be awarded a diploma that lists their legal name, which may not be the name they go by, so that they endure a final act of disrespect before leaving college.

This hypothetical day in the life of trans-spectrum college students is far too often their reality. In this essay, we examine recent research on the experiences of trans-spectrum students and, using the findings of these studies, suggest ways for colleges and universities to become more trans-inclusive, focusing on two often overlooked areas: the classroom and athletics. While the number of students openly identifying and expressing themselves as gender nonconforming has grown rapidly over the last decade, their presence on campuses is still commonly ignored, and they are rarely included in college research or supported by administrative policies.

## RESEARCH ON TRANS-SPECTRUM COLLEGE STUDENTS

The dearth of studies on the identity development of trans-spectrum people, particularly trans-spectrum youth, led us to undertake the research that became *The Lives of Transgender People* (Beemyn and Rankin 2011). Working with trans college students, we had observed that they often understood their identities and came to identify as trans in ways that were quite unlike previous generations of trans people, and the study confirmed our perceptions. Based on data collected from nearly 3,500 surveys and more than 400 interviews with trans-masculine, trans-feminine, and gender-nonconforming individuals in the United States, the study found pronounced differences in how people experienced being trans by age, which resulted largely from the rise of the Internet and the greater visibility of trans people in the media and pop culture over the past decade.

The participants indicated that they first recognized feeling "different" from others because of how they perceived their gender at four to five years of age, on average, or from their earliest memories. But while the older respondents found little or no support, and many of the trans women were punished if their gender difference was revealed or discovered, the respondents in their teens and early twenties grew up being able to turn to the Internet and find support online if they did not receive it from their families and friends. Because of greater exposure to trans people through the media, more parents today are willing to embrace their trans children, including male-assigned kids who identify as female, so that young trans people less often have to hide or deny who they are. Many were out in high or middle school, and some even in elementary school, whereas many of the participants who grew up from the 1940s through the 1980s repressed their gender identities until later in life, when they could no longer ignore their "true selves," or when the Internet became available to them and they recognized that they were "not the only one" who felt as they did.

Another generational difference was in how the participants identified. Many of the older MTF (male-to-female) respondents first thought of themselves as cross-dressers because it initially seemed to make sense; only later did they recognize that they did not want to stop presenting as female. Similarly, many of the older FTM (female-to-male) respondents who were attracted to women first thought of themselves as butch lesbians, because that, too, seemed to fit, before they realized that they were indeed men. With access to greater resources, the younger trans-masculine and trans-feminine respondents did not experience this sense of misidentification at all or for very long.

The participants in their teens and twenties also more readily recognized that there was not one way to be trans. While the older respondents felt limited to identifying themselves as cross-dressers or transsexuals, depending on their desire for gender-affirming surgeries, the younger individuals envisioned and created a wide range of gender possibilities. One of the most striking findings of our research was that the survey respondents provided more than a hundred different descriptions of their gender identity, ranging from the general ("I am me") to the very specific ("FTM TG stone butch drag king"). Most of the younger people identified outside of a gender binary; they saw themselves as both male and female, as neither male nor female but as a completely different gender, or as somewhere in between. Some also went by gender-inclusive pronouns, most commonly using "ze" or "sie" and "hir," or "they" and "them" as singular pronouns to refer to themselves.

Having accepted and sometimes having lived as their gender identity from childhood or their early teens, the younger individuals in our study entered college looking for—but typically not finding—support and resources. Other research, which focuses specifically on campus climate, describes how trans students frequently experience an unreceptive or even hostile college environment. The largest of these studies, the 2010 *State of Higher Education for Lesbian, Gay, Bisexual, and Transgender People* (Rankin et al. 2010), involved more than 5,100 students, staff, and faculty, including almost 700 trans-spectrum individuals. Among the trans respondents, 417 (60%) identified as gender nonconforming, 174 (25%) as transmasculine, and 104 (15%) as transfeminine.

The 2010 *State of Higher Education* study found that discrimination and a fear of discrimination were commonplace among the trans-identified participants. Among the three trans-spectrum groups, 31–39 percent reported experiencing harassment on campus, with 65 percent of the transmasculine students and 55 percent of the transfeminine students stating that they did not disclose their gender identity because of a fear of negative consequences. An even greater number of the trans-spectrum students of color sought to hide their gender identity in order to avoid intimidation or because they feared for their physical safety. Thus most of the respondents had either experienced harassment or remained closeted in the hope of avoiding harassment, which shows that students who are out on most colleges today will be discriminated against at some point. Because they found the climate on their campuses so antagonistic, more than a third of the trans-spectrum participants seriously considered leaving their schools, with some having already transferred to other institutions. But, at the same time, more than half indicated that they felt comfortable or very comfortable with the overall campus climate at their colleges and universities, demonstrating that some schools are much more trans-supportive than others.

Another recent study (Dugan, Kusel, and Simounet 2012) confirmed that many trans students are faced with a hostile campus climate, which can adversely affect their educational experience. Comparing ninety-one trans-identified and intersex-identified students with matched samples of cisgender (non-transgender) LGB-identified and cisgender heterosexual-identified students, the researchers found that the trans students "reported more frequent encounters with harassment and discrimination as well as a significantly lower sense of belonging within the campus community" (2012, 732), even though the trans students were no less engaged in educational activities, such as participating in internships, working with faculty members, and volunteering for community service. The trans students also had significantly lower scores than their cisgender LGB and heterosexual peers on measures of gains in complex cognitive skills and capacity for socially responsible leadership, which may reflect the difficulties they experienced in developing a positive sense of self in an often negative environment.

The work of Brent Bilodeau (2009) demonstrates the extent to which colleges and universities can be hostile places for trans-spectrum students. Bilodeau considered the experiences of trans students at two large midwestern public universities that have implemented some trans-supportive policies and practices and found that genderism still permeated every aspect of campus life: the academic classroom, campus employment and career planning, student organizations and communities, and campus facilities. The students interviewed for the study who identified or expressed their gender outside of a binary had an especially difficult time finding campus support, as the institutions remained firmly entrenched in a gender system that assumes students are either male or female. It is noteworthy that these were schools that had made progress in recognizing and addressing the needs of trans people; colleges and universities that have done little or nothing to support trans-spectrum students create an even more toxic environment.

## TRANS-SUPPORTIVE COLLEGE POLICIES

Colleges and universities can be supportive of trans students by implementing the policies and practices that have been suggested by educators and advocates in the field (Beemyn 2005; Beemyn, Curtis, et al. 2005; Beemyn, Domingue, et al. 2005; Bilodeau 2009). These changes include adding "gender identity and/or expression" to the institution's nondiscrimination policies; creating gender-inclusive bathrooms, locker rooms, and housing options; enabling trans students to use a chosen first name and a non-assigned gender on campus records and documents; covering hormones and surgeries for transitioning students as part of student health insurance; requiring all student affairs professionals, public safety officers, and other staff who work daily with students to attend a trans-focused training session; and regularly sponsoring trans speakers, performers, and other programs that include the perspectives of trans people. Campus Pride, a national support and advocacy group for LGBT college students, tracks and maintains lists of the colleges and universities that have enacted many of these trans-inclusive policies and suggests best trans-supportive practices. The organization also produces the LGBT-Friendly Campus Pride Index, which measures the supportiveness of colleges and universities by examining institutional resources and policies (see the resource list at the end of the article for Web links).

According to Campus Pride's Trans Policy Clearinghouse (2014), more than 150 colleges and universities offer a gender-inclusive housing option (housing in which students can have a roommate of any gender), and more than 115 enable trans students to use a chosen first name rather than their legal first name on campus records and documents such as identification cards, course rosters, and directory listings. But fewer colleges and universities have done much work to address two large aspects of campus life: the academic classroom and athletics. In both these areas, trans-spectrum students face a rigid gender binary and regularly experience discrimination that interferes with their ability to participate fully.

## CREATING A TRANS-INCLUSIVE CLASSROOM

Fostering a trans-inclusive classroom involves both establishing an environment in which trans-spectrum students are supported and welcomed and educating cisgender students about the experiences of trans-spectrum people. To begin to make trans students feel included from the first day of classes, instructors should not presume the gender of their students or that they go by their given name, especially if the institution does not allow students to use a first name other than their legal one on course rosters and other campus records. Instead, teachers should ask the students to indicate the first name and pronouns by which they want to be known, either by introducing themselves to the class or by providing the information to the instructor in writing. This exercise would mean that some trans-spectrum students would be faced with having to decide whether to come out and may not feel comfortable doing so, especially to a faculty member who is going to grade them or to a room full of their peers. But the option is important for the trans students who are open about their gender identity and who want to be acknowledged as how they see themselves.

For the classroom to be a truly trans-inclusive environment, the curriculum must also be changed so that trans-spectrum people are not erased by the assumption of a gender binary and are specifically represented. A number of studies have shown the benefits of "teaching trans" to both trans-spectrum and cisgender students. Caitlin L. Ryan, Jasmine M. Patraw, and Maree Bednar (2013) discuss how making gender diversity a recurring theme in an urban, public elementary school classroom over the course of a year affected the third- and fourth-grade students. The teacher, who was one of the study's authors, used four lesson plans of increasing complexity to familiarize students with the concepts of gender nonconformity and transgender. Contrary to critics who say that young children are not ready for such topics, the researchers found that the students were receptive and engaged. From their experiences, the students better recognized restrictive gender norms, developed a broader understanding of gender identity and expression, and were able to apply the knowledge they learned to situations not directly about gender.

The Ryan, Patraw, and Bednar study is the only published research to date on the implementation and assessment of a trans-inclusive elementary school curriculum. Several more studies have been conducted at the college level, but research remains very limited here as well. Kim A. Case and Briana Stewart (2013) examine the impact of introducing three different trans educational interventions (a letter from a transsexual teen to his parents, a list of facts about transsexuality, and a clip from a documentary about transsexual college students) to a group of 132 students at an urban state university in Texas. The results of the study indicate that all of the interventions significantly lowered the participants' negative attitudes and stereotypical beliefs about transsexuality, but no significant difference was found between the respondents' pre-test and post-test mean scores for predictions of discriminatory behaviors. The students had become more supportive, but this change had yet to be incorporated into how they might treat trans people. The participants, who were recruited from different social sciences courses, were almost all female and their average age was thirty-one years old; research involving a younger, more gender-diverse sample may have led to different results, because youth are generally more likely to support trans rights, while men are generally less likely to do so.

In another study, BJ Rye, Pamela Elmslie, and Amanda Chalmers (2007) found that having a MTF guest speaker talk about her experiences to students in upper-level human sexuality courses at a Canadian college resulted in the participants' expressing more positive attitudes toward transsexual people. For many of the students, this class program was the first time they had "met" an out trans individual, and according to the authors, "the effect was remarkable." Written feedback indicated that the students developed a greater understanding of transsexuality as a result of the speaker talking about herself and about trans-spectrum people in general, and for some students, the experience changed their conception of diversity and inclusion. While a more involved or sustained intervention similar to Ryan, Patraw, and Bednar's research may have had an even greater effect, these two college-level studies demonstrate that even a small step to educate cisgender students about trans-spectrum people can make a big difference.

At the same time, what Kate Drabinski (2011) refers to as the "special guest" model is limiting, as it continues to treat trans-spectrum people and their experiences as peripheral. A class is devoted to a trans speaker or panel; otherwise, their perspectives fail to inform the curriculum. Framing Transgender Studies as a set of practices rather than simply as an identity, Drabinski offers an approach that enables the insights that can be gained from an examination of the lives of trans people to remain foregrounded in the Women's and Gender Studies classroom.

But if trans-spectrum experiences are considered only within Women's and Gender Studies, then academia will continue to operate from a gender binary and be biased against trans people. To create more comprehensive and lasting curricular change, all disciplines must engage in "gender-complex education"—education that recognizes the existence and experiences of trans-spectrum and gender-nonconforming people (Rands 2009). As Kat Rands (2013) offers, even a field like mathematics, which has traditionally not addressed issues of social justice, can seamlessly incorporate gender diversity. Ze presents a series of exercises for middle-school students using statistics related to anti-trans discrimination from the Gay, Lesbian, and Straight Education Network's National School Climate Survey (Kosciw et al. 2010). The students then design and carry out an action plan based on what they have discovered about the value of peer intervention in anti-trans-bias incidents. From these lessons, the middle school students further develop critical mathematical and statistical skills, and they learn how to apply these skills in practical ways in order to address an issue that is relevant to their lives. A similar approach, with more complex exercises, could be used in high school and college math classes.

## CREATING A TRANS-INCLUSIVE ATHLETIC PROGRAM

Until recently, the inclusion and support of trans-spectrum students in athletics had been a largely unexplored topic. In part, the lack of discussion was a matter of priorities: trans students and their supporters focused initially on advocating for the more immediate needs of having safe places to live and to go to the bathroom on campuses and being able to receive appropriate care at college counseling and health centers. Typically, only after these issues have been addressed at their institutions have trans students considered the inclusiveness of campus recreational facilities and sports teams.

Another reason that athletic programs have received little attention is the paucity to date of out trans-spectrum student athletes. For example, the *Student-Athlete Climate Study* (Rankin et al. 2011), which involved nearly 8,500 college student athletes from 164 NCAA-member institutions, had only 7 trans-identified respondents. An earlier study (Rankin et al. 2008), which sampled more than 1,300 athletes from six institutions, included no trans-identified students.

In the last few years, though, the issue of trans participation in athletics has received greater consideration and much more visibility as a result of several trans-spectrum student athletes having come out. Most well known is Kye Allums, a starting guard for the George Washington University women's basketball team, who became the first openly trans Division I athlete in 2010. He was able to remain on the team after he began to identify as male because, in compliance with NCAA guidelines (Griffin and Carroll 2011), he did not begin to take hormones until after ending his college playing career. Other out FTM college athletes have included Keelin Godsey, an All-American women's track and field athlete at Bates College in 2005, and Taylor Edelmann, the captain of the men's volleyball team at SUNY Purchase in 2013. Like Allums, Godsey was able to compete on a women's team because he had not begun to transition, while Edelmann started taking testosterone and switched from the women's to the men's team (DeFrancesco 2013; Torre and Epstein 2012).

Even fewer MTF college athletes have come out, and their ability to play sports in keeping with their gender identity has been much more controversial, despite research showing that any possible physical advantage disappears after taking hormones. The NCAA allows MTF athletes to compete on women's teams if they have been on hormone therapy for at least a year (Griffin and Carroll 2011). Nevertheless, there has yet to be an NCAA-level female athlete who is openly transgender. Currently, the only out trans woman participating on a women's sports team is Gabrielle Ludwig, a basketball player at Mission College, a community college in Santa Clara, California (Prisbell 2012).

The NCAA's policies for transgender athletes are more inclusive and realistic than the International Olympic Committee's policies, which require MTF competitors to have at least two years of hormone therapy and all transgender people to undergo gender-affirming surgery and to change documents to be legally recognized as their gender identity. But the NCAA needlessly excludes transgender women who have not taken hormones for more than a year from participating on women's teams, assuming that male-bodied athletes automatically have a physical advantage over female-bodied athletes. The most trans-inclusive athletic policy would enable students to participate on the team that is consistent with their gender identity, irrespective of whether they are taking hormones or have changed the gender listed on their legal records (Buzuvis 2012).

There is also a movement underway to include trans athletes in K–12 programs. As of 2013, two states have enacted formal policies that allow elementary and secondary school students to join teams based on their gender identity (Massachusetts and California) and one state does so just at the high school level (Washington). Two recent legal settlements (Office for Civil Rights 2014; "Resolution Agreement" 2013) between the U.S. Department of Education and school districts in California, which affirm that anti-transgender discrimination is covered under Title IX, may lead other school districts and colleges to enact trans-supportive athletic policies to avoid possible lawsuits.

While colleges and universities are bound by the rules of the NCAA and the governing bodies of club sports, a growing number of campus athletic programs are developing policies that ensure that trans-spectrum athletes are accommodated as best as possible within these expectations. In addition, institutions are creating trans-inclusive policies for their intramural and recreational sports teams, which enable trans students to compete based on their gender identity. Among the campuses with such policies are Bates College, Emory University, Miami University (Ohio), and the University of Vermont (Campus Pride Trans Policy Clearinghouse 2014).

## CONCLUSION

Trans-spectrum people are not new to our campuses, but institutional policies, attitudes, procedures, and facilities often keep them isolated and invisible (Rowell 2009). With more and more trans-spectrum people coming out to themselves and others during childhood and adolescence, many colleges and universities are witnessing a steadily growing number of openly trans students. These students are expecting to be recognized and to have their needs met by their institutions. However, campuses have been largely unprepared to meet these needs and now are scrambling to provide support services and to create more inclusive policies and practices.

The vast majority of college students, faculty, student affairs educators, and administrators have a tremendous amount to learn about gender diversity. For this majority and for trans-spectrum students and educators, opportunities are all but untapped to leverage this diversity to enhance learning, as well as to support and celebrate these individuals. At the same time, every day that students and educators remain ignorant about this population is another day that trans-spectrum students face overt or unintentional harassment and discrimination that may result in their departure from the institution.

Colleges and universities can be supportive of trans-spectrum students by implementing the trans-inclusive policies and practices that have been suggested within this article and through the resources provided on best practices at the end of the work. However, the changes needed cannot end there. Having a process whereby students can change the male/female designation on their college records, for example, is of little value to gender-nonconforming students who fit into neither box. Gender-segregated co-curricular activities (e.g., fraternities, sororities, and athletic teams) and "women's" health and support services likewise ignore and exclude the growing number of genderqueer, gender fluid, agender, and androgynous students. Only after a complete transformation of institutional cultures will colleges and universities become truly welcoming to trans-spectrum students.

## NOTE

1. We use *trans-spectrum* and *trans* to refer to the wide range of individuals whose gender identity or expression is sometimes or always different from the gender assigned to them at birth.

## REFERENCES

Beemyn, Brett-Genny. 2005. "Making Campuses More Inclusive of Transgender Students." *Journal of Gay and Lesbian Issues in Education* 3(1): 77–89.

Beemyn, Brett, Billy Curtis, Masen Davis, and Nancy Jean Tubbs. 2005. "Transgender Issues on College Campuses." In *Gender Identity and Sexual Orientation: Research, Policy, and Personal Perspectives*, edited by Ronni L. Sanlo, 41–49. San Francisco: Jossey-Bass.

Beemyn, Brett-Genny, Andrea Domingue, Jessica Pettitt, and Todd Smith. 2005. "Suggested Steps to Make Campuses More Trans-Inclusive." *Journal of Gay and Lesbian Issues in Education* 3(1): 89–104.

Beemyn, Genny, and Sue Rankin. 2011. *The Lives of Transgender People*. New York: Columbia University Press.

Bilodeau, Brent. 2009. *Genderism: Transgender Students, Binary Systems, and Higher Education*. Saarbrücken, Germany: Verlag Dr. Müller.

Buzuvis, Erin. 2012. "Including Transgender Athletes in Sex-Segregated Sport." In *Sexual Orientation and Gender Identity in Sport: Essays from Activists, Coaches, and Scholars*, edited by George B. Cunningham, 23–34. College Station, TX: Center for Sport Management Research and Education.

Campus Pride Trans Policy Clearinghouse. Last modified November 20, 2014. http://www.campuspride.org/tpc.

Case, Kim A., and Briana Stewart. 2013. "Intervention Effectiveness in Reducing Prejudice against Transsexuals." *Journal of LGBT Youth* 10(1–2): 140–158.

DeFrancesco, Dan. 2013. "Volleyball Eases Transgender Player's Transition." *USA Today*, May 8.

Drabinski, Kate. 2011. "Identity Matters: Teaching Transgender in the Women's Studies Classroom." *Radical Teacher* 92: 10–20.

Dugan, John P., Michelle L. Kusel, and Dawn Simounet. 2012. "Transgender College Students: An Exploratory Study of Perceptions, Engagement, and Educational Outcomes." *Journal of College Student Development* 53(5): 719–736.

Grant, Jaime M., Lisa A. Mottet, and Justin Tanis. 2010. *Injustice at Every Turn: A Report of the National Transgender Discrimination Survey—Executive Summary.* Accessed September 20, 2013. http://www.thetaskforce.org/static_html/downloads/reports/reports/ntds_full .pdf.

Griffin, Pat, and Helen Carroll. 2011. *NCAA Inclusion of Transgender Student-Athletes.* NCAA Office of Inclusion. http://www.ncaa.org/sites/default/files/Transgender_Handbook _2011_Final.pdf.

Kosciw, Joseph G., Emily A. Greytak, Elizabeth M. Diaz, and Mark J. Bartkiewicz. 2010. *The 2009 National School Climate Survey: The Experiences of Lesbian, Gay, Bisexual, and Transgender Youth in Our Nation's Schools.* New York: Gay, Lesbian, and Straight Education Network.

Office for Civil Rights, U.S. Department of Education. "Letter to the Downey Unified School District." October 14, 2014. http://www2.ed.gov/documents/press-releases/downey -school-district-letter.pdf.

Prisbell, Eric. 2012. "Transsexual Gabrielle Ludwig Returns to College Court." *USA Today,* December 5.

Rands, Kat. 2009. "Considering Transgender People in Education: A Gender-Complex Approach." *Journal of Teacher Education* 60(4): 419–431.

———. 2013. "Supporting Transgender and Gender-Nonconforming Youth through Teaching Mathematics for Social Justice." *Journal of LGBT Youth* 10(1–2): 106–126.

Rankin, Susan, Dan Merson, India McHale, and Karla Loya. 2008. *Student-Athlete Climate Study Pilot Project.* University Park: Center for the Study of Higher Education, Pennsylvania State University.

Rankin, Susan, Dan Merson, Carl H. Sorgen, India McHale, Karla Loya, and Leticia Oseguera. 2011. *Student-Athlete Climate Study (SACS): Final Report.* University Park: Center for the Study of Higher Education, Pennsylvania State University.

Rankin, Susan, Genevieve Weber, Warren Blumenfeld, and Somjen Frazer. 2010. *2010 State of Higher Education for Lesbian, Gay, Bisexual, and Transgender People.* Charlotte, NC: Campus Pride Q Research Institute in Higher Education.

"Resolution Agreement between the Arcadia Unified School District, the U.S. Department of Education, Office for Civil Rights, and the U.S. Department of Justice, Civil Rights Division." 2013. Accessed August 9, 2013. http://www.justice.gov/crt/about/edu/ documents/arcadiaagree.pdf.

Rowell, Elizabeth H. 2009. "Promoting Dialogue on the Transgender Experience in College Courses through Films and Literature." *Human Architecture: Journal of the Sociology of Self-Knowledge* 7(1): 87–92.

Ryan, Caitlin L., Jasmine M. Patraw, and Maree Bednar. 2013. "Discussing Princess Boys and Pregnant Men: Teaching about Gender Diversity and Transgender Experiences within an Elementary School Curriculum." *Journal of LGBT Youth* 10(1–2): 83–105.

Rye, BJ, Pamela Elmslie, and Amanda Chalmers. 2007. "Meeting a Transsexual Person: Experience within a Classroom Setting." *Canadian Online Journal of Queer Studies in Education* 3(1). http://jqstudies.library.utoronto.ca/index.php/jqstudies/article/view/3269.

Torre, Pablo S., and David Epstein. 2012. "The Transgender Athlete." *Sports Illustrated,* May 28.

## RESOURCES

Campus Pride Trans Policy Clearinghouse: http://www.campuspride.org/tpc.

Johnson, E., and A. Subasic. 2011. *Promising Practices for Inclusion of Gender Identity/Gender Expression in Higher Education.* http://www.umass.edu/stonewall/uploads/listWidget/ 25137/promising-practices.pdf.

LGBTQ-Friendly Campus Pride Index: http://www.campusprideindex.org.

Trans Checklist for Colleges and Universities: http://www.campuspride.org/tools/trans gender-checklist-for-colleges-universities.

# 2 · TRANSGENDERING THE ACADEMY

## Ensuring Transgender Inclusion in Higher Education

PAULINE PARK

As more and more transgendered and gender-variant people seek to participate fully in the life of their institutions as faculty members, staff, and students at colleges and universities across the United States, the issue of transgender inclusion has become increasingly important in higher education, sparking lively and often heated discussion about everything from curriculum to faculty hiring to gender-neutral student housing to restroom construction on campus.[1] My objective here is to provide a comprehensive assessment of the issues that arise when institutions of higher education attempt to address the impediments to the full participation of transgendered students, faculty, and staff members in the life of the academy. My perspective is informed by work in the academy in both faculty and staff positions (and, of course, as a student) as well as work within the community, most intensively with Queens Pride House, which I co-founded in 1997, and the New York Association for Gender Rights Advocacy (NYAGRA), which I co-founded in 1998. Queens Pride House is the only LGBT community center in the borough of Queens, and we offer support groups (including a transgender support group), free mental health counseling for members of the community, and other services; our advocacy program has included public policy forums focused on advocating for members of the community, such as our public forum on policing in March 2015, which focused on police harassment and brutality directed against transgendered women of color and other LGBT people and people of color.

In 2009 NYAGRA published the first directory of transgender-sensitive health care providers in the New York metropolitan area. Directories of this kind have been posted online for cities such as Los Angeles, Boston, and Minneapolis–St. Paul, but the NYAGRA directory was the first such directory in the United States ever published in a print edition. It is now available online as well at transgenderrights.org.

NYAGRA is a co-founding member of the coalition seeking enactment of the Gender Expression Non-Discrimination Act (GENDA), the transgender rights bill currently pending in the New York state legislature.[2] I represent NYAGRA in that coalition, as I did in the coalition that secured enactment of the Dignity for All Students Act (DASA) in 2011. The Dignity Act came into effect in July 2013 and prohibits discrimination and bias-based harassment in public schools throughout the state of New York. The New York state DASA legislation includes comprehensive lists of "protected categories," which include race, religion, ethnicity, and disability as well as sexual orientation and gender, defined to include gender identity and gender expression. Safe schools legislation such as DASA can help move us out of a purely "identitarian" conceptual framework, which can be limiting. Instead of focusing on a single group of students (whether transgendered, gay, or LGBT), the DASA law focuses broadly on safety from bullying and bias-based harassment across the entire student population, while at the same time it specifically and explicitly includes transgendered and gender-variant students in its provisions. The campaign for this legislation thus provided an ideal opportunity for collaboration between LGBT and non-LGBT organizations.

My thinking is also informed by my experience as coordinator of the transgender support group at Queens Pride House as well as my work on the board of directors and staff of the only LGBT community center in the borough of Queens, the most diverse county in the United States. The clients we serve through our mental health program—which provides free counseling to members of the community as well as support groups for men, transgendered people, youth, and elders—are a strikingly diverse population, a substantial proportion of whom are immigrants (including undocumented immigrants, primarily from Latin America and Asia). In the context of work for such a community center, notions of "multiple oppressions" and "intersectionality" become very real and are manifest in a transgender support group that is diverse in terms of race and ethnicity as well as gender identity and expression.[3] It should be obvious—but may not be to everyone—that making higher education more LGBT-inclusive must also mean tackling the problem of bullying and bias-based harassment in elementary and secondary schools, since so many LGBT students drop out of school because of such bullying and never make it to college; based on anecdotal evidence (in the absence of any comprehensive study of the problem), that is especially true of transgendered students.

In addition to my work on behalf of NYAGRA in the legislative arena, an important component of my work is transgender sensitivity training. I have conducted sessions for a wide range of social service providers and community-based organizations, ranging from one-hour workshops to full-day trainings. A small part of my training work has been with academic institutions, focused on issues related to transgender inclusion—including, for example, gender-neutral housing, which has become a major issue on many campuses.

## TRANSGENDER INCLUSION: THE NEED TO RECOGNIZE THE FULL DIVERSITY OF THE COMMUNITY

So here is the question I would like to address: If our goal is to make higher education fully transgender-inclusive, how would we go about achieving that objective? The first step would have to be to gain a full understanding of just what "transgender" means; and there may be as many different definitions of "transgender" as there are transgendered people (see, for example, Winter 2010). An online search will yield hundreds of different terms used by transgendered and gender-variant people to self-identify. Conversely, many transgendered people do not identify with the term *transgender*. Clearly, the almost bewildering diversity of the transgender community constitutes one of the biggest challenges in attempting to include and serve this population, whether in higher education, health care, or social services. The main point is to avoid the narrowing of discourse around gender identity that is constantly rearticulated and reinforced by the mainstream media (the over-reliance on what I call the classic transsexual transition narrative), which focuses almost obsessively on a linear medical transition from male to female through hormone replacement therapy (HRT) toward the end point of sex reassignment surgery. Some do follow that path, but most transgendered people do not. Any effort to establish fully transgender-inclusive programs and services on a college campus will falter unless this effort is based on a recognition of the full diversity of transgender identity.

## TRANSGENDERING THE ACADEMY: CAMPUS POLICIES, CURRICULUM, STUDENT SERVICES, AND FACULTY AND STAFF DEVELOPMENT

Having situated myself as an activist and ex-academic, and having attempted to describe the diversity of the transgender community, I would now like to set out what I see as four crucial elements in what I call "transgendering the academy." These include, first, establishing campus policies and protocols that explicitly prohibit discrimination based on gender identity and expression; second, constructing curricula and building academic programs and departments that advance the study of transgender in the academy; third, advancing transgender entry into faculty positions within academia; and fourth, establishing an institutional infrastructure of services for transgendered students, faculty, and staff. One of the tasks that must be undertaken in order to effect what I call the "transgendering of the academy" is the adoption by colleges and universities of policies explicitly prohibiting discrimination based on gender identity and gender expression as well as sexual orientation. There is a curious paradox here: where campuses are situated in jurisdictions that currently include gender identity and expression in antidiscrimination law, explicit policies that do so are somewhat redundant, as such colleges and universities are already under legal mandate to enforce nondiscrimination. But I argue that campus policies are still useful, even in cities, counties, and states with gender identity and expression in human rights law, as these policies represent an explicit commitment on the part of the college or university to transgender inclusion. These policies send a signal to transgendered students, faculty, and staff that their presence and participation in campus life are valued and also send an important signal to those who would discriminate against transgendered members of the campus community.

Of all the items in the project of transgendering the academy, this is, on the face of it, the easiest: simply add either gender identity and expression to the college or university antidiscrimination policy or, better still, add a definition of gender that includes identity and expression and that requires no elaborate wordsmithing or lawyering but merely expresses a commitment on the part of the administration to do so. The difficulty comes when applying such a non-discrimination policy to specific situations such as sex-segregated facilities, including those where there is the possibility of unavoidable nudity (to use a legal expression). Restrooms, dormitories, gyms, and locker rooms are the most significant "sites of contestation." Some institutions, such as New York University (NYU), have adopted policies that specifically require the construction of at least one gender-neutral restroom per new building (Minter 2007; Seedman 2013); at the same time that NYU adopted this policy in 2005, the university senate approved the adoption of a general policy prohibiting discrimination based on gender identity or expression, recognizing (albeit belatedly) that the university had been under a legal mandate from the City of New York to avoid such discrimination since the enactment of the transgender rights law by the New York City Council in 2002 (Senate of New York University 2005).

Explicit campus-wide policies ensuring full access to campus facilities for transgendered students as well as faculty and staff are important, but these must be drafted in ways that address the potentially thorny issues that arise when it comes to sex-segregated facilities. The rule should be one of reasonable accommodation, backed by an aggressive effort by the administration to ensure full access to such facilities. The prohibition of discrimination based on gender identity and expression must be explicitly included in faculty, staff, and student handbooks along with prohibition of discrimination based on other characteristics such as race, ethnicity, religion, national origin, disability, and so on. Above all, the prohibition of discrimination based on gender identity or expression must be included in legal documents that ensure the right of the student or faculty or staff member to litigate a dispute if necessary; only then can the institution be held accountable, especially in jurisdictions that do not include gender identity or expression in state or local non-discrimination law.

Single-sex colleges must also address the issue of admissions policies, a particularly thorny issue for women's colleges; but the inclusion of both transmen and transwomen in women's spaces is an issue that will not go away, much as many administrators at women's colleges may wish it to. Clearly, the principle of empowering women through education needs to be subjected to scrutiny, as does the very definition of what constitutes a woman, and what provisions must be made to accommodate and ideally to fully include in the life of the college those female-born individuals who transition to male over the course of their undergraduate careers at women's colleges, as well as those male-born individuals who seek admission to a women's college as women. In 2014, Mills College in Oakland adopted a transgender-inclusive admissions policy that could well become a model for women's colleges throughout the country (Mills College 2015b). Under that policy, "Mills College admits students of all genders to its graduate programs, and 'self-identified' women to its undergraduate programs. Mills shall not discriminate against applicants whose gender identity does not match their legally assigned sex" (Mills College 2015b).

The policy adopted by the college is explicitly based on self-identification and includes transgendered women but does not exclude those who transition from female to male during the course of their studies, as long as they have not transitioned before applying for admission to the college. "One of the women's schools, Mills College in Oakland, California, relies on self-identification for gender. This is clearly the direction in which our society is moving, jurisdiction by jurisdiction and agency by agency," Kiera Feldman wrote in an op-ed in the *New York Times* in May 2014 (Feldman 2014). The development of this pioneering policy was the work of many people at Mills, including the members of the Gender Identity and Expression Subcommittee, which met 2012–2013 to address the issue of transgender inclusion (Park 2010). In April 2013, Professor Julia Oparah invited me to speak at Mills. I addressed faculty, staff, and students—including the president of the college and senior administrators—on issues of transgender inclusion that have arisen at women's colleges, including Mills itself.[4]

Colleges and universities should also mandate transgender sensitivity training for all faculty and staff—and where feasible, for students as well. Where mandatory diversity training already exists for race, ethnicity, religion, and disability as well as sex or gender, this training should include sexual orientation and gender identity and expression as well. In other words, "diversity" needs to be redefined campus-wide in order to include diversity of sexual orientation and gender identity and expression.

Another mechanism for enhancing inclusion would be to conduct a campus-wide census of students, faculty, and staff—especially those in leadership positions—that includes self-identification by sexual orientation and gender identity. No doubt such a proposal could meet resistance even at the ostensibly more progressive colleges and universities. But at the very least, surveys of "campus climate" should include questions about climate for LGBTQ students, faculty, and staff. And participation in the census should be purely voluntary, even if this means incomplete data. (Incomplete data would be better than no data on gender identity at all, which is the current situation at most colleges and universities in the United States.) Gender and Sexuality Resources at Mills College reported that "in 2012, 34.7% of seniors self-identified as lesbian, bisexual, queer, or transgender/genderqueer" (Mills College 2015a). When done in a non-intrusive and sensitive manner, the collection and dissemination of such statistics can help empower transgendered students, and LGBT students more generally, and can also help them and their allies advocate for more on-campus resources.

The second element in the project of transgendering the academy is the inclusion of transgender-relevant courses in the curriculum of institutions of higher education. Inclusion of a course on transgender issues as a requirement for completing a major or a minor in LGBT Studies would represent a significant advance for transgender inclusion in the curriculum. On the curricular front, at least, there has been some progress over the course of the last few decades, as the number of courses offered at colleges and universities in the United States and Canada—and increasingly outside North America—that include a substantial component on transgender issues has grown exponentially, albeit from a small base. Once again, there seems to be no comprehensive list, which would be very useful for LGBT campus professionals as well as for students and faculty. All too often, even where transgender-inclusive courses are included in a college course catalog, those courses are offered irregularly and by graduate students or adjunct professors with little institutional influence and limited ability to ensure continuity in course content from semester to semester. But where such courses exist, they are primarily in the humanities and to a lesser extent in the social sciences. In other fields, significant transgender- or even LGBT-specific content in curricula is rare. In schools of medicine, for example, transgender-specific content is sparse, and what little there is focuses almost exclusively on the medical aspects of transsexual transition—even though familiarizing physicians and other health-care providers with what might be termed the "psychosocial" aspects of health-care provision may be as important in ensuring transgender access to quality health care as "cognate" knowledge of the surgical and endocrinological aspects of gender transition. I would suggest that a minimum of two hours of transgender sensitivity training should be required at every school of medicine that offers an MD.

However, the asymmetry in institutional power between transgender-identified students and faculty who develop and teach so many transgender-inclusive courses but lack decision-making power over curriculum development and the tenured faculty who wield decision-making power over them poses a serious issue for academic institutions. And inextricably linked with the issue of curriculum development is that of faculty and staff development. Certainly, one of the biggest challenges in advancing a project of transgendering the academy will be that of transgendering the faculty of colleges and universities, few members of which are openly transgendered; even fewer transgender-identified faculty members obtain tenure after having been hired while openly transgendered; and still fewer obtain tenure primarily for research focused on transgender issues. Most theorists who focus substantially on transgender issues are in the humanities, with only a scattering in the social sciences.

Indeed, one of the most remarkable facts about what might be termed "Transgender Studies" is that many—if not most—tenured faculty members in the field are not themselves transgender-identified; those who are for the most part are graduate students and adjunct faculty. What if the faculty of a program or department of Women's Studies at a college or university were almost entirely male? Or consider for a moment a comparison with Ethnic Studies: imagine for a moment if faculty in a program or department of African American, Asian American, Native American, or Latino Studies on a given college campus were mostly or even entirely white; such a situation would be regarded as controversial if not unacceptable by many students, faculty, and administrators alike. However, Transgender Studies—depending on how one defines the field—may be very close to that situation today. There are, of course, significant differences between race and ethnicity, on the one hand, and sexual orientation and gender identity or expression, on the other, and it would be risky indeed to make too glib a comparison between them. And yet, entertaining the analogy for the moment may be useful in pointing out the striking asymmetry in power relations between the majority of those who participate in this nascent field called Transgender Studies who are students, untenured faculty, and independent scholars as well as activists and the minority who, as tenured faculty members, constitute the privileged elite of this small society of largely white and upper-middle-class academicians. Even more problematic is the tendency of Transgender Studies as a field to mirror the larger academic society's tendency to construct and rigidly enforce orthodoxies of thought as well as hierarchies of power, both within and outside the academy. The clinical literature is dominated by psychiatrists, psychoanalysts, and psychotherapists, with some participation by social workers and other members of the "helping professions," but the transgendered people whose lives are profoundly affected by the determinations of those professionals are largely excluded from participation in the construction of that literature for lack of the professional credentials required for that participation.

If transgendered people have made little headway in attempting to secure tenure in traditional academic departments, they have made even less progress in schools of medicine where psychiatrists earn their MDs. The American Psychiatric Association (APA) is possibly the least open association in the "helping professions" to transgendered people. Despite the vast influence that the psychiatric profession wields over the lives of transsexual, transgendered, and gender-variant children, youth, and adults, this profession is also the most resistant to public or LGBT community input of any kind.

Then there is the question of institutional infrastructure, especially of student services. Here, the Consortium of Higher Education Lesbian, Gay, Bisexual, Transgender Resource Professionals (hereafter "the Consortium") and its members have played a leading role in developing LGBT student services offices at campuses around the United States. And one of the most important keys to serving undergraduate and graduate students on campus is a fully funded LGBT student services office with at least one or more full-time staff members, which is the minimum needed to effectively serve transgendered and gender-variant students. Support groups for those coming out and transitioning are also crucial. Support and guidance in navigating the physical infrastructure of a campus are especially important, including access to restrooms and locker rooms in gyms. Housing is also an important issue, and single-sex institutions—especially women's colleges—are increasingly confronted with issues of access. Health care is a particularly important and sensitive issue for transgendered students, who face multiple and significant impediments when they attempt to access procedures and care both related to gender transition and not directly gender-related, both on and off campus. Offices of LGBT student services can also play a role in assisting transgendered and gender-variant students navigate what might be called the "semiotics of campus life," including negotiating classroom etiquette related to names and pronouns and even posting transgender-affirming signage around campus.

One of the challenges frequently faced by offices of LGBT student services is the "silo-ing" that often results from the construction of offices of multicultural affairs along identitarian lines—such that the office of LGBT students primarily serves white queers, with little engagement with the offices of African American, Latino, or Asian American students, which in turn are inadvertently relieved of the obligation to serve LGBT students of color within their constituencies. Housing the LGBT student services office within the same complex as those serving students of color can help foster collaboration and collaborative programming. Colleges and universities must work to ensure that LGBT students of color—and especially transgendered students of color—do not fall between the cracks. "Intersectionality" must not be simply a slogan; it must be a principle upon which student service professionals at colleges and universities operate.

Finally, let me mention something of particular interest to me as the alumna of three different academic institutions, and this is the role of alumni in the lives of their alma maters. As anyone working on staff at a college or university will know, alumni wield enormous influence with administrators, above all because of their financial contributions to the institutions they once attended. In this regard, it seems to me that the development of LGBT alumni associations represents one of the most promising recent developments in higher education. I would encourage us as a community to think in terms of LGBT alumni associations that are able to exercise some degree of autonomy from the general alumni associations and the college and university administrators who run them. Such LGBT alumni associations may be positioned to undertake initiatives that would enhance transgender inclusion in the academic institutions with which they are associated. Just to suggest a few such ideas, an LGBT alumni association should consider creating a transgender-specific scholarship fund and perhaps at some point even funding an endowed chair dedicated to transgender-related research.

## CONCLUSION

My own experiences in the academy, in social services provision and community-center work, and in activism and advocacy work have led me to conclude that we are in the process of bringing about significant, possibly even transformational, change in how our society views gender, but to make the academy truly transgender-inclusive will require much more work. It seems that academic institutions need to focus on four crucial aspects of this work: first, colleges and universities need to adopt policies and protocols that explicitly include gender identity and expression; second, they need to develop transgender-inclusive curricula that are fully supported by academic programs and departments; third, they need to advance openly transgendered faculty into tenure-track positions and eventually tenure those who deserve it; and fourth, they need to develop an infrastructure to support transgendered faculty, staff, and students. Academic institutions need to do so through an approach informed by the broadest possible conception of gender identity and expression. And those institutions that identify themselves as women's colleges need to articulate standards for admission and graduation that are as transgender-inclusive as possible, along the lines of Mills College in Oakland and other women's colleges that have begun to create fully inclusive admissions policies. The project that I have called the transgendering of the academy will ultimately benefit not only the transgendered but all the students, faculty, and staff as well as helping to advance the pursuit of a progressive vision of social justice and social change that will help transform our society for the better.

## NOTES

This article is based on a keynote address given at the colloquium on "Trans Politics: Scholarship and Strategies for Social Change," organized by the Institute for Research on Women at Rutgers, the State University of New Jersey, and held at Rutgers University's New Brunswick campus on April 18, 2013.

1. For an explanation of the usage of *transgendered*, see Park 2011.
2. The Gender Expression Non-Discrimination Act (GENDA) (A.4226/Gottfried) (S.195/Squadron) would add gender identity and expression as a category in New York state human rights law, thereby protecting transgendered and gender-variant New Yorkers from discrimination in employment, housing, public accommodations, education, and credit; see, for example, the Empire State Pride Agenda website for more information: http://www.pride agenda.org/igniting-equality/current-legislation/gender-expression-non-discrimination-act.
3. I might add parenthetically that I am the first and so far only openly transgendered executive director of an LGBT community center in the state of New York and one of only two in the United States—as well as the first and so far only Asian American executive director of an LGBT community center in the state of New York and one of only two in the country. I am also the only openly transgendered Asian American executive director of an LGBT community center in the United States, which may say more about the lack of diversity in the leadership of LGBT community centers in this country than about me.
4. Julia Oparah (chair of the Ethnic Studies Department) was a leading figure in the drive for transgender inclusion and generously credits me with serving as a catalyst for her own involvement in that work. I was one of the keynote speakers at the very first Expanding the Circle conference on LGBT inclusion in higher education (February 28, 2010), and Professor Oparah has told me that this speech and subsequent conversations with her persuaded her to spearhead the efforts at Mills to address the issue of transgender inclusion at the college. Professor Oparah and other members of the subcommittee credited my speech and my conversations with faculty, staff, and students with helping to advance the process that led to the adoption of the most progressive policy on transgender inclusion at any college or university in the United States (Park 2013).

## REFERENCES

Feldman, Kiera. 2014. "Who Are Women's Colleges For?" *New York Times*, May 24. http://www.nytimes.com/2014/05/25/opinion/sunday/who-are-womens-colleges-for.html?_r=0.

Frazer, Somjen M. 2009. *LGBT Health and Human Service Needs in New York State*. Albany, NY: Empire State Pride Agenda Foundation.

Mills College. 2015a. "Diversity and Social Justice at Mills: Gender and Sexuality Resources." Accessed March 19, 2015. http://www.mills.edu/diversity/gender-sexuality-resources.php.

———. 2015b. "Mills College Undergraduate Admissions Policy for Transgender or Gender Questioning Applicants." Accessed March 19, 2015. http://www.mills.edu/academics/undergraduate/catalog/admission_applying.php#transgendered_policy.

Minter, Shannon. 2007. *Advancements in State and Federal Law Regarding Transgender Employees: A Compliance Guide for Employers and Employment Law Attorneys*. San Francisco: National Center for Lesbian Rights and the Transgender Law Center.

Park, Pauline. 2003. "GenderPAC, the Transgender Rights Movement, and the Perils of a Post-identity Politics Paradigm." *Georgetown Journal of Gender and the Law* 4.2: 747–765.

———. 2006. "S/he's Not Heavy, Zie's My Non-Gendered Sibling: Why Gender-Neutral Pronouns Don't Work for Me." *Big Queer Blog*. Accessed, March 19, 2015. http://www.bigqueer.com/index.php?/archives/196-Shes-Not-Heavy,-Zies-My-Non-Gendered-Sibling-Why-Gender-Neutral-Pronouns-Dont-Work-for-Me.html.

———. 2010. "Transgendering the Academy: Transforming the Relationship between Theory and Praxis." Keynote speech at Expanding the Circle: Creating an Inclusive Environment in Higher Education for LGBTQ Students and Studies, San Francisco, February 28.

———. 2011. "GLAAD Is Wrong on 'Transgender' vs. 'Transgendered.'" Accessed March 19, 2015. http://www.paulinepark.com/2011/03/glaad-is-wrong-on-transgender-vs-transgendered.

———. 2013. "Transgendering the Academy: Transgender Inclusion at a Women's College." Accessed March 19, 2015. http://www.paulinepark.com/2013/04/transgendering-the-academy-transgender-inclusion-at-a-womens-college-mills-college-4-1-13.

Ray, Nicholas. 2006. *Lesbian, Gay, Bisexual, and Transgender Youth: An Epidemic of Homelessness*. New York: National Gay and Lesbian Task Force Policy Institute and National Coalition for the Homeless.

Seedman, Alexander. 2013. "NYU Launches Gender Neutral Bathroom Awareness Campaign." *NYU Local*, April 19. Accessed March 19, 2015. http://nyulocal.com/on-campus/2013/04/19/nyu-launches-gender-neutral-bathroom-awareness-campaign.

Senate of New York University. 2005. "Minutes of a Stated Meeting of the Senate of New York University." Accessed March 19, 2015. http://www.nyu.edu/content/dam/nyu/adminMgmtCouncil/documents/November-3-2005-Senate-Meeting-MINUTES.pdf.

Winter, Claire Ruth. 2010. "Understanding Transgender Diversity: A Sensible Explanation of Sexual and Gender Identities." Charleston, SC: CreateSpace Independent Publishing Platform.

# PART II TRANS IMAGINARIES

# 3 · "I'LL CALL HIM MAHOOD INSTEAD, I PREFER THAT, I'M QUEER"

## Samuel Beckett's Spatial Aesthetic of Name Change

LUCAS CRAWFORD

"And when a name comes, it immediately says more than the name: the other of the name and quite simply the other, whose irruption the name announces."   —Jacques Derrida, *On the Name*

The modernist writer Samuel Beckett has never been discussed in relation to transgender experience, even though his notoriously cryptic text *The Unnamable*—by performing an ambiguous series of name changes—lands so closely to a ubiquitous event of contemporary transgender life. This text, the third portion of what is often called Beckett's first trilogy, appeared in English in 1958. It is a monologue of sorts that does not meet any realist expectations of plot, character, or setting; for that reason, it very effectively resists being summarized. In short, the voice of the text continues speaking mercilessly even when it would like to stop. The voice imagines other "character" types through acts of naming and renaming, but it is unclear if these are names he is trying on himself, if he is naming parts of himself, if he is naming some imagined Others, or if he is naming parts of himself as Other. The animating force of the text is the voice's commitment to cast off all markers of human subjectivity, especially a name, a history, and a gender. Yet, the voice's speech becomes a highly ambivalent gesture insofar as talking about these categories necessarily leaves traces of them—reaffirms them—in the very act of trying to leave them behind. The text continues by virtue of this paradox; it is, after all, impossible to become unnamable by naming oneself so. The text ends with pages of disjointed and difficult run-on sentences, finally ending with a statement about the inability of naming to ever end: "You must go on, I can't go on, I'll go on." Although this is a very complex text indeed, for the purposes of this chapter, it is best to imagine *The Unnamable* as a long existential (perhaps tortured) speech about wanting to stop speaking but being unable to do so. Although the sense of exhaustion and continuation may well resonate with transgender readers, what could possibly be made of this odd voice's penchant for renaming? In response to what I have perceived as a transgender-focused imperative to name, I suggest here that *The Unnamable* shows not only profound understanding of the ambiguous quality of name change but also that Beckett regards un-naming or renaming as queerly spatial acts. Specifically, I argue that Beckett represents name change as a spatial act that necessitates losing one's "ground" in discourse—or, in other words, losing the stable self from which one is assumed to speak.

## WHY BECKETT? WHY NAMES?

It may well seem surprising that a non-trans writer such as Beckett would be granted any ground in this discourse. Yet, in one of only several attempts to theorize Beckett's queerness, it becomes clear that Beckett was a haunting presence at one of the earliest moments of queer theory—a moment that had everything to do with name change. That is, at his inaugural lecture at the Collège de France in 1970, queer thinker Michel Foucault began by wishing it were possible for him to disown the authorial voice of his own discourse, as if the very name Foucault were posing a difficulty to the task at hand. It is fitting, then, that Foucault expressed this desire by beginning his famous lecture series with an extensive citation of *The Unnamable*, since this text underlines the aporia (or puzzling impasse) between the necessity of speaking of (and as) one's self and the very impossibility of speaking from such a settled location of self. Here is Foucault's opening gambit from that day:

> I wish I could have slipped surreptitiously into this discourse which I must present today, and into the ones I shall have to give here, perhaps for many years to come. I should have preferred to be enveloped by speech. . . . I should have preferred to become aware that a nameless voice was already speaking long before me, so that I should only have needed to join in, to continue the sentence it (*lui*) had started and lodge myself . . . in its interstices. . . . I should have liked there to be a voice behind me which had begun to speak a very long time before, doubling in advance everything I was going to say, a voice which would say, "You must go on, I can't go on, you must go on, I'll go on, you must say words, as long as there

are any, until they find me, strange pain, strange sin, you must go on, perhaps it's done already, perhaps they have said me already, perhaps they have carried me to the threshold of my story, before the door that opens on my story, that would surprise me, if it opened." (qtd. in Mowitt 1996, 139)

As we see above, Beckett's skewing of the norms of naming has already—if fleetingly—been put to use for queer purposes; Foucault hangs Beckett's work (but not Beckett's name) like a banner over his entire lecture series. In his reading of Foucault's citation of Beckett, John Mowitt suggests that Foucault's wish to "lodge" in the voices of others is inherently queer, owing to its "interpenetration of voices" (Mowitt 1996, 144). Foucault, he suggests, is "being addressed from behind by a voice without a name" (139), a spatial figure he reads as an act of anal sex translated into authorial voice and narrative. Mowitt decodes a number of supposedly queer images and references elsewhere in *The Unnamable*: for instance, the name Basil—"clearly a[n Oscar] Wilde allusion"—and the unnamable's spatial descriptions of what it means to be spoken by discourse: a voice "issues forth from me, came back to me, entered back into me" (Mowitt 1996, 144–145). Foucault's desire to deemphasize his own name, identity, and authorial voice is, for Mowitt, tantamount to anonymous queer sex. If these narrative postures are indeed akin to sexual positions as Mowitt has it, then what kind of act is the event of name change? As a formal version of the un-naming that Foucault effects above, what kind of spatial and sexual act is the insertion of a new name into one's own voice? Is name change, following Mowitt's allegorical reading, an auto-erotic act of fucking oneself—of triumphantly delivering a new voice from within oneself?

This may appear to be the case for transgender people, for whom name change is often considered the "threshold," signifier, or decisive event of one's trans narrative. No other moment, it seems, could be more indicative of one's agency and sovereignty (or contained self-ownership) than of rewriting the beginning (archive or *arkhē*) of one's entrance into language. This is often how trans names are received by allies in queer and trans communities: in ways that emphatically attribute to the trans person the power of self-determination and authority. The main reason this attribution of agency has taken shape is, I suggest, the serious difficulty trans people face with regards to our new names in social worlds beyond (and within) trans and queer spheres. And, this is a good reason. What we already understand as bad behavior in response to trans name change may be summarized by a story relayed by Kate Bornstein: at the DMV, Bornstein struggled to be taken seriously as she tried to procure a new driver's license. The officer flirted and asked if Bornstein had been recently married or recently divorced; Bornstein stood under surveillance, as two officers were "looking at me, then the paper, then me, then the paper" (Bornstein 1995, 29) trying to figure her out. This model of response—one based on confusion, disbelief, lack of imagination, and a stubborn attachment to normalcy—does not position the trans person as the sovereign author of their new name and narrative. These are obviously problematic responses, ones that cause inconvenience (at best), shame, anger, and other pains in the lives of trans people. However, is it possible that in our fight against these denials of trans agency—in our assertion of trans autonomy—we have over-invested in the presumed primacy and naturalness of names? Have we taken for granted that we know precisely how names work, and why?

In my experience of name change, the most flummoxing (though well intentioned) responses came from within trans and queer scenes rather than from without. I felt from others an overwhelming (and sometimes stifling) desire to respect my new name by attributing various normative narratives to me. Some supportive people sought to continually affirm (what they perceived to be) my true and underlying gender, as though the name had "solved" the mystery of my ambiguous gender and had thereby granted a new and straightforward interpretive code through which to understand me. I had instead thought of my name change, first, as what Jacques Derrida might call "a sweet rage against language" (Derrida 1995, 59) and second, as a vehement disarticulation of my name from any coherent or unchanging category of self; yet, I found myself called to answer to much more than a new name. I grew increasingly uncomfortable with the sense that answering to Lucas also meant answering to interpellations to theories of subjectivity and gender with which I strongly disagreed. To this day, my name change—unaccompanied by what we tend to define as the official body modifications of transgender—seems to encourage acquaintances and strangers alike to force a strict and constraining story of gender conformity onto me. Finding Beckett's text was, for me, a way of finding someone else who thought that names could do the opposite; they could help us cast off normative expectations, including expectations of having a coherent self and story, which are expectations I sometimes sense very strongly within queer and trans scenes and conversations.

It is useful to note that some critics have construed Beckett's practices of naming in precisely the opposite way. For instance, Rubin Rabinowitz, in *Women in Beckett*, suggests that Beckett "often changes the names of the characters . . . to hint that they are not people in the outer world but surrogates of an underlying persona" (1990, 112). In the case of *The Unnamable*, it is in fact the very lack of any underlying persona that the voice is at pains to point out: as the voice says, referring to both himself and his narrative, "the subject doesn't matter, there is none" (qtd. in Rabinowitz 1990, 112.). While Beckett does not suggest that treating names as merely "real" is somehow regressive or normative, he does show us that the naturalization and sanctification of new names demands a convergence of rhetorical and affective norms of property and propriety. In stark contrast to the agency with which we might associate new trans names, Beckett muddies the sovereignty of the renaming subject by figuring self-definition as a chorus act: "the self-accompaniment of a tongue that is not mine" (Beckett 1997, 348). As such, renaming ourselves inevitably entails the Other—as corroborator of the name and, with all positive and negative connotations, as a voice that we sometimes hear or speak as our own. Renaming is, in Derrida's terms, both a repetition and a reminder of the unavoidable absence at the heart of the name and also a break from the necessary repetition of the name, which Derrida characterizes as traumatic experience: "renaming (*renomment?*) [as] repeated severance from the originary severance" (Derrida 1995, 12).

In this chapter, therefore, I depart from Mowitt's allegorical queer interpretation (in which the "pen" in Beckett's hands becomes "penis" when emerging from Foucault's mouth) and linger on the spatial economy that generates the possibility of namelessness in Beckett's text. In so doing, I show that transgender, at least as much as queerness, has a place in studies of Beckett. Likewise, Beckett also helps us see how transgender acts such as renaming can exemplify, anticipate, and perhaps exceed queer theories of language.

## IMPROPER NAMES

First, I analyze the tenuous "ground" of the human subject in the text in order to suggest that losing one's ground in discourse (rather than protecting it) is the spatial metaphor (or "architectonic") of name change that may best capture a transing politics of language. As Derrida makes clear throughout his oeuvre, proper names are underpinned by implicit concepts of both property and propriety, inasmuch as names gather together what "belongs" to one. "Title," it is no coincidence, refers both to names and to documents that prove ownership or one's "entitlement" (all implications intended). Following Derrida's assertion that proper names, property, and propriety—each a derivative of the Latin *proprius*, which means "own" in the adjective sense—are mutually implicated, Mark Wigley suggests in *The Architecture of Deconstruction* that giving a name to something is inherently both a spatial act and a repressive one: "To name something is always to locate it within a space. The sense of the proper name is that of the proper place. Names are always place names. By designating something as 'art' or 'law,' for example, is already to resist its subversive qualities and to make a place for it in a conceptual scheme, marking its site, delimiting its domain" (Wigley 1995, 155). Proper names, in this sense, both "give place" to something within a system and also, in assigning such a conceptual place, inaugurate a sense of what is proper and improper to the phenomenon at hand. Changing a proper name, then, could entail a transformation of propriety and our sense that to be human is to treat one's self as sovereign property. It is my contention, however, that the rupture of a new name is too often neutralized because, in the manner that Jacques Lacan describes, the name is treated as a social pact upon which we have all agreed in advance. As Judith Butler puts it, we "simultaneously" agree to recognize the same object (man, woman, trans-woman, trans-man, etc.) under one sign. This social pact, she suggests, "overrides the tenuousness of imaginary identification and confers on [the sign] a social durability and legitimacy" (Butler 1993, 152) that a transing subject may or may well not desire.[1] There is much at stake in simply and silently accepting a new name through the etiquette and assumption of this kind of "social pact." Not only do such norms of naming, including when they are taken up by queer and trans scenes, sometimes work against the desires of some trans people, but the desire to abject the very newness or novelty of a name illustrates the way in which we tend to attribute worth to things that are—or are able to feign—fixity, longevity, and tradition. To locate the "realness" of names in an illusion of origin or stability would be to eschew any sense of changeability, the very principle against which gender norms strive.

Beckett's text works against this devaluation of novelty by having its narrative voice undergo many name changes. Indeed, readers follow the unnamable through a series of insufficient names: Basil, Mahood, Jones, and Worm. The levity and speed with which the unnamable changes names—"Decidedly Basil is becoming important, I'll call him Mahood instead, I prefer that, I'm queer" (Beckett 1997, 351)—offers a stark alternative to transgender conventions of name change: he changes names without the validating narratives of memory, in other words, without an archive. As Jonathan Boulter suggests, the unnamable is without *arkhē*, without beginning.[2] Many critics, including Boulter, interpret the unnamable's name changes as "desperate attempts to assert a kind of agency" (Boulter 2008, 128). I would like to suggest that, in fact, the opposite may be true. The unnamable may change names precisely to escape the imperative to accept (and equate himself with) a past and a subjectivity. Throughout the text, voices from above try to force a past onto him in order to pull him up into their world of nameable and proper humanity, but he ultimately does not capitulate. Such a resistant practice of name change certainly desanctifies the process.

## THE UNNAMABLE'S NAMES

This desanctification of the event of name change reflects Beckett's ambivalence with regards to agency and the subject. As Asja Szafraniec puts it in *Beckett, Derrida, and the Event of Literature*, the two main names (Worm and Mahood) between which the narrative voice shifts are "meaningful for Beckett's project of questioning the conditions of the possibility of the subject" (Szafraniec

2007, 128). On this point, Szafraniec suggests, the choice of the particular name Mahood is telling, as it bears resemblance both to "minehood"—a sense of property, sovereignty, self-ownership—and, of course, "manhood." Yet, the missing "n" leaves these two intimately related properties compromised. Since the ultimate goal for the voice of *The Unnamable* is to be able to stop speaking, Szafraniec suggests that self-naming is the unachievable act that would "cure" this compromise and that would attain this pure silence for the voice: "To silence the clamor of voices, the 'I' should become the owner of those voices, to thereby saturate the flow of words with its (the 'I''s) own intentions. Should the "I" identify itself, reject that which is its other, and therewith take full possession of the speaking voice—should it say "I"—it would be free to go silent" (Szafraniec 2007, 124).

Becoming the "owner" of the voice would entail all three of Derrida's interpretations of *proprius*: a proper name, a location for oneself within discourse (a property, a "ground"), and the propriety of speaking like a subject, acting like a subject, and claiming a past like a subject. (Here we hear *proprius*'s overarching meaning of "own," in the sense of having something of one's own. We may ask, does owning entail an identifiable owner?) Refusing all three of these versions of ownership does indeed leave the Beckettian voice, as Boulter puts it, "homeless" (2008, 128), as his "inability to name himself, that is, his inability to identify his language as his own" leaves him "in a space where it is impossible to locate oneself within discourse" (2008, 124). (Boulter's own careful diction here shows us exactly how difficult it is to speak of the non-subjective voice of this text: he locates the voice in "a space" in the very gesture of suggesting that he has no proper place.) It is therefore commonplace among innovative Beckett critics to interpret the voice of this text as fulsomely seeking to "own" these voices—Szafraniec also reads the names as the voice's "vain attempts to establish its own identity" (2007, 128). We can instead read the voice as struggling to resist the "ownership" of a name, to resist the benefits of peace, ease, and approval that would accompany modes of language and feeling. Accepting a new nameable life and subjectivity "up there in their world" (Beckett 1997, 339), in the light, is a resolution that would end the pain of the unnamable's compelled speech, yet he ultimately resists.

Indeed, the condition of feeling in excess—or adrift—of one's name is in fact the definitive spatial quest of Beckett's text. As Szafraniec points out, the fact that "Where now?" is the first sentence of *The Unnamable* suggests that spatial dislocation is the meager "plot" that the reader can expect in the text and is therefore constitutive of the felt experience of becoming unnamable. For this reason, Szafraniec interprets the name Worm "as a calque, a loan translation from the Latin *ubi sum* [where/am], since it sounds like the 'where'm' in [the later line of] 'where'm I?'" (2007, 129). As the voice recounts, "Where am I? That's my first question, after an age of listening." In contrast to the inquisitive "Where am I?" of Worm, the name Mahood in the text "is the embodiment of the gesture of substantialization that produces the subject, subject as substance, 'my selfhood' or 'minehood'" (Szafraniec 2007, 128–129). In Szafraniec's reading, then, the difference of the names is a spatial one: Worm (where'm) doesn't know where he is while Mahood (minehood) partakes of the "ownership" of self that we associate with safety and security. The unnamable's oscillation between the two names therefore implies a correlative oscillation between the imperative to own and the impossibility of even knowing where one "is" in discourse.

But what does Worm's lack of discursive location imply about names and space in general? Butler and architectural theorist Sanford Kwinter both question the way in which the rhetoric of "owning a place" in discourse relies upon a certain spatialization of the human subject. Together they remind us that the spatial metaphor of a "ground" (for time and for sex) that we use to anchor subjectivity is "indeed a gendered corporealization of time" (Butler 1990, 141). As Kwinter writes, "matter, form, and subjects ('doers') come only later, reintroduced at a second order level, not as ground but as produced effect" (Kwinter 2001, 40). The unnamable is a fragile subject who lives with this very knowledge: he exists in a "world of pure discourse without ground, without *arkhē*" (Boulter 2001, 104). Beckett does not describe this discursive ground as in any way metaphysical or otherwise immaterial. Rather, the groundlessness of the self is equated specifically with actual shifting territory, as though the firmness of one's environment is a required condition for the firmness of one's self. The voice of the text explicitly questions the makeup of the material beneath him. As he reports, "I may add that my seat would appear to be somewhat elevated, in relation to the surrounding ground, if ground is what it is. Perhaps it is water or some other liquid" (Beckett 1997, 338). If, as Szafraniec argues, the question of "Where'm I?" is the felt condition of namelessness, then these two kinds of domestication—having a proper ground for the self (in discourse) and the body (in space)—are not just related but are in fact mutually implicated.

## WHAT'S GROUND GOT TO DO WITH IT?

Later in the text, the voice suggests that the underpinning of this tenuous self is comprised of a stickier situation than merely "water or some other liquid." In this excerpt, the voice attributes Worm's inability to enter the enlightened human world (or his capability to resist it) to the specific makeup of his groundless turf:

> Worm should have fled, but where, how, he's riveted, Worm should have dragged himself away, no matter where, towards them, towards the azure, but how could he, he can't stir, it needn't be bonds, there are no bonds here, it's as if he were

rooted, that's bonds if you like, the earth would have to quake, it isn't earth, one doesn't know what it is, it's like sargasso, no, it's like molasses, no, no matter, an eruption is what's needed, to spew him into the light . . . it's like slime, paradise, it would be paradise, but for this noise, it's life trying to get in, no trying to get him out, or little bubbles bursting all around, no, there's no air here, air is to make you choke. (Becket 1997, 417)

Here, readers learn that Worm's compromised ground is like sargasso (masses of brown algae that float atop some ocean waters), molasses, or slime. In the first instance, Worm's milieu is described as a marine environment. Algae is a suitable metaphor for the consistency of names without grounds: algae is, of course, underpinned only by the diverse and dangerous body of the ocean itself. Worm's sargasso ground is an illusory and slippery one that rises to the top only because of its lightness (its ability to float) rather than because of the heaviness with which we associate ground and substantiality. In the case of molasses and slime, Beckett introduces both the slowness and the malleability of this sticky ground. This surface is quaggy and sticky rather than solid. It is not easy to move on a ground that moves along with you or holds you back: Worm is "rooted," but not with "bonds" like gravity—by the gummy quality of the ground itself. This space is not meant to describe a prehuman condition from which the voice will eventually emerge according to plan; only an eruption, a sudden paradigm shift rather than a natural progression of self-knowledge or enlightenment, would propel him into the "light" of the world above.

What, then, is the subject to do who lives in a world with such a slippery ground for one's name and one's discourse? Beckett's text presents a series of responses to this question that, while certainly nonprescriptive, approach the tone of aphorism. In what might be regarded as a thesis statement for Beckett's theorization of naming, the voice of the text suggests that "the essential is never to arrive anywhere, never to be anywhere, neither where Mahood is, nor where Worm is, nor where I am, it little matters thanks to what dispensation. The essential is to go on squirming forever at the end of the line." In this spatial rendering of name change, the key direction is to not be where one's name is located, which entails never "arriv[ing] anywhere," a proposition that might understandably throw the pilots of even the queerest trajectories for a loop (Beckett 1997, 386). As Boulter suggests, the elimination of telos (end) from the equation of name change suggests that renaming is not only an endless act but also one that entails distance. Indeed, it is from "this condition of distance," this distance "from desire, power, and language" that the voice is compelled to speak (Boulter 2008, 128). But how might distance from one's own name be accomplished? For the voice, "squirming forever at the end of the line" is both his suggestion and also an apt description for his own actions throughout the text.

Even at the end of his (quasi-)life, the text's voice continues to "squirm" rather than finally ascend to self "ownership" in language, name, and body.

Beckett makes a deceptively simple point: we can never reach the location of our names. Our bodies cannot ever be, in the end, a word. The translation of body to language is never simple, complete, or without remainder. Names, in this sense, are not trajectories or destinations but are, instead, decoys that disrupt our linear path to self "ownership" or discovery. As the text continues a page later, "perhaps it's by trying to be Worm that I'll finally succeed in being Mahood, I hadn't thought of that" (Beckett 1997, 387). For Beckett, then, names—in effecting more than what they intend or appear to name—exceed themselves, in the sense that their performativity moves the object (intended to be merely labeled) into new territory.

This complex image, "squirming forever at the end of the line," may resonate for some activists and academics with the recent turn to the politics of refusal. One way to define this politics is as an opposite to a politics of recognition; while the latter would guide us to seek access to the mainstream (be that of a nation-state, or an institution such as marriage, etc.), the former refuses precisely that.[3] The resemblance of *The Unnamable* to this increasingly articulated politics of refusal leaves a few questions for those seeking clear bridges between Beckett's work and activist praxis. If the image of squirming insinuates physical discomfort, neither moving forward nor turning away, and moving almost imperceptibly in place, then what does it mean to "squirm" in the face of seemingly unconquerable forces? How will we respond to others and to political situations if we do so in the manner of "squirming"? Closer to the matter at hand: we tend to think of a name as that which ought to make us feel fully comfortable and like ourselves. What are the possibilities of a name that makes us or others squirm? How is a name a method of physically affecting others?

## WHAT'S IN A NAME?

The result of Beckett's suggestion that one name can help you better become a different name problematizes how we tend to think about how language refers to things. In other words, the performativity of names in the text causes a crisis in the structure of referentiality. Butler and Derrida have each addressed this crisis in turn, and I turn briefly to their work in order to show the stakes of Beckett's extension of this crisis of referentiality to new names in particular.

Derrida suggests in *Limited Inc.* that the intended authority of names is self-destructing. As he puts it, "the signature is imitable in its essence. And always has been. In French one would say that *elle s'imite*, a syntactical equivocation that seems to me difficult to reproduce: it can *be* imitated, and it imitates *itself*"

(Derrida 1988, 34). In other words, although names are meant to be unique and distinguishing, it is their very iterability—and therefore vulnerability to counterfeit—that gives them their meaning. Butler elaborates on this point in *Bodies That Matter*, where she argues (through her refutation of Slavoj Žižek's sense that names effect permanence) that "identity is secured precisely in and through the transfer of the name, the name as a site of transfer or substitution, the name, then, as precisely what is always impermanent, different from itself, more than itself, the non-self-identical" (Butler 1993, 153).[4] Butler also points out that the changeability of women's names is precisely what secures the "illusory permanence" (Butler 1993, 153) of patrilineal structure, which requires women to bear the new name that operates as a sign or signature for the transfer of (female) property. That women's names are required as prostheses for a transfer between men suggests that names attempt to "seal a deal" that is otherwise lacking a performative. As Derrida suggests in his analysis of Claude Lévi-Strauss, proper names are in fact impossible: "nonprohibition, the consciousness or exhibition of the proper name, only makes up for or uncovers an essential and irremediable impropriety. When within consciousness, the name is called proper, it is already classified and is obliterated in being named. It is already no more than a so-called proper name" (Derrida 1997, 109). For Derrida, then, two things are true. First, the relentless saying and confirming of a proper name is a means by which one may simultaneously practice and hide a name's performativity. Second, the name of "proper name" itself changes the currency of the name; when its designation as proper is so emphasized, the propriety of the name suffers even more: "it is already no more than a *so-called* proper name" (Derrida 1997, 109, emphasis added).

As the voice of Beckett's text suggests, a name (as well as a pronoun) is a "matter of habit" (Beckett 1997, 391), a repeatable linguistic token that becomes meaningful and adheres to a subject only through time, repetition, and habit—a phenomenon that Beckett, in his book *Proust*, defines as the polar opposite of art. In *The Unnamable*, the voice discloses the open secret of renaming, and in so naming the process of naming, turns his name(s) into, in Derrida's words, "no more than a so-called proper name." Below, following a tale about Mahood's refusal to learn that the human is a higher mammal, the voice flaunts the impropriety of renaming: "but it's time I gave this solitary a name, nothing doing without proper names. I therefore baptize him Worm. It was high time. Worm. I don't like it, but I haven't much choice. It will be my name too, when the time comes, when I needn't be called Mahood any more, if that happy time ever comes" (Beckett 1997, 385). The unnamable does precisely what Derrida suggests; it brings forth the impropriety of naming. By naming the proper name as a name, readers are (despite the voice calling Worm a "solitary") "restored to the obliteration and the non-self-sameness [*non-propriété*] at the origin" (Derrida 1997, 109). The mock solemnity ("baptize") and sarcasm ("nothing doing") with which this name change is announced only sharpen the voice's critique as it calls out the conventions of naming. That this new name is specifically a nonhuman one indicates, in Boulter's reading, that the non-self-sameness of *The Unnamable* is indeed a post-human existence (Boulter 2008, 124). Quite contrary to common conceptions of trans naming, Worm is configured here not only as a name he doesn't like but as one over which he has limited choice, even though "he" appears to have "chosen" it. In a culture where one cannot choose not to have a self, the "choice" of a new name for the self is not exactly choice. Renaming in Beckett's text, therefore, is anything but a moment of the sovereign agency of the human; it is, rather, an occasion that draws the voice into conversation with his other names, even an occasion on which the voice assesses his own process— his own failure—to stop narrating himself into existence.

Instead of speaking names as though they are successful at describing what we already are, then, we might theorize renaming, as Derrida does, as a potential "expansion of self" made possible precisely through "the ability to [like the unnamable] disappear in your name" rather than "return [the name] to itself" (Derrida 1995, 13) and to its own constructed stability. The "your" in Derrida's account seems to denote a parent (he begins, "that which bears, has borne, will bear your name seems sufficiently free, powerful, creative, and autonomous to live alone and radically to do without you and your name" [Derrida 1995, 13]), but his sense of disappearing "in" a name suggests that renaming can indeed become a mode of imperceptibility in which one has the transient and compromised freedom to change. Elsewhere in his text, however, Derrida claims that a name is too often a "post-scriptum" that "comes after the event" (Derrida 1995, 60) of change. Indeed, this is precisely how new trans names are often interpreted: as a definitive sign that something has already changed in the bearer's self-perception and/or body.

Again, Beckett flips this temporality inside-out: if by trying to be one name, one becomes another name entirely, then an act of naming is itself an event that announces the irruption of novelty and unprecedented change. Naming becomes "a gesture of renunciation" (Szafraniec 2007, 94) rather than a tool of recognition; a performative rather than an expressive statement; a generator of, rather than a postscript to, material change; and a means to "expose the name as a crisis in referentiality" (Butler 1993, 139). Naming, in the very simplest terms, reveals how incomplete and slippery is the attachment of words to bodies.

## THE NEGATIVITY QUESTION

Even though renaming hereby has many seemingly negative connotations (exposing, evacuating, critiquing, renouncing), name changes also comprise events in their own right by generating change. The misunderstanding of Beckett's work as inherently and absolutely negative and unprincipled (that is, as nihilistic) is premised on the implicit belief that critique and rupture do not generate anything novel.[5] For Beckett and Derrida alike, however, it is a certain negative ontology of the self that allows for and demands change. (A negative ontology of the self is simply the process of defining oneself by what one is not—hence the "negative.") Derrida's collection *On the Name* takes negative theology as one of its main concerns. It is "impossible," he suggests there, "to give a univocal sense to the 'I'" (1995, 13). This is too true in *The Unnamable*, in which "I" marks quite explicitly both its own fictionality and its transferability among names. Even the text's first page marks out this narrative pattern: "I, say I, unbelieving" (Beckett 1997, 331). Here, the speaker addresses himself as "I," telling "I" to "say I," a formulation that shows his knack for acknowledging the fictionality of both his own rhetoric and his own self-presence. Derrida formulates this sense of multiplicity clearly: "sorry, but more than one, it is always necessary to be more than one in order to speak, several voices are necessary for that . . . this voice multiplies itself, dividing within itself: it says one thing and its contrary" (1995, 35). Derrida's description of contradiction and multiplicity is explicitly true for the voice of *The Unnamable*, who begins by asking: "how proceed? By aporia pure and simple? Or by affirmations and negations invalidated as uttered, or sooner or later?" (Beckett 1997, 331). In a discursive world in which the voice of the text eventually disowns all statements he makes about himself, the reader's sense of him as a character is indeed comprised of a series of erasures and negations only. This negative mode of self-definition is explicitly labeled by the voice as a tool of the voices above in the social world. Here is another excerpt in which this negative ontology of the first-person perspective is presented: "First I'll say what I'm not, that's how they taught me to proceed, then what I am, it's already under way, I have only to resume at the point where I let myself be cowed. I am neither, I needn't say, Murphy, nor Watt, nor Mercier, nor—no, I can't even bring myself to name them, nor any of the others whose very names I forget, who told me I was they, who I must have tried to be, under duress, or through fear, or to avoid acknowledging me, not the slightest connection" (Beckett 1997, 371). To circle back, we see most clearly here that the unnamable is defined through negation, or more precisely through "owning" nothing of his own save for his displaced names—emptied husks that name only the absence of ground. This sounds "negative," but it is only by virtue of this absence that multiple names can emerge and that the voice can change. Later in the text, the voice claims that this absence is his only constitutive feature: "I'm all these words, all these strangers, this dust of words, with *no ground* for their settling, no sky for their dispersing, coming together to say, fleeing one another to say, that I am they, all of them" (Becket 1997, 443; emphasis added). This apparent evacuation of names is a gesture toward what Derrida in *Of Grammatology* calls "the irremediable absence of the proper name" (Derrida 1997, 106–107) or, in other words, the recognition that at its origin any name—like any gender—is grounded in a performative speech act that can never attain full presence.

## CONCLUSION: DOING THE IMPOSSIBLE

In this chapter, I offer Beckett's performed literary theory of name change, in which names are described as groundless signs that both (1) function as linguistic prostheses of the always-already fragile subject and (2) prop up the always necessarily incomplete privatization of the subject. This spatial rhetoric derives from Beckett's own emphasis on the slippage between material and linguistic "grounds" and spaces. It is precisely the voice's lack of location in discourse—his lack of narrative "property" and a proper name—that permits his always compromised but absolutely constitutive impropriety. Given that Beckett's oeuvre works quite specifically against the assumptions of literary realism (his work does not desire or feign a direct representation of, or even relationship to, lived reality), the connection between his modernist work and a contemporary praxis of transgender name change is complex.

In my own life, finding kindred thinkers such as Beckett has led me to see that there are larger matters at stake in my desire to find a little space for impropriety with regards to my own name. Prescribing a new "proper" way to use names would be antithetical to this desire, and to Becket's work, but perhaps it's possible to suggest that we proceed with the knowledge that names are affective, spatial, and intimately reflective and generative of ideas about ownership, land, and language. Indeed, I suspect that few transgender people wish to call themselves "Worm" or actually try to live without a name; as texts of experimentation and limit cases, Beckett's works do not imply that we ought to. They ask us to do something harder, which is to continually, and with necessary failure and tenuousness, keep going and keep renaming and reforming what threatens to settle.

Although Beckett's ideas have been very empowering for me (inasmuch as we can and must regard the abilities to dissent and to create as important ones), it is necessary to end by addressing again the seeming negativity or critical focus of this argument. Indeed, does this "negative ownership" of discursive ground imply anything affirmative? For Derrida, the language of negative ontology is affirmative of something much more radical than finally finding one's "real" identity, that is, the very ethical imperative to do impossible things. Here, Derrida insists that the language of impossibility can, in fact, be deeply ethical and affirmative:

> And the language of ab-negation or of renunciation is not negative: not only because it does not state in the mode of descriptive predication and of the indicative proposition simply affected with a negation . . . but because it denounces as much as it renounces; and it denounces, enjoining; it prescribes overflowing this insufficiency; it mandates, it necessitates doing the impossible, necessitates place, again. I shall say in French, *il y a lieu de* (which means *il faut*, "it is necessary," "there is ground for") rendering oneself there where it is impossible to go. Over there, toward the name, toward the beyond of the name in the name. . . . Going where it is possible to go would not be a displacement or a decision, it would be the irresponsible unfolding of a program. The sole decision possible passes through the madness of the undecidable and the impossible: to go where . . . it is impossible to go. (Derrida 1995, 59)

There are three points that require emphasis in this excerpt. First, Derrida allows us to see that seemingly negative language and denunciation of existent paths or programs is precisely the kind of thinking that mandates novelty—that leads to the dissatisfaction that calls for continual transformation and change. Second, we see that the ethical imperative—"il faut"—that results from this language of mutual denunciation and ethics is once again an explicitly spatial imperative. In effect, Derrida suggests that the formulation of "there is ground for" is only ethical inasmuch as it leads us into impossible, groundless, territory. Third, the impossibility that Derrida champions here is precisely how, in "On a Certain Possible Impossibility of Saying the Event," he (negatively) defines "the event," a model of action that, in closing, I suggest could characterize future name changes and scholarly considerations of name changes. Here, Derrida suggests that an "event" is defined precisely by its impossibility: "this impossibility is not simply negative. This means that the impossible must be done. The event, if there is one, consists in doing the impossible. But when someone does the impossible, if someone does the impossible, no one, above all the doer of the deed, is in a position to adjust a self-assured, theoretical statement to the event and say 'this happened.' . . . A decision should tear—that's what the word decision means; it should disrupt the fabric of the possible" (Derrida 2007, 231, 237). If Derrida defines the event as a singular emergence that cannot be owned or perhaps even effected by any one subject, then the event of name change is not (at least not exclusively) about agency and self-assertion. Rather, it may consist in the necessary impossibility of tearing through one's own self-ownership. The "impossible" for Beckett is, as the title of the text suggests, to become unnamable (precisely through a proliferation of names)—to become something other than one's name, to have one's name move one beyond oneself. More precisely, undergoing name change in the mode of "the event" requires that one's name effect something that was not previously possible to do or to think and that is not possible to plan *per se*; it is, in short, a theory of a "new name" actually doing something new.

In this reading, the seemingly negative aporia and denunciations of *The Unnamable* remind us of something radically affirmative: names, including new names, could instead move (us) toward the Other in unexpected ways, could dislocate us from that which we feel is our "ground" and our affective "property" and propriety, and could motivate us to take changing names as a reminder that we could—rather than unfold identities and proprieties that are already possible—pursue the impossible instead. Perhaps this is what Foucault imagined when introducing his lecture series by placing his own (quasi-celebrity) name under erasure. Foucault's use of Beckett's *The Unnamable* was a desire to renounce vocal agency and the tight grips of the conceptions of authorship and subjectivity, something that Foucault's own work acknowledged as both impossible and necessary. For Mowitt this is a quintessentially queer moment. However, given that the story hinges on a series of name changes, it may be more accurate to view Foucault's introduction as a crucial moment at which transgender desire could be heard speaking through—speaking in the name of—queer academic history.

## NOTES

An extended version of this chapter appears in my book *Transgender Architectonics: The Shape of Change in Modernist Space.*

Thank you to the editors and reviewers of this collection for their invaluable comments and support.

1. For more on Butler's critique of Lacan, see *Bodies That Matter: On the Discursive Limits of "Sex,"* especially the fifth essay, "'Dangerous Crossing': Willa Cather's Masculine Names." Here, Butler critiques "Lacan's notion that the name confers legitimacy and duration on the ego" (Butler 1993, 209). Against his sense that names are "nominal zones of phallic control" (153) always based on the Law (and name) of the Father, Butler suggests instead that, for women, propriety is all about having a *changeable* name. As she puts it, "the durability of the subject named is not, then, a function of the proper name, but a function of a patronym, the abbreviated instance of a hierarchical kinship regime" (154).

2. Boulter follows Edward Said in his description of beginning (which he equates with ground and *arkhē*): "to begin . . . is to circumscribe a space. . . . Articulating or inscribing a beginning is thus an act of profound epistemologico-hermeneutic consequences: it is the logic of beginning as ground (*arkhē*) that presupposes the movement toward end (*telos*). But

the unnamable's narrative calls on a kind of thinking about the logic of beginning that he will acknowledge to be defunct" (Boulter 2001, 99–100).

3. Critical theorists of race have, arguably, led this turn to the politics of refusal. Such work ranges from Jasbir Puar's "Celebrating Refusal," an online analysis of Judith Butler's refusal of Berlin Pride's Zivilcourage Award in favor of highlighting the work of queer of color groups who have protested Israeli apartheid and who educated Butler on the issues. Another example can be found in Audra Simpson's 2014 *Mohawk Interruptus: Political Life across the Borders of Settler States*, in which the author describes the quality and outcomes of the Kahnawà:ke Mohawks' refusals of Canadian and American citizenship.

4. Žižek, Butler suggests, implies that names have the "power to confer durability" (Butler 1993, 153) even though they have no content. That is, for Žižek, names are referential but not descriptive. For more, see again "'Dangerous Crossing': Willa Cather's Masculine Names" in *Bodies That Matter*.

5. For a tour de force of the currency of nihilism in Beckett's work and Beckett criticism, see Shane Weller's monograph, *A Taste for the Negative: Beckett and Nihilism*.

## REFERENCES

Beckett, Samuel. 1997. *Molloy, Malone Dies*, and *The Unnamable*. Toronto: Alfred A. Knopf.
Bornstein, Kate. 1995. *Gender Outlaw: On Men, Women, and the Rest of Us*. New York: Vintage Books.
Boulter, Jonathan. 2001. *Interpreting Narrative in the Novels of Samuel Beckett*. Gainesville: University Press of Florida.
———. 2008. *Beckett: A Guide for the Perplexed*. New York: Continuum.
Butler, Judith. 1990. *Gender Trouble: Feminism and the Subversion of Identity*. New York: Routledge.
———. 1993. *Bodies That Matter: On the Discursive Limits of "Sex."* New York: Routledge.
Crawford, Lucas. *Transgender Architectonics: The Shape of Change in Modernist Space*. Surrey, UK and Vermont, USA: Ashgate, 2015.
Derrida, Jacques. 1988. *Limited Inc*. Translated by Samuel Weber and Alan Bass. Evanston, IL: Northwestern University Press.
———. 1995. *On the Name*. Edited by Thomas Dutoit. Translated by David Wood, John P. Leavey Jr., and Ian McLeod. Stanford, CA: Stanford University Press.
———. 1997. *Of Grammatology*. Translated by Gayatri Chakravorty Spivak. Baltimore: Johns Hopkins University Press.
———. 2007. "A Certain Impossible Possibility of Saying the Event." In *The Late Derrida*, edited by W.J.T. Mitchell and Arnold I. Davidson, 223–244. Chicago: University of Chicago Press.
Kwinter, Sanford. 2001. *Architectures of Time: Toward a Theory of the Event in Modernist Culture*. Cambridge, MA: MIT Press.
Mowitt, John. 1996. "Queer Resistance: Michel Foucault and Samuel Beckett's *The Unnamable*." *Symploke* 4.1–2: 135–152.
Puar, Jasbir. 2010. "Celebrating Refusal: The Complexities of Saying No." Blog post. *Bully Bloggers*, June 23. https://bullybloggers.wordpress.com/2010/06/23/celebrating-refusal-the-complexities-of-saying-no.
Rabinowitz, Rubin. 1990. "Stereoscopic or Stereotypic: Characterization in Beckett's Fiction." In *Women in Beckett*, edited by Linda Ben-Zvi, 106–116. Champaign: University of Illinois Press.

Simpson, Audra. 2014. *Mohawk Interruptus: Political Life across the Borders of Settler States.* Durham, NC: Duke University Press.

Szafraniec, Asja. 2007. *Beckett, Derrida, and the Event of Literature.* Stanford, CA: Stanford University Press.

Weller, Shane. 2005. *A Taste for the Negative: Beckett and Nihilism.* London: Legenda.

Wigley, Mark. 1995. *The Architecture of Deconstruction: Derrida's Haunt.* Cambridge, MA: MIT Press.

# 4 · EXCRUCIATING IMPROBABILITY AND THE TRANSGENDER JAMAICAN

KEJA VALENS

Colonialism and its legacies constitute the Caribbean as we know it and continue to set the terms through which the Caribbean subject is understood to exist and to have a race, nationality, gender, and sexuality. Although mestizaje, créolité, hybridity, and other Caribbean literary and critical movements underscore the creative as well as the destructive forces of colonialism, Caribbean literature and theory tend still to imagine the colonial period and its legacy as oppressive, in contrast to a liberated and liberating postcolonial present or future.[1] For those who object to the gender binary that underwrites the heteronormative patriarchy on which colonialism rests, transgender relations and subjects figure a more recent transgressive break with and departure from the oppressive colonial model along with hope for a better and decolonized future. Yet Jamaican author Patricia Powell's novel *The Pagoda* (1998) suggests an account of transgender Caribbean subjects and relations that not only survive colonialism, as if in spite of it, but also enable and are enabled by colonialism. Indeed, I argue that by probing the enduring violence of colonial structures and the insidious totality that renders any claim to a space outside of them impossible, *The Pagoda* offers the recognition—both less and more hopeful—that "transgressions" of the colonial order are always already present in it and thus provide an opening not to a utopian future but to an improbable present.

Set in nineteenth-century Jamaica, *The Pagoda* recounts lives not easily accounted for in histories of the Caribbean. Sociologist Mimi Sheller observes that "one of the greatest silences in Caribbean historiography is the invisibility of queer subjectivities" as a result, in large part, of the ways that "existing approaches to nineteenth-century Caribbean history have largely ignored the methodological problems raised by subaltern studies, postcolonial theory, and, especially, queer theory" (Sheller 2012, 3). To find the stories of how transgender Caribbeans have struggled with, survived, and supported the colonial Caribbean requires creative engagement. As Powell draws her historical fiction from the contradictions and absences of the colonial archive as well as from the logical and fantastic imagining of a Jamaican past from the perspective of the present moment, she engages in the kind of invention that is necessary in order to consider the "real" histories of transgender Caribbean subjects.

Caribbean cultural critic Édouard Glissant's *Poetics of Relation* guides my understanding of Powell's novel as forging and revealing connections between the pain of colonial experience and resistance to it, between resistance to the colonial order and the colonial order itself, among bodies and stories and histories that are not neatly separable into any binary, be it colonizer/colonized, black/white, or male/female. Relation, Glissant notes, comes from "the human spirit's striving for a transversal relationship, without universalist transcendence" (Glissant 1989, 98; translation modified).[2] Transversal relationships as Glissant presents them operate along a lateral principle of organization; they cut across transcendence, heading not up and out but shifting sideways between and across hierarchies. As I understand them, transversal relationships provide an account of relation beyond the binarism of colonial heteronormativity, eschewing the sameness of the latter even as they recognize its power (to divide, for example, whites and blacks, men and women, and then join them under various forms of the dominance of white masculinity). As I will argue, the relations that Powell's *The Pagoda* writes into existence—among a transgender Chinese Jamaican, his octoroon wife, the human trafficker who brought him to Jamaica and arranged his marriage, and the members of the rural Jamaican village in which he lives—are transversal relations. They lie across, mix up, repeatedly redivide, and recombine people and positions.

In Glissant's compellingly un-idealistic vision, the role of the writer involves "reopening the wound [of colonialism] and escaping the numbing power of Sameness" (Glissant 1989, 104). Colonialism—structured by what the feminist philosopher María Lugones calls "heterosexualism and the colonial/modern gender system" (Lugones 2007, 186) and what Sheller describes as "corporeal forms of private and public embodiment that reproduced racial, gender, sexual, and class hierarchies," (Sheller 2012, 9) and which I term the heterocolonial order—is perhaps the constitutive wound of the Caribbean. The heterocolonial order enforces an interlocking series of divisions and connections between civilized and savage, white and black, man and woman, chaste and perverse, normal and abnormal, among other things, which derive from the combination of the norms of heterosexuality and the principles and practices of colonialism and subject the Caribbean to their (often contradictory and destructive) orders even as they create the Caribbean and its subjects as we know them.

If the Caribbean is constituted by multiple wounds and sutures, as St. Lucian Nobel laureate Derek Walcott's powerful image of a vase broken and reassembled illustrates (Walcott 1993, 69), Caribbean nationalisms and identity politics search, either in the past or in the future, for unified, "true" Caribbean identities, scarred but healed. From this perspective Glissant's call to reopen the wound bespeaks the recognition that the concepts of nation, identity, and individual belong themselves to the colonial legacy. To escape these constructs may be as undesirable as it is impossible, yet this recognition allows the composition of a national literature that, as Glissant notes, "serves two functions: the first is that of demythification, of desecration, of intellectual analysis, whose purpose is to dismantle the internal mechanism of a given system, to expose the hidden workings, to demystify. It also has a hallowed purpose in reuniting the community around its myths, its beliefs, its imagination or its ideology" (1989, 99–100). One part of my argument is that the excruciatingly improbable stories of transgender Caribbeans—not as new unified identities for the new Caribbean nationalisms but, as in Powell's work, figures who expose, suffer, and benefit from both the persistence of the heterocolonial order and their persistent transgressions of it—exemplify this national literature whose unworking is, as it were, its work.[3]

Powell belongs to a generation of Caribbean writers who, at the turn of the twenty-first century, produce narratives that witness and mourn the enduring injuries of colonial and patriarchal structures (Francis 2004). Powell's first two novels, *Me Dying Trial* and *A Small Gathering of Bones*, depict late twentieth-century Jamaican state and social structures that perpetuate colonial and Christian ideologies and construct homosexuality as foreign, disowning or destroying local persons and traditions that embrace same sex desires and practices even as those local persons and traditions offer alternative and loving spaces for a variety of sexualities and genders. Powell's third novel, *The Pagoda*, joins a smaller but rapidly growing set of Caribbean literary representations of transgender subjects and relations.[4] While *The Pagoda* is Powell's first historical novel and presents her first transgender character, like her other works it opens the enduring wounds of heterocolonialism in Jamaica and reflects on the ways that order has always been traversed by multiple practices and relations.

Jamaica stands out in the Caribbean, along with Trinidad and Tobago, Barbados, and Guyana, as particularly intolerant of transgressions of heteronormativity.[5] The August 2013 murder of Dwayne Jones, a transgender teenager in Montego Bay, and the discussions that followed it display the persistent and profoundly homophobic and transphobic elements of postcolonial Jamaica.[6] The case underscores the unhopeful part of my claim that "transgressions" of the colonial order are always already present in it, for if Jamaican law and the Dwayne

Jones case exemplify the integration of transgender throughout the Caribbean, it does not look very good for transgender subjects or relations. The more hopeful part builds on the fact that *The Pagoda* does not stop there. It allows us to examine not only how transgender and queer subjects have long been mistreated but also how they have survived and even been integral to colonial, postcolonial, and neocolonial heteropatriarchy.

In what follows I will first briefly outline the story and the setting of *The Pagoda* and consider what it means to call the protagonist, Lowe, transgender. Then I will examine the coercive forces of patriarchy and colonialism on Lowe's identification. Showing how the experience of coerced gender, racial, and sexual identification connects Lowe to those around him, I analyze the relationships that Lowe has with his wife, Miss Sylvie, and Cecil, the captain who brought Lowe to Jamaica, arguing that the heterocolonial order ironically enforces as much as it excludes trans relations. Turning to the cast of background characters in *The Pagoda*, in the final section I argue that they offer to both Lowe and the reader an alternative model in which trans relations are integrated in the heterocolonial order as a set of transversal relations that simultaneously belong to and transgress that order.

## *THE PAGODA* AND TRANS TERMINOLOGY IN THE CARIBBEAN CONTEXT

*The Pagoda* is set in colonial Jamaica after the 1834 abolition of slavery and in the midst of the subsequent expansion of the "coolie trade" that brought Chinese and Indian workers to the Caribbean (Walters 2010; Yun 2004). Powell explains in an interview with Faith Smith that she planned to write about a Chinese woman in colonial Jamaica, "but while doing research, I found out in one article that Chinese laws did not permit women to emigrate until later than the time I had anticipated for my characters; and because I still wanted a female protagonist, I decided to have her cross-dress. . . . She cannot be one thing or another, but at all times must wear myriad costumes and selves" (Smith and Powell 1996, 326). If Lowe is thus born out of a doubled necessity, Powell's references to Lowe with feminine pronouns in the interview and with masculine ones in the novel only further underscore the gender crossings that Lowe's story entails.

As *The Pagoda* outlines, Lowe's life begins in China, where he spends his early years as a little copy of his father. At puberty Lowe suddenly becomes a girl and is married off to an old man. He escapes by dressing as a boy and stowing away on a ship bound for Jamaica. Cecil, the ship's captain, discovers him, rapes him, and forces him to spend the voyage as his sex slave. Lowe ends up pregnant by Cecil. In Jamaica Lowe delivers in secret a daughter named Elizabeth and continues to live as a man, fathering the baby. Cecil sets Lowe up with a shop and then a wife, Miss Sylvie. Lowe and Miss Sylvie live together, raising Elizabeth as their own, for thirty years. Cecil continues to make sporadic appearances, during which he carries on sexual relationships with both Lowe and Miss Sylvie. About ten years before the start of the novel, Elizabeth marries and becomes estranged from Lowe. The novel begins as, anticipating his death, Lowe attempts to write Elizabeth a letter in order to tell her "of what I am in truth" (Powell 1998, 8). Shortly thereafter, Lowe's shop burns down. Cecil, who is visiting, dies in the fire. Lowe increasingly revisits his past, especially his rape-filled passage from China to Jamaica. He discovers in himself a great desire to reconnect with the Chinese community in Jamaica and to build a pagoda that will serve as a Chinese Jamaican cultural center. He begins to share his story with others and to explore the possibility of relationships that might not rest on either "playing" or "being" a particular gender, race, or sexuality, becoming increasingly connected—whether or not he realizes it—to a community full of characters whose myriad transgressions of the colonial order seem to always already be a part of it.

Most studies of *The Pagoda* examine various ways in which Lowe exemplifies the intersections of gender, sexual, racial, and national identification. Although they disagree on whether to call Lowe a man or a woman, they have until recently concurred in determining that Lowe is "really" one or the other (Chin 2007; Francis 2004; Harrison 2009; Lezra 2008; Misrahi-Barak 2012; Yun 2004; Walters 2010). I join a small but growing number of critics who understand Lowe as transgender (Frydman 2011; Prater 2012; Woodhull 2004). Although I remain wary both of the Euro-American conceptions of gender and sexuality that adhere to the term "transgender" and of concepts of identity writ large, I find compelling the associations with many terms deeply rooted in Caribbean Studies that are evoked by the word.[7] The *trans* of *transgender* invokes the transatlantic and transnational movements that so profoundly mark the Caribbean and whose connection to Euro-American hegemony render their use both so problematic and so appropriate. *Transgender* also evokes an ensemble of related words that share the prefix, including *translation, transformation, transgression,* and Glissant's "transversal relations." Indeed, using the term *transgender* and the prefix *trans* ought to compel us to ask, in a paraphrase of K. Anthony Appiah, whether the *trans* in *transgender* is the same as the *trans* in any of these other terms (1991), and further, how we can combine the dislocation of *trans* (inherent in its root, the Latin "across, beyond, over") with the localization of any or all of these *trans*es in the Caribbean.[8]

## COERCION AND THE IMPOSSIBILITY OF ESCAPING THE HETEROCOLONIAL ORDER: LOWE, MISS SYLVIE, CECIL

Caribbean literary critic Rosamond King finds that, because Lowe's gender change is coerced, he is a character who reinforces "the belief that unconventional genders are not indigenous to the region" and that he does not represent transgender Caribbean experience (King 2008, 584). However, it is precisely in the coerced nature of Lowe's transgender that I find one of the most salient links to Caribbean experience. Any gender of any Caribbean subject—whatever the degree of "indegeneity" and however postslavery or postcolonial—emerges from colonial coercion.[9] Colonialism, as Lugones notes, "introduced many genders and gender itself as a colonial concept and mode of organization of relations of production, property relations, of cosmologies and ways of knowing" (Lugones 2007, 186). This heterocolonial order imposes "a" gender, race, sexuality, and class on all subjects.[10] The "many genders" in this system specify lines of separation (codifying the distance for example between black women and white women), rather than acknowledging the possibility of belonging to multiple categories or that of passage between categories. At the same time, the imposition and policing of this complex array of gender, racial, and sexual categories coerce both belonging to and transgression of their boundaries. Lowe's position as a protagonist searching to tell "who I am in truth" suggests that he himself may not understand, but *The Pagoda* demonstrates that what Lowe's gender is, and what its changes mean, has much less to do with Lowe as an individual with personal desires than it has to do with him as a colonial subject, as a body subjected to multiple political and economic orders.[11]

Lowe arrives in Jamaica on a ship full of Chinese who, like the Africans before them, got there because "people like Cecil . . . could . . . pay little or nothing to men desperate for food and work, to kidnap anyone they could find" and take them across an ocean and sell them "to the highest bidder in the West Indies" (Powell 1998, 17). That Lowe ran away from a forced marriage and, passing as a man, became a stowaway on Cecil's ship makes me want to claim that coercion alone did not determine his path but that some particular personal desire led him to choose a transgender escape. However, as Sam Chen says in the novel when Lowe and the other Chinese Jamaicans discuss the "choice" of immigration: "when you don't have one grain of rice to eat, you not free. When you don't have money, you not free. You turn slave to your stomach. Desperation drives you. Is either immigration or death, no!" (44).

Perhaps what led Lowe to understand that the stifling femininity of "a wife weighted down by tradition" is the kind of impending death that impels emigration could explain the source of his transgender existence. Indeed, *The Pagoda* proceeds through revelatory flashbacks as if it might lead to an original personal identity, but the search turns into a dizzying endless regress. Each step back requires another, and each time we land on something that seems like it must be the "true" Lowe, we find only someone else's coercive construction. Lowe realizes that "Nobody had ever asked him. He had just lived out all their fantasies. There was his father, who used to dress Lowe the same way he dressed himself.... Then it was Cecil's fantasies and his grand plans for both Lowe and Miss Sylvie" (Powell 1998, 99). But it is not just Cecil or Lowe's father, not just exceptional individuals with individual power over Lowe, who enforce their peculiar gender-crossing fantasy categories onto Lowe. Lowe's father represents Chinese patriarchy, a system where only boys were valued in the family and girls became the wives of others. Moreover, Cecil's questions to Lowe, "You know what them do with the Chinese woman in British Guinea. In Cuba. In Trinidad? Bring them to whorehouse. Is that you wanted?" require answers recognizing that not only Cecil but also the heterocolonial order both construct and coerce Lowe's manhood in Jamaica (99). The Pagoda does not tell the story of an "indigenous" and "free" Caribbean transgender identification but, by telling the story of a coerced transgender Chinese Jamaican identification, reveals how the patriarchal and heterocolonial orders that strip Lowe of the subjective agency to choose a gender ironically force him not only to conform to their norms but also to transgress them.

Lowe experiences his double bind as unique and individual, but the novel displays that Lowe is not exceptional, neither in his subjection to coercive gender orders nor in his transgression of them. The Pagoda opens with what seems to be a simple hierarchy with the coercively transgendered Chinese Jamaican Lowe at the bottom, his relatively free rich white wife, Miss Sylvie, next, and the white trafficker in human flesh, Cecil, at the top and in control of all. Each position in this hierarchy turns out, however, to be equally and forcibly assigned to a particular gender, race, and sexuality, even as each of these positions also exercises control over the gender, race, and sexuality of other positions.

Because Miss Sylvie looks white and rich, Lowe assumes that she operates freely in the heterocolonial order. His descriptions of her directing the building of the house they live in, profiting handsomely from the estate, and controlling the servants, all establish his view of her freedom and power. When he is faced with the ways that Miss Sylvie had to be white to marry her first husband, a rich white politician, and had to have white children to be white, Lowe insinuates that she had a kind of choice that was unavailable to him, asking her, "But why'd you marry him, then" (Powell 1998, 146). Miss Sylvie's answer shows that, while the particulars are different, her choices were just as proscribed and prescribed as his: "He like me. He pursue me. And I could pass. . . . A powerful man as that? Is every girl's wish. I mean what women have, Lowe, if it ain't what the father give them, what the husband give them?" (146). Like Lowe, Miss Sylvie cannot articulate her own desire. She married not because it was her wish but because it was "every girl's wish," the wish that is part of being a (colored) girl, the wish "given" by the (white) father and the (white) husband as much as everything else is given by them. So when her children are born brown, Miss Sylvie gives them away, and when her husband calls her a "nigger," she strangles him. For Miss Sylvie, as for Lowe, the strictures of the heterocolonial order force and exclude belonging to the very same categories.

Although Lowe and Miss Sylvie are both forced to occupy and to change positions in the heterocolonial order, their parallels do not create a space of mutual resistance. They are connected to each other through the coercive structure itself, in a marriage designed to keep each one in a proper place. Each one's attempts to "help" the other into a "better" position only illustrate Sheller's observation that "being more deeply inscribed into particular gender, racial, and moral orders" is often the result as well as the cause of attempts to challenge them (Sheller 2012, 9).

Miss Sylvie repeatedly attempts to share an emotional and sexual relationship with Lowe: "she removed the strips of cloth that banded the chest and swallowed at once the knobby red nipples. She murmured into his chest. She knew! She murmured into his belly. She knew!" (Powell 1998, 112). But it is not exactly clear what she knew, and indeed her knowledge seems to be of his womanhood, a knowledge that would simply force him back into that category rather than make any space across or through categories. Lowe never responds to Miss Sylvie's touch, and as Miss Sylvie touches him, his mind repeatedly returns to his onboard rape by Cecil. Lowe recognizes that Miss Sylvie's attentions subject him to one more person's desires and put him into one more category in the heterocolonial order. For even though "secretly in his heart he yearned for her embrace, and often he wished he could small himself up into her lap and sleep there," he senses "she always wanted more. He heard it in her frenzied breathing, he could smell it like danger on her skin, he could taste it at the back of his throat, and it was always there in the pressure of her fingers kneading him. He didn't feel as if he had agency, as if he had voice. For who is to say she wouldn't fold up her fantasies into him and turn him further into something he wasn't, as his father had done and then Cecil?" (114).

Lowe, for his part, attempts to help Miss Sylvie become the biological mother he thinks she "really" is and reconnect with the children she gave away. When Lowe suggests to Dulcie, the housekeeper who has been with Miss Sylvie since her first marriage, that they find the children and "invite them," Dulcie tries to explain that to do so would be to force Miss Sylvie into a role she never occupied and has not asked for, "she was a like a grip for them, a carrying vessel" (Powell 1998, 195). But Lowe insists. And only when one of the children arrives and

Miss Sylvie refuses to respond to the appellation "mother" and instead looks at the now grown child "with pure hate," does Lowe see "how very wrong he had been. How so damn wrong" (207–208).

When Lowe realizes his mistake, he opens one of the excruciatingly limited windows into the improbable possibility of non-heterocolonial, transversal relations where family relationships need not be biological or reproductive and biological connections need not define family or identity, where motherhood is not a requirement of womanhood, and where there are many roles outside of or unrelated to the "mother" that women who have given birth can take up. Another such window opens when, later in the novel, Miss Sylvie falters in her suggestion that Lowe become a woman, "Maybe you wouldn't even have to be like this anymore . . . you wouldn't have to dress up like that, you wouldn't have to look like a . . ." and finishes awkwardly, "I mean unless you want to" (Powell 1998, 140), allowing that Lowe might want to do something else that she can't quite name. These openings occur, however, less as positive possibilities for transversal relations than as recognitions of a failure or incapacity to conceive of them.

If Lowe and Miss Sylvie find it impossible to escape reifying the heterocolonial order, Cecil is the visible and tangible embodiment of those who actively establish and enforce it. Cecil literally imposes heterocolonial family structure by giving Lowe a daughter and a wife—and Miss Sylvie a husband and a daughter—and also by exercising his ability to have sexual relationships with women and nonwhites at any time. Cecil embodies the colonial white male's sexual power over female and nonwhite bodies and his social power over the lines of lineage on the island. That he is not only the biological father of Lowe's daughter, Elizabeth, but also (the novel strongly hints) of the man Elizabeth eventually marries, demonstrates how that power is perpetuated through the inequality of its structure—a structure in which nonwhites and women are both forced into a patrilineage and set up, by the indiscriminate impregnation of nonwhite women, to transgress its rules not only through subjection to coercive sex but through an almost inevitable transgression of the incest taboo.

That Cecil dies in the first pages of *The Pagoda* might suggest the fall of the heterocolonial order and a path in the rest of the story to peeling away the layers of colonial history to finally find the "real" Lowe. Cecil's reach, however, exceeds his death—not through his personal power but because he was only a vessel of a vast structure that he represented but did not control. Cecil's own status as a white Jamaican man, his economic and social power, his intimate relationships, his ability to parent, and his ability to live are no more individual expressions of personal desire than are Lowe's.

As Lowe comes to terms with the insignificance of Cecil's personal power in the heterocolonial order, he shifts from trying to escape from Cecil's coercive power to trying to understand Cecil's position. Lowe asks Omar, the overseer of Miss Sylvie's estate and a probable object of Cecil's sexual attentions, "Did you know Cecil? . . . I mean, really know him?" Omar's initial response, "Yes, sir," is followed by a description of Cecil that shows that to really know Cecil is to know how he too was subjected to heterocolonial power:

> "He was a man with his hands in everything. He was best friends with Miss Sylvie's husband. His family some of the richest on the island. But must be he fell out with them, they cut him off, so he run the coolie trade. . . . Plenty Chinese and Indian people and some Negro people he set up in business, if he take a fancy to them, but he was a man with his hands everywhere."
>
> "And he never marry," Lowe said.
>
> "No sir, not as far as I know."
>
> . . .
>
> "And children?"
>
> There was the silence again, and outside, frogs and cicadas went wild in the night.
>
> "Who is to tell, sir?" (Powell 1998, 226–227)

In spite of, or perhaps precisely in, his role as a rapist and a trafficker in human beings, Cecil's life is rife with silences and suggestions of desires, choices, that could not find expression as open truths or identities in the heterocolonial order that he also enforces.

The "plenty Chinese and Indian people and some Negro people" to whom Cecil "take[s] a fancy," his long-term sexual relationships with Lowe and Miss Sylvie and probably Omar suggest that he has a particular desire for nonwhites and men. And inasmuch as nonwhite men in the heterocolonial order are themselves positioned as either more or less male than white men, with Chinese maleness in particular always already somehow effeminized, Cecil's desire for nonwhite men can be read as a kind of transgender desire—either a desire for a transgender person or a desire that changes Cecil's own manhood. Furthermore, Cecil's desire for Lowe appears to be a desire for him *as* transgender. On the ship when they meet, it appears to be the combination of dressing and fighting him like a man and possessing "woman's flesh" that so attracts Cecil to Lowe (Powell 1998, 48–49). Aided and perhaps guided by the colonial positioning of all Chinese women as prostitutes, Cecil works to maintain Lowe as a man and as the object of his sexual attention once they arrive in Jamaica. Nonetheless, Cecil can only have suspect and forced liaisons with Lowe, Miss Sylvie, Omar, and the others, and he can only uncle or absentee parent any children he fathers with them, for his ability to access nonwhites, men, and transgender people for sex does not include an ability to marry or form families with them. Cecil's strange kindness, for a trader in human flesh and a rapist, or his strange cruelty, for a lover of nonwhites, reveals the contradictions of his situation and suggests that, like Lowe and Miss Sylvie, Cecil also is caught between his inability or lack of desire to conform to the heterocolonial order and his inability to do anything but conform.

Cecil's death does not remove the power structures of which he was both representative and victim, but with Cecil finally gone, Miss Sylvie says to Lowe, "it's just us now," and once "the strange combination they were" sinks in to Lowe, he realizes the tremendous possibility that represents (Powell 1998, 138). Finding himself "suddenly terrified by the possibility of more dreams, more fantasies," Lowe also realizes that the power of just the two of them together is that there is no clear order into which they fit; he has to ask, "What you mean, exactly?" (Powell 1998, 138). Miss Sylvie responds with another question, a question that has never been asked of Lowe, "Well, what is it you'd like, Lowe?" (138). If early in the novel Lowe would have tried to articulate what he wanted to *be*, now he answers with what he would like to *have*, outlining for Miss Sylvie his dream of the pagoda (139). Lowe seems to recognize that it is pointless to try to claim an identity when you do not control the structures in which that identity is articulated. So his dream, what he wants, is to create his own structure. Miss Sylvie echoes James Baldwin and Dionne Brand when she suggests that Lowe's new structure could be built on "another island." Lowe insists on staying in Jamaica, and so the pagoda is deferred in time rather than in place. Lowe's words in his final letter to Elizabeth, "the center is there, maybe next year we can open it with a big ceremony," express both the continued hope and the continued uncertainty for its completion (240).

## TRANS RELATIONS: SHARMILLA, JOYCE, PRETTY, OMAR, AND JAKE

If in the foreground of *The Pagoda* the stories of Lowe, Miss Sylvie, and Cecil reopen the wounds of the heterocolonial order and leave them to bleed out in pain, in the background a whole other cast of characters hold out the bandages that have always bound them, transversally. As Lowe struggles to find "what I am in truth" and a new structure for an integrated identity, Sharmilla, Joyce, Omar, Jake, Pretty, and any number of other characters understand Lowe's, and their own, gender and sexuality in alternative ways. Jason Frydman argues that "the proliferation of queer intimacies" in *The Pagoda* articulates a "utopian vision of a simultaneously creole and pluralist Jamaican nationalism" (Frydman 2011, 96). I see a less radical and both more and less hopeful position rooted in the inescapability of heterocolonialism's wounds and the necessity of remaining in relation with them. *The Pagoda*'s Jamaica is neither utopian nor new—which I will show as I turn my attention to the improbable, imperfect, and unoriginal future that the background characters hold out. These characters and their relationships to and with Lowe evince spaces for transgender lives and loves that permeate all aspects of Jamaican life, surviving and resisting but also supporting and perpetuating the heterocolonial order.

Shortly after Cecil's death, Lowe travels to the city to reconnect with the Chinese Jamaican community, centered around the successful businessman Kywing. There, Lowe sees Kywing's Indian-born wife, Sharmilla, to whom he feels a deep connection, "for it was as if she knew exactly what lay behind the costume" (Powell 1998, 35). Lowe takes Sharmilla primarily as knowing something about the body under his clothes and the identity that body conveys. But he also recognizes something else: "Once, for a brief and furtive moment, he thought perhaps she desired him, but he found the idea so worrisome, so marked with frustration and distress, that he wiped it completely from the shelves of his mind" (35–36). The suggestion that Lowe, in his search for singular and true identity, cannot grant is that Sharmilla recognizes and desires him as transgender. Indeed, each time Lowe acknowledges a trans relation he appears surprised, confused, and scared and expects others to feel likewise.

Lowe's outlook, however, is not that of *The Pagoda*. Throughout the novel, relationships between men and relationships between women as well as crossings of the gender binary appear as common and as common knowledge, even if always marginal. There are "the Chinese men, from the neighboring villages and towns, . . . the ones married to the Indian and Negro women, to the low-class creoles and hybrids; . . . the ones still basking in the sweet waters of bachelorhood and those who patronized whorehouses and those who took each other in love," and when "their conversations grew heated, they drank heavily, they sweated," all of the Chinese men "groped at each other's groins and at their own, they exchanged soft laughs and knowing glances" (Powell 1998, 42, 46). Then there are "the spindly and rotund women with crocus-bag bundles on their heads who stepped in [to the shop] just to ease the load. . . . They would always talk and laugh in spirited voices and argue about the elections, the lying and thieving politicians, about education for their children, family planning, the women loved on the side, about their wayward husbands. . . . He liked it most when they lowered their voices and talked about their garish sexual lives and laughed deep, throttling laughs that revealed secrets and insatiable cravings" (56–57). And Miss Cora's shop, on Sunday evenings, is filled with "Men with merriment. Men who beat their wives and fucked their daughters. Men with good intentions. Generous and kind men. Men who loved him and other men" (134).

The policeman's wife, Joyce, goes so far as to show a way out not only of the male-female binary but of gender or even the subject as a relevant category. When Lowe becomes confused by his increasing awareness of the complex network of coerced and masqueraded lives surrounding him, "he decided he would go and see his friend Joyce" (Powell 1998, 148). She invites him to spend the night, explaining "Fine [her husband] down at the station . . . he sleep there most nights" (150). When Lowe wakes up naked in Joyce's bed, he says to her, "So you know, then." She answers, "I always knew" (152), and explains, "It wasn't anything in you clothes or you gestures . . . it was just in your laugh" (153). Joyce gestures away from knowledge about Lowe's body or from biological determinism, even as she hints at some kind of essence. When Lowe persists, "but what if I wasn't that way . . . I mean what if, suppose I didn't like it, suppose . . ." the topic of conversation shifts from knowledge about what Lowe *is* to knowledge about what Lowe *wants*. Joyce's answer keeps the subject in suspension: "I never been wrong yet," she said, and smiled. "Forty years now. . . . Sometimes is a walk, a look, sometimes is a silence, a dis-ease. But you know, Lowe, everybody seduceable. Man or woman" (153). Joyce proffers first that there might be forty years' worth of trans lovers in the village but then shifts from identifying particular seducible subjects to a suggestion that what categorizes people is not who they are or even what they want but the multiple seductive ways in which they can relate to one another. This alternative categorization seems not just against but completely distinct from the heterocolonial order.

Joyce's position as the policeman's wife is crucial to *The Pagoda*'s argument, however, and should not be overlooked. Her alternative categorization does not dismantle the town's order but, rather, enables and is enabled by it. Joyce's transverse seductions occur literally in the bed of the law, not while the law is sleeping but while the law is on duty. Her husband's spending most nights at the station may be cause or effect of Joyce's activities, but his name, Fine (by which Joyce refers to him), conveys his tacit approval of the setup. Indeed, while Lowe refers to him as Mr. Fine, when Joyce drops the title, her sentence "Fine down at the station" conveys both that it is fine down at the station—all is in order with the colonial administration—and that Fine, her husband, is down at the station and will not interfere with their relationship.

Following on the experience with Joyce, Lowe begins to go to town without his moustache. The villagers

> commented on what they called his smooth and unblemished skin, his childish baby face . . . , and one of them, an effeminate one they call Pretty, who had a penchant for impregnating young girls, then always crying that they just wanted to saddle him with bastards, for none of them was his, even went as far as to say

Lowe looked like a woman he used to know. And at that they stormed into laughter, hammering their feet on the pavement. . . . Did they know? he had wondered.
And if so, was it that it didn't matter to them? He had noticed that even with all
their comments, they seemed not to harbor any bad feelings against him. (Powell
1998, 172)

Pretty identifies something trans about Lowe, but from the position of one who
also crosses gender lines in a way that is familiar to the community to which he
belongs. At the same time whatever the villagers do or do not know about Pretty
or Lowe remains vague, and no one finds any need to ask for more precision than
that he has smooth skin and reminds Pretty of a woman. Lowe is like others who
cross gender categories, and those crossings occur in multiple and complex ways.
At the same time, most of the villagers are married to people of the opposite gender and some refer to the "nasty . . . ungodliness" of the homosexual relationship
they suspect between Cecil and Lowe (15). Pretty and Lowe, emblematizing the
very broad range of trans relations, are related to one another by the ways that
they are both denigrated by *and* integrated into dominant social structures.

It might seem as if Lowe's subsequent sexual encounter with Omar is a step
in his return to heterosexual femininity, but when Omar and Lowe lie naked
together, we find instead another character accepting Lowe's transgender in ways
that exceed Lowe's own understanding. Omar's actions convey a tender, if somewhat awkward, treatment of Lowe's body as between or across male and female.
After touching Lowe's breasts and waist, Omar seems both surprised and com-
prehending that Lowe is to be treated as neither or both or something different
yet from a man or a woman: "'Shh,' said Lowe. He did not want to face him, he
did not want to read the astonished eyes, he did not want to kiss him, he did
not want to talk to him. There was the organ between them, the throbbing hard
thing between them. With stubby fingers Omar drew circles on Lowe's back. He
soothed the stringy edges of Lowe's hair, he blew into Lowe's neck and rustled
the fuzz that grew there at the nape, he hummed low jerky tunes of his youth,
and his chest lay still against Lowe's curving back" (Powell 1998, 226). Although
Lowe still expects Omar to be "astonished" at seeing his unbound breasts and
curved hips, Omar's earlier refusal to look at Lowe's unclothed chest suggests
that he already knew something of the morphology he might see and does not
reduce the "truth" of Lowe's gender and sexuality to that morphology. Attracted
to and aroused by Lowe, Omar operates in an exploratory and relational mode,
not trying to give to or take something from Lowe, not trying to follow standard
expectations of sex between men and women or between men but, rather, trying
to figure out how to relate their two bodies and their various desires. The description of "the organ, the throbbing thing between them" without a possessive pronoun to identify "the organ" allows that it may be Lowe's or Omar's organ, that

what Omar may be offering Lowe (or vice-versa) is an organ that they can share or that can equally belong or be foreign to both of them, even if neither is quite sure how to do that. Facing Lowe's back, Omar offers an intimacy of naked touch unattached to any traditionally gendered or sexualized body part or bodily act.

In spite of the many villagers' different ways of understanding Lowe through their own transgender desires that they either have or recognize for him or others, the problem of how to designate Lowe in a language where names, titles, and personal pronouns reinforce a gender binary plagues the characters of *The Pagoda* as much as it does the narrator and critics of the novel. Omar's insistence on calling Lowe "Mr. Lowe," even when Lowe has demanded "Call me A-yin, damn it. Call me by my blasted name" (Powell 1998, 222), even when he has just lain naked with Lowe, reinforces the novel's suggestion that to locate Lowe in any one gender is both to misidentify him and almost inevitable.

Near the end of *The Pagoda*, the carpenter Jake figures out if not Lowe's true-true name then a most appropriate way to refer to him: "ma'am Mr. Lowe" (Powell 1998, 241). The novel never settles, however, on one "right" way to articulate Lowe's status—Jake's and Omar's appellations figure as equally valid, and the narrator's mode of referring to Lowe always with male pronouns but sometimes as a girl or a woman, and sometimes as Lau A-yin repeats the multiplication effect. There is no single true gender or sexuality for Lowe to "be," and so no single true name or pronoun with which to designate him. Lowe emerges in and out of the heterocolonial order's denial and creation of him, and its reliance on and challenge by others (who) like him.

I read the trans relations in *The Pagoda* as offering ways around, through, and under heterocolonial patriarchy that do not destroy it or point to any move out of or beyond it. That *The Pagoda* reveals an increasing number of trans relations shows not that the trans relations themselves are on the rise but, rather, that Lowe's—and the reader's—awareness of them is. This does not guarantee that Lowe's letter to Elizabeth will be completed or sent or that the pagoda he wants to build for her and his grandchildren will be finished or used. But it requires the recognition that trans relations have always and everywhere been present, lived, and negotiated. Trans relations and transgendered subjects, subjected to coercion, incompletion, and imperfection, proliferate not only before or after heterocolonialism but persist throughout it. They emerge when we reopen the wounds of colonialism and their excruciatingly improbable poetics of relation transgress and transfigure the gender binary that occasions them.

## NOTES

1. Thanks to Rhonda Cobham-Sanders for her remarks to this effect at the 2013 International Conference on Caribbean Literature.

**2.** I use J. Michael Dash's translation with one modification: Dash uses "cross-cultural" for Glissant's "transversale" (Glissant 1989, 98; Glissant 1997, 327). I use "transversal" for "transversale" in order to underscore the repetition of the prefix *trans* (repeated in Glissant in both "transversale" and "transcendence" and repeated in this chapter in *transgender*, among other things) and in order to convey the general idea of being in a position of crossing or of cutting across that is contained in the idea of "transversale" rather than the specification of the cross-cultural of Dash's translation.

**3.** That Glissant's work demonstrates occasional difficulty placing figures that do not conform to heterocolonial gender and sexual structures does not prevent such figures from embodying his model of Poetics of Relation.

**4.** Notably Michelle Cliff's *No Telephone to Heaven* in Jamaica (1987), Shani Mootoo's *Cereus Blooms at Night* in Trinidad (1996), Mayra Santos-Febres's *Sirena Selena vestida de pena* in Puerto Rico (2000), and Nalo Hopkinson's *Skin Folk* in Jamaica (2001).

**5.** Articles 76 and 77 of Jamaica's Offences Against the Person Act make "the abominable offense of buggery" illegal and punishable by up to ten years in prison. Article 79 states that "Any male person who, in public or private, commits, or is a party to the commission of, or procures or attempts to procure the commission by any male person of, any act of gross indecency with another male person, shall be guilty of a misdemeanor," punishable by up to two years in prison. Although "gross indecency" is not defined in the law, it has been interpreted to include any kind of physical intimacy between consenting adults. For more information, see J-Flag, "Know Your Rights" (2013). In Barbados and Guyana, sodomy is illegal and punishable by life in prison. In Trinidad and Tobago, the 1986 "Sexual Offenses Act," strengthened in 2000, makes both male and female homosexuality punishable by up to twenty-five years in prison, and the Immigration Act makes it illegal for homosexuals to enter the country. In October 2013, a challenge to the constitutionality of Jamaica's "Buggery Laws" was brought to Jamaica's Supreme Court. As of the writing of this chapter, the challenge is ongoing and no ruling has been made.

**6.** Newton Duncan's "Dressed for Murder," in *Jamaica Gleaner*, August 4, 2013, sympathetic to Dwayne Jones, for example, mentions that "to the overwhelming majority of Jamaicans, cross-dressers are homosexuals who deserve the full wrath of the righteous." Carolyn Cooper, in her "Dressed for Murder" and "Sexual Falsehood Top to Bottom," in *Jamaica Gleaner*, August 4 and August 11, respectively, gives similar analyses of Jamaican public opinion.

**7.** For discussion of the problems of the vocabulary of gender and sexuality in the Caribbean and in critical work about the Caribbean, see Natasha Tinsley (2010, 5–15).

**8.** I am grateful to Melvin Rahming for asking this second question when I presented an early version of this chapter at the 2013 International Conference on Caribbean Literature.

**9.** The appeal to Caribbean indigeneity is itself interrogated in *The Pagoda* through evocations of the colonial history that eradicated indigenous Jamaicans and populated the island with colonizers, slaves, and emigrants from India, China, and the Middle East—brought by very different forces but all from elsewhere.

**10.** Mimi Sheller's conception of embodiment and sexual citizenship in the Caribbean analyzes the imbrications of coerced gender, racial, and sexual categorizations (2012).

**11.** Albert Memmi and Frantz Fanon's analyses of the effects of colonialism on the self-conception of the colonized lay the foundations for this understanding (Memmi 1965; Fanon 2008). Saidiya Hartman's attention to the endurance of the structures of slavery post-emancipation and Sheller's analysis of "erotic agency," among others, develop its many valences (Hartman 1997; Sheller 2012).

## REFERENCES

Appiah, K. Anthony. 1991. "Is the Post- in Postmodernism the Post- in Postcolonial?" *Critical Inquiry* 17.2: 336–357.

Chin, Timothy. 2007. "The Novels of Patricia Powell: Negotiating Gender and Sexuality across the Disjunctures of the Caribbean Diaspora." *Callaloo* 30.2: 533–545.

Cliff, Michelle. 1987. *No Telephone to Heaven*. New York: Dutton.

Fanon, Frantz. 2008. *Black Skin, White Masks*. Translated by Richard Philcox. 1952. New York: Grove Press.

Francis, Donette. 2004. "Uncovered Stories: Politicizing Sexual Histories in Third Wave Caribbean Women's Writings." *Black Renaissance/Renaissance Noire* 6.1: 61–81.

Frydman, Jason. 2011. "Jamaican Nationalism, Queer Intimacies, and the Disjuncture of the Chinese Diaspora: Patricia Powell's *The Pagoda*." *Small Axe* 15.1: 95–109.

Glissant, Édouard. 1989. *Caribbean Discourse, Selected Essays*. Translated by J. Michael Dash. Charlottesville: University Press of Virginia.

———. 1997. *Le discours antillais*. Paris: Gallimard.

Harrison, Sheri-Marie. 2009. "'Yes Ma'am Mr. Lowe': Lau A-Yin and the Politics of Gender and Sexuality in Patricia Powell's *The Pagoda*." *Anthurium: A Caribbean Studies Journal* 7.1–2. http://scholarlyrepository.miami.edu/anthurium/vol7/iss1/7.

Hartman, Saidiya. 1997. *Scenes of Subjection*. Oxford: Oxford University Press.

Hopkinson, Nalo. 2001. *Skin Folk*. New York: Aspect.

JFLAG. 2013. "Know Your Rights." *jflag.org*. Accessed September 28, 2013. http://jflag.org/resources/lgbt-communities/know-your-rights.

King, Rosamond S. 2008. "Re/Presenting Self and Other: Trans Deliverance in Caribbean Texts." *Callaloo* 31.2: 581–599.

Lezra, Esther. 2008. "[Ab]Errant [Ab]Erring Stories/Remembering Bodies/Disordering Stories in *The Pagoda* and *The Sand Child*." In *African Diasporas: Ancestors, Migrations, and Borders*, edited by Robert Cancel and Winifred Woodhull, 80–106. Trenton, NJ: Africa World Press.

Lugones, Maria. 2007. "Heterosexualism and the Colonial/Modern Gender System." *Hypatia* 22.1: 186–209.

Memmi, Albert. 1965. *The Colonizer and the Colonized*. Translated by Howard Greenfeld. New York: Orion Press.

Misrahi-Barak, Judith. 2012. "Looking In, Looking Out: The Chinese-Caribbean Diaspora through Literature—Meiling Jin, Patricia Powell, Jan Lowe Shinebourne." *Journal of Transnational American Studies* 4.1. https://escholarship.org/uc/item/0pn2w8cs.

Mootoo, Shani. 1996. *Cereus Blooms at Night*. New York: Grove Press.

Powell, Patricia. 1998. *The Pagoda*. New York: Harcourt.

Prater, Tzarina. 2012. "Transgender, Memory, and Colonial History in Patricia Powell's *The Pagoda*." *Small Axe* 37: 20–35.

Santos-Febres, Mayra. 2000. *Sirena Selena vestida de pena*. London: Punto de Lectura.

Sheller, Mimi. 2012. *Citizenship from Below: Erotic Agency and Caribbean Freedom*. Durham, NC: Duke University Press.

Smith, Faith, and Patricia Powell. 1996. "An Interview with Patricia Powell." *Callaloo* 19.2: 324–329.

Tinsley, Natasha. 2010. *Thiefing Sugar: Eroticism between Women in Caribbean Literature*. Durham, NC: Duke University Press.

Walcott, Derek. 1993. *The Antilles: Fragments of Epic Memory*. New York: Farrar, Straus, and Giroux.

Walters, Wendy. 2010. "Archives of the Black Atlantic: Postcolonial Citation in *The Pagoda*." *Novel: A Forum on Fiction* 43.1: 163–168.

Woodhull, Winifred. 2004. "Margin to Margin, China to Jamaica: Sexuality, Ethnicity, and Black Culture in Global Contexts." *Revista Canaria de estudios ingleses* 48: 119–127.

Yun, Lisa Li-Shen. 2004. "An Afro-Chinese Caribbean: Cultural Cartographies of Contrariness in the Work of Antonio Chuffat Latour, Margaret Cezair-Thompson, and Patricia Powell." *Caribbean Quarterly* 50.2: 26–43.

# 5 · TRANSCODING THE TRANSNATIONAL DIGITAL ECONOMY

JIAN CHEN

This chapter focuses on the trans embodied, transnational digital media of Cheang Shu Lea. For more than thirty years, Taiwan-born queer digital nomad Cheang has produced new media art that highlights and plays with the boundaries of gender, racial ethnicity, sexuality, nationality, cultural genre, and technological medium.[1] In particular I look at her post-porn digital film *I.K.U.* (2000), which rips off Ridley Scott's analog film *Blade Runner* (1982), and *I.K.U.*'s sequel *UKI* (2009–2012), a live video performance and online game.[2] These coupled pieces, along with Cheang's other work in the 2000s, make visible the digital technologies that had linked cultural mediums, media technologies, and media industries (film, television, newspapers, books, radio, performance, games, photography) nationally, regionally, and globally by the conclusion of the twentieth century. Using *I.K.U.* and *UKI* as examples of her larger body of work, I argue that Cheang's attention to networked media technologies and their new interfaces with viewers, who become users and players, urges us toward an investigation of the structural impact of digital technologies in mediating transnational neoliberal capitalism. As a crucial part of this argument, I show how Cheang's work compels us to think about and experience racially gendered/sexed embodiment and biogenetics as motive forces in the restructuring and globalizing of political economies of the United States, Western Europe, and the global North.

My chapter begins with a discussion of Ridley Scott's *Blade Runner* (1982) and the racialized anxieties that shape the film's nostalgia for the human and American liberal society in the urban rubble of high-tech de-industrialization.

It follows with a focus on *I.K.U.*'s playful trans recoding and subversion of *Blade Runner*. Cheang's digital film *I.K.U.* highlights the racially binary gender/sex/ sexual cultural economies that underpin *Blade Runner*'s post-apocalyptic vision of high-tech, which the 35mm film projects at a moment when the U.S.-based Hollywood film industry is undergoing transformation by a new, digitally powered global economy. While *I.K.U.* intervenes in the representational politics of *Blade Runner* and dominant visions of high-tech, *I.K.U.*'s sequel performance and game *UKI* breaks away from the representational politics of visibility and viewing by wiring us to the invisible off-sites of the digital economy, including electronic and biogenetic dumping sites that give birth to live trans genetic, species, and media forms. Against neoliberal accounts of the digital economy driven by technological, economic, and social determinisms, *I.K.U.* and *UKI* suggest that *racially* binary systems of gender, sex, *and sexuality* fundamentally structure the new political economy. In the chapter's conclusion, I explore the implications of Cheang's trans subversions in producing critical trans practices that build on and shift the textual politics of counter-cultural interpretation and meaning-making.

## NOSTALGIA FOR THE HUMAN "RACE" IN RIDLEY SCOTT'S *BLADE RUNNER*

Ridley Scott's *Blade Runner* (1982) opens with the radioactive landscape of Los Angeles 2019. Rising high above this landscape of fiery ethers, acid rain, and blinking electromagnetic surfaces, we are given a view of Tyrell Corporation's pyramid headquarters. Wide shots of the LA cityscape are intercut with close shots of a disembodied eye that mirrors an image of the city on its surface. Moments later we associate these images of an eye with the interrogation tool developed by the Tyrell Corporation to distinguish between real humans and human clones, called Replicants. The tool is used by Blade Runners (human police agents trained to kill Replicants) to measure the eye movement and other involuntary bodily reactions (or lack thereof) of suspected clones as they are asked emotionally charged questions. In *Blade Runner*'s LA 2019, the Tyrell Corporation's genetic engineering of Replicants represents the final frontier of high tech's encroachment on nature, divine creation, and human society. The human clones were originally produced to explore and colonize planets beyond Earth as slave laborers. But when a more intelligently designed Nexus 6 generation of Replicants starts a revolt on an off-planet colony, Replicants are banned from returning to Earth under threat of death. Scott's film follows weathered Blade Runner Deckard (Harrison Ford) as he is forced out of retirement to hunt down a group of Replicants who have returned illegally to Earth to confront their creators at the Tyrell Corporation. As Deckard terminates these illegal Replicants one by one, his ambivalent identification with the human clones grows. He "falls

in love" with Rachael (Sean Young), a Nexus 6 female Replicant employed by
the Tyrell Corporation, and his life is saved by the prized leader of the renegade
Replicants, Roy (Rutger Hauer). Deckard's identification with the Replicants is
secured by the conclusion of the film when he escapes with Rachael. Viewers are
left questioning Deckard's status as human or clone.

As argued by neo- or post-Marxist social critics, *Blade Runner* gives a visually
and narratively engrossing indictment of the degrading effects of high-tech-ruled
postindustrial global society. Postmodern geographer David Harvey mourns the
loss of the human exemplified by Deckard's falling in love with Replicant Rachael
(Harvey 1990, 313–314). Feminist film scholar Vivian Sobchack emphasizes the
film's spatial excess, which displays the decay and allure of post-consumer materials that have lost their use-value (Sobchack 2001, 262–263). These social critiques tend to match *Blade Runner*'s own suspension between melancholia and
erotic awe, except that the film has no memory of human life before the intru-
sion of bio-tech.[3] For Harvey and Sobchack, new intimacies between humans,
enslaved clones, and perhaps also the discarded refuse that is the city, all signal
humanity's degradation by a high-tech corporate state that has remade humans
into exploitable, consumable "things." These critiques, however, fail to address
the racial politics of the film's vision of Los Angeles 2019.

*Blade Runner*'s dystopian view of postindustrial techno-bio-science relies on
the racialized imagining of Los Angeles as transnational capital of the future. As
racial theorist and media scholar Adilifu Nama suggests, "the historical model
of black-white binary race relations symbolized by the Replicant 'other' is juxtaposed against the impending multicultural future signaled by the Asian iconography that has displaced all that is 'American'" (Nama 2008, 58). Nama situates
the film's anxiety about the human within the racialized crises of American
national identity and global dominance in the 1980s, following the Black Power
and women's movements and the U.S. defeat in the Vietnam War and newly facing the growing economic power of the Pacific Rim. I would add that the human-
clone relationship in *Blade Runner* not only is premised on the historical model
of binary race relations between blacks and whites but also displaces the *cultural
memory* of embodied racial communities affected by histories of systematic cap-
tivity, racism, and forced migration through the analogy (analog) of social class.[4]
Replicants (who are all white, it seems) are coded as the enslaved and exploited
"black" and migrant underclasses of the future. To be clear, I am not arguing that
Hollywood films need to mirror social histories and experiences of violently
imposed inequality. Rather, I am arguing that *Blade Runner*, like most films in
the conventional science fiction Hollywood genre, participates in the cultural
encoding of whiteness as a race at risk of becoming an underclass and, ultimately,
an extinct species (standing for the human). This encoding of whiteness bor-
rows from histories of dispossession, exploitation, and violence experienced by

nonwhite social groups, even as it displaces the possibility of remembering the histories borrowed. In *Blade Runner*'s exchange between race and social class, Black Americans and the African diaspora are disappeared from all social positions within the global landscape of LA 2019. This emphatically white-to-white alliance between human and clone is then juxtaposed with Asian-styled market multiculturalism, the liminal mestizo figure of police agent Gaff, and the high-tech corporate state rulers of the city-state-world.

*Blade Runner*'s iconography of Asianness signals not only what Nama identifies as the rival threat of an Asian-inflected global multicultural economy in the heart of LA but also the decline of an American mass industrial society equated with rational pragmatism. In its place is a street market of sensory delights that includes bazaar vendors who sell rare or synthetically made animals, a subcontracted genetic engineer who makes human eyes, and a bar that features female performers with snakes. The commodities exchanged in this postindustrial market are severed from "proper" productivity and use, as they return to their neo-primitive or technologically induced "natural" state. The wild market replacing the rational geography and public life of America's metropolis for mass industrial capitalism is racially coded as ethnic Asian. Contributing to Hollywood's Orientalist archive, Asianness itself is perceived as a collection of ethnic surface-substances compliant with the demands of the primal market or state.[5]

Despite the floating signifiers of Asian-centered multiculturalism, the only visible human embodiment of multicultural hybridity in Scott's *Blade Runner* is the blue-eyed Mexican European Japanese cop Gaff (Edward James Olmos), who is charged with looking after Deckard (Ford). Although he speaks the Spanish German Japanese hybrid "Cityspeak" of the street market, Gaff is a liminal character who also occupies the corporate and police offices above the street. He appears to be the only nonwhite human or clone that crosses into above-street LA in *Blade Runner*. Gaff's embodied hybridity builds on the racialization of Latina/o Americans as mestiza/o, with its overdetermined dimensions (Anzaldúa 2012, 99–113; Fiol-Matta 2002, 7–15). Considered native to the precolonial Americas and, at the same time, fundamentally mixed with "Old World" Spanish (Hispanic) ancestry prior to British colonial settlement, Latina/o Americans are claimed by the white-dominant American nation in envisioning a multiracial hybridity original to U.S. territories (especially in the Southwest), while retaining ties to Western European empires. This racial hybridity, however, must always be policed and managed by the nation-state (Anzaldúa 2012, 99–113; Fiol-Matta 2002, 7–15). It poses the threat of an irretrievable, unmeasurable Western European ancestry mixed irreducibly with indigenous peoples— and other peoples colonized by Western European and American empires—to form modern Chicana/o and Latina/o racial identities, communities, and nationalities with indigenous ties to the U.S. landmass and social histories. In *Blade Runner*, therefore, Gaff appears as an "authentic" embodiment of racial and ethnic hybridity. But his hybridity and border-crossing between street market and corporate state towers remain hermetically sealed in his lone, vanishing presence in the future city-world of LA 2019.

*Blade Runner's* racialized geography of disappeared Africans, Asianness equated with the neo-primitive market, and policed Latina/os provides the visual and visceral detail through which the film delivers its dystopian commentary on high-tech twenty-first-century dictatorship. Within this racial geography, the white European American humans in the film are placed in the ambivalent position of risking substitution or even extinction by human clones while also identifying and finding kinship with the cloned image of themselves—however artificial. Blade Runner Deckard's "romantic" escape with Replicant Rachael at the conclusion of the film represents an ambivalent tactic for racial (coded as human) survival in a world imagined to be relentlessly globalized, de-natured, and un-(white) American. Although the technocratic rulers in *Blade Runner* are also white, Dr. Tyrell and the Tyrell Corporation are already hopelessly transnational and transhistorical. The palatial design of the Tyrell Corporation headquarters and the aristocratic extravagance of Dr. Tyrell's bedroom mimic the style of Western European monarchies, intermixed with pyramid-structures associated with early Egyptian civilization.

## RACIAL TRANS EMBODIMENT AND CULTURAL LABOR IN CHEANG SHU LEA'S *I.K.U.*

Described as a riff-porn-sequel to Ridley Scott's *Blade Runner* (1982) and set in the near future 20xx (approximately 2030), Cheang Shu Lea's digital film *I.K.U.* begins where *Blade Runner* ends. We find human Blade Runner man and clone Replicant woman getting inside an elevator. But *I.K.U.* is not at all about human and clone falling in love and fighting to survive in a hostile new world under techno-corporate dictatorship. *I.K.U.* trades love for sex and sex for sexual simulation, and human and clone remain within the confines of high-tech corporate ruled systems, if only to exploit them toward other aims. Cheang's rip-off exposes and remembers the racially gendered/sexed bodies and histories that have made transnational postindustrial cultures, technologies, and capital possible.

In *I.K.U.'s* opening scene, sex between masculine human Runner and feminine human clone—called the Coder—programs the clone to obtain "ecstasy data" through sex with humans of all genders and sexual desires:

RUNNER: Say kiss me.
CLONE: Kiss me.

RUNNER: I want you.
CLONE: I want you.

Activated, the Coder moves through different scenarios that make up the film's futurist urban landscape in search of sexual transactions. These scenarios located in a subway, strip club, highway overpass and underpass, theater bar, underground parking lot, and sushi bar never provide a complete cinematic mise-en-scène of the cityscape. Instead, they revisualize the city as a series of decontextualized internal window-worlds that could be anyplace. In each of *I.K.U.*'s scenarios, the feminine Coder's body and sexual practices mutate to match the sexual desires and bodies of human sexual partners. The Coder's arm turns into a virtual prosthetic phallus that penetrates both male and female human partners.

While clone-human interactions in *I.K.U.* could be described as playfully pan-sexual and pan-gender, the commands that flash onscreen to direct the Coder to "her," "their," or even "its" (referring to the Coder's status as "non-human" clone) next sexual assignment suggest otherwise. The Coder's sexual interactions and polymorphous sexual body have less to do with agency, desire, and diversity than with command, programming, and modulation. Both Coder and human Runner are agents of the Genom Corporation, which has combined IT and genome technology to produce and mass market ecstacy [*sic*] data that provides "sexual excitement without sexual friction." Users of different sexualities and genders plug into this audiovisual sexual data with an I.K.U. chip and wearable computer. The Coder, human Runner, Genom Corporation, and humans who provide raw sexual experience simulate positions within an informalized economy of sex work (sex worker, pimp, transnational network, and johns). Yet, the technological enframing of *I.K.U.*'s future world overrides what might otherwise be a representation of exploitation within an advanced capitalist economy that has made sex, desire, and intimacy into commodities. *I.K.U.* does not presume that sex and sexuality *ever* were expressions and measures of individual self-possession, freedom, and choice. Neither utopian or dystopian in tone, Cheang's film operates on the flat, smooth techno-scientific register of the pregiven, where capital and its exploits are preprogrammed as natural impulse, biology, genetics. Resistance, conflict, and contradiction exist only through mutation and modulation. The lone outlaw in *I.K.U.*'s world, the Tokyo Rose virus, operates *internally within* the system produced and circumscribed by the Genom Corporation. As mutated code and sexual performer, Tokyo Rose turns the Genom Corporation's networks of data transmission into a literally embodied "net," used in performance to seduce and hack into the only male Coder in *I.K.U.*

In Cheang's *I.K.U.*, the neoliberal ideology of the Internet as the meta-network of networks becomes the object of play, exploitation, and subversion. The film makes it impossible to interpret the Internet and the IC networks it enables in the objective, rational, and neutral terms of technology as pure mediator. *I.K.U.* "worlds" the Internet and networked technologies by embodying them through the representational orders shaped by sexual, racial, and colonial histories. The sexual mutability of *I.K.U.*'s inhabitants remains confined to racially gendered forms of embodiment, imagined within colonial fantasies. Humans who provide raw, pre-data sexual experience are unchanging in their binary gender expression as biologically culturally sexed males and females. Their sexual practices are tied to the heterosexual or homosexual coding of binary gendered sexualities, except when they have sex with the human clone Coder.

While the feminine Coder and masculine human Runner also seem to take binary gender forms, their binary gender expressions are in a constant state of deconstruction and reconstruction through the redistribution of biological signs for sex into "secondary" cultural expressions of gender and sexuality.[6] The femininity of the Coder does not rely on "female" sexual organs to sex gender but, rather, displaces the overvaluation of the vagina and breasts in their sexual (and reproductive) "function" and gender representation of femaleness. The Coder's virtual prosthetic phallus-arm, other erogenous body parts, and the Coder's entire body provide multiple gender/sexual surfaces. The Coder's femininity is a disarticulated mix of female and male gender signs and sexual practices that remain suspended in relay between binary genders and sexualities, never able to wholly symbolize one or the other sex or sexuality. The masculinity of the Runner similarly displaces the overvaluation of the "male" sexual organs in representing sexual (and reproductive) "function" and engendering maleness. The Runner's mixed gender signs and sexual practices, which include the use of a dildo-gun for downloading sexual data from the Coder, denaturalizes not only the presumed correspondences between sex, gender, and sexuality but the *differences between* sex as nature or biology, gender as social construction, and sexuality as cultural expression. Sex, gender, and sexuality become delinked, ungrounded, and mixed in the crossing of the bio-social-cultural.

The *trans* gender/sex/sexual embodiments and sexual practices of *I.K.U.*'s Coder and Runner are far from pure expressions of freedom, fluidity, or choice. Their bodies and interactions remain under command and control of the networked technologies of the Genom Corporation, which has incorporated not only sex/gender/sexuality but also race and ethnicity as technologies for extracting information capital. The trans mutability of the human clone Coder draws on her coding as racially ethnic Asian. Within an increasingly transnational American Orientalist imaginary, the racialization of Asian-ness continues to work through attributing ethnic detail and gendered sexual deviance, while generalizing racially. Ethnic racialization authenticates a fantasy of particularized ethnic "foreignness" based on a cultural location elsewhere. Simultaneously, it de-authenticates this specificity through a joint fantasy of the de-particularized multitude, displaced from any delimited culture, history, or geographic place. Within this relay of racial ethnic fantasies, gender and sexuality become viral signs without material substance in what is perceived as the "normally" binary white sexed body and its sexual practices. In *I.K.U.*, the Coder's Japanese sounding techno-gibberish and morphing Asian features express forms of Orientalist racial ethnic coding that disarticulate gender/sex signs and sexual practices from anything like "normal" subjectivity with interior depth and agency. The Coder's femininity and sexuality are merely plastic, surface expressions that respond elastically (though unpredictably) to the desires of desirers. *I.K.U.*'s clone Coder is the embodied image of racialized Asian femininity.[7]

As a co-dependent prototype, the human *I.K.U.* Runner is coded as a racially ethnic black American within the transnational imaginary of American neoliberal—or neo-racist—multiculturalism. Speaking in clearly identifiable American English (in contrast to the speech-fragments of the Coder), the Runner as Genom agent with a dildo-gun embodies the image of militarized black hypermasculinity produced by the U.S. state and American dominant culture. Racialized blackness is coded as an assimilating ethnic who "belongs" to America, thus being capable of representing an exportable multicultural American national identity made for global circulation. Simultaneously, racialized blackness is coded as an unassimilable ethnic, bearing the ever-present threat to overturn the veneer of multiculturalism based on erased histories of racism, apartheid, enslavement, and forced migration. The anxiety between "inside" and "outside" produced by racial ethnic fantasies of blackness is expressed and managed through gendering and sexuality. Black bodies are attributed with liminal or ambiguous sexual features in excess or failure of "properly" sexed white American subjects (Mercer 1994, 131–170).

Yet, Cheang's *I.K.U.* does not attempt to break from these transnational American racial fantasies in order to recuperate humanized subjects with "normal" racial gender and sexual embodiment. Instead, the film shows that the culturally and biologically encrypted *relationship between* sex, gender, and sexuality is shaped—even enframed—by racial imaginaries. The encoding of sex, gender, and sexuality within white Euro-American dominant culture relies on hetero- and homo-binary logics of male/female sex, masculine/feminine gender, and opposite-sex/same-sex sexuality. On the other hand, different expressions of sex, gender, and sexuality—and of their relationship with one another—within subjugated non-white racial cultures remain displaced from any naturalized sense of binary origins. Non-Western expressions of sex, gender, and sexuality are perceived as inauthentic, substituted, failed, excessive, and/or without origins, except in relationship to naturalized whiteness as the primary origin from which one is already displaced. Thus, racial trans embodiment in Cheang's *I.K.U.*

does not merely expose and play with the Western binary gender/sex/sexuality system. The film highlights the primacy of binary conceptions of gender, sex, and sexuality as products of dominant global racial imaginaries that shape worlds, bodies, and experiences through digital technologies and programming at the genetic molecular level. Black American masculine human Runner and Asian feminine clone Coder both transgress binary gender, sex, and sexual boundaries, but their transgressions remain constrained by techno-biologically programmed dominant culture, managed by the Genom Corporation. Nevertheless, the *trans* bodies of *I.K.U.* derive pleasure, connection, experience, and productivity in the pockets of autonomy enabled precisely by the corporation's reliance on transnational technological networks for control and management.

In sharp contrast to the nostalgic tone of Scott's *Blade Runner*, Cheang's *I.K.U.* has the flat yet live feel of viewing an information feed that becomes interactive. As viewers watch the Coder extract, store, and transmit sexual data in different scenarios, we become implicated in these communicative acts as if we are intercepting the scenarios and data as live performances. For example, viewers are given a virtual "internal" view of the Coder's prosthetic phallus-arm as it penetrates different humans and extracts orgasmic data. The thrill or shock of getting this impossible view is undercut by the informational representation of the internal body as a grid-surface and the viewers' alignment with the bio-technological apparatus of the Genom Corporation. In the absence of any feeling of loss, rage, or fulfillment, Cheang's *I.K.U.* does not engage in *Blade Runner*'s depth-models of cinematic narrative, identification, and interpretation. While *I.K.U.* shows the penetration of bio-tech capitalism into the innermost recesses of the human body and subjectivity (the cell, sexual organs, desire, agency), it also shows the pleasures and potential of the autonomous experiences, relationships, and subversions enabled by transnational high-tech corporations' over-reliance on technological networks. With the Genom Corporation nowhere to be seen in *I.K.U.*'s world, the Coders, Runner, Virus, and humans who do all the work (and anti-work) of sexual data extraction run astray from their bio-tech programming and use digital technologies of command, control, and communication in unintended ways. *I.K.U.* remakes the technologically facilitated globalization that *Blade Runner* mourns as the loss of the American nation-state, liberal society, and the human.

It is striking that, in *I.K.U.*, resistance and subversion always remain circumscribed by the Genom Corporation's dislocated yet controlling presence. The absence of pure transgression speaks less to its impossibility than to the urgency—or what *I.K.U.* presents as flat living fact—of understanding and responding to the new material conditions that frame and shape the politics of cultural representation by the conclusion of the twentieth century. Cheang's *I.K.U.* not only exposes, intensifies, and modulates racially binary gender/sex/

sexual Euro-American imaginaries but, just as important, shows how these imaginaries newly relate to mediated political economies at the moment of transition from analog to digital cultures. Following more than two decades of unprecedented social mobilization for racial, gender, sexual, and economic justice and an end to war, the American culture wars of the late 1970s highlighted the centrality of culture to politics in the post–civil rights era. In particular, the debates on sexual morality that were part of the culture wars illustrated the ability of the formal state apparatus and corporations to co-opt and manage the sexual and racial countercultures produced as part of 1960s and 1970s social movements (Everett 1996; Hunter 2006; Rubin 2011, 137–181). They also exemplified the partial entry of previously barred and segregated racial, gender, and sexual communities into a new "multicultural" public sphere of cultural contention, restructured in response to mass movements.[8] Counter-cultural and leftist critical strategies shaped by post–World War II and post–civil rights American neoliberalism and empire, including cultural studies, poststructuralism, and postmodernism, have tracked the increasingly decentralized forms of ideological production within a political economy newly mediated by culture and dislodged from institutional foundations. Yet, these cultural and critical strategies have only barely addressed the cultural technologies and economies that mediated the American culture wars and that have continued to transform the industrial foundations of the capitalist political economy.

*I.K.U.* documents the transition from the analog Hollywood film industry that produced Scott's *Blade Runner* to the digital technologies that enable Cheang's irreverent sequel. Without nostalgia, *I.K.U.* shows the shift from the cumulative storytelling (montage) of narrative analog film to the dispersed composite images of computerized digital media.[9] This shift also moves viewing practices away from the more passive depth perception and consumption of the industrial film complex (Fordist Hollywood production, distribution, and theatrical reception) toward the personalized, interactive use of perceived images as windows for information, communication, and action. Without sentimentalizing, *I.K.U.* reminds us that these transitions remain tied to cross-sector corporate, state, military, and bio-techno-science institutions that have created and continue to manage and profit from a de-centralized transnational Internet-based economy. *I.K.U.* shows us that there is nothing "new," "postindustrial," or "global" about the digital economy. The Internet-based economy builds on and expands the *cultural modes* of economic development that gave Third World countries marginal, unequal entry into transnational economies dominated by Western European and Japanese empires before World War II and the United States and the USSR after World War II. The culturally-driven development of Third World economies exacerbated the violence, displacement, and structural inequalities of colonization, war, poverty, and hetero-patriarchal nationalisms. They also offered contingent work and mobility, especially to low-income gender and sexually nonconforming people, girls, and women, through service, leisure, entertainment, and sex industries that provided "secondary" intimate labor to formal industrial state economies in First and Second World countries and to developing formal economies in Third World countries.[10]

For instance, Cheang's *I.K.U.* poses connections between the Internet-based digital economy and Japanese and American militarized corporate sex, service, entertainment, and leisure industries in Northeast and Southeast Asia during World War II and the Cold War (Shigematsu and Camacho 2010). *I.K.U.*'s feminine Asian Coders were originally nursing robots. They were then recruited to work in a twenty-four-hour live porn show on Internet TV before becoming sexual data collectors. *I.K.U.* also links the high-tech economy to the pre-1990s analog American film and media industry through the image of the masculine Black American human Runner. The Runner documents the co-optation of the militarized masculine image of the Black Power movement by American mainstream media and policymakers starting in the mid-1960s (Ferguson 2003, 1–29; Keeling 2007, 95–117). This co-optation culminated in Hollywood's Blaxploitation films in the 1970s and then transnational Hollywood's mainstay images of black urban life by the end of the 1990s (Harris 2006, 63–78; Keeling 2007, 95–117). Both Coders and Runner perform forms of cultural labor considered tangential to the "hard" political economy. Yet, Cheang's film suggests that these disavowed cultural modes of labor not only sustain formal political economies but *drive* the material foundations of political economies.[11] Rather than trying to undo these images of exploitation, *I.K.U.* resituates these images within their cultural economies of production and poses the possibility of autonomy, pleasure, relationship, and subversion at the very edges of overextended, technologically facilitated transnational networks.[12]

## TRANS GENETICS, SPECIES, AND MEDIA IN CHEANG SHU LEA'S *UKI*

*UKI* (2009–2012) is Cheang's inverted sequel to *I.K.U.* While *I.K.U.* focused on the clone Coder's sexual data collection according to the Genom Corporation's programming, *UKI* focuses on the viral byproducts of Genom's intensified efforts to harness human sexual experience as data for profit. In *UKI*, the Internet-based bio-tech and media networks used to extract, store, and transmit sexual data crash and are abandoned by Genom. The corporation bypasses the embodied world of I.K.U. Coders, Runner, humans, digital technologies, and urban scenarios for programming at the micro-cellular level. Genom creates BioNet, a network of microcomputing cells that recode human orgasm into "self-sustaining pleasure" (Cheang 2000). In the transition from embodied

to intracellular networks, outdated I.K.U. Coders and networked digital technologies are dumped at electronic trash sites, off the visible urban grid. In these
e-dumps, junked I.K.U. Coders, Genom agents and Runners, UKI viral muta-
tions, and their offspring and co-habitants steal, swap, inject, lick, suck, and
ejaculate bits of code and bio-parts to form trans genetic mutants such as
part-human-clone and part-fly UKI Mosca and the code junkie Coder XQ.
This wasteland orgy of viral coding gives "birth" to the UKI virus. The UKI
virus tries to overtake the city and the human body, infiltrate the Genom Corporation's BioNet, and sabotage and reclaim its cellular orgasm data.

Together, *I.K.U.* and *UKI* have something to say about the so-called global
civil societies or public spheres facilitated by networked high-tech economies
in the twenty-first century.[13] *I.K.U.* envisioned a future controlled by a bio-tech-
media conglomerate and populated by the conglomerate's agents, workers, raw
material for extraction, and markets. In *I.K.U.*'s totalized networks of extraction, viewers are situated as interactive users positioned both inside and outside
*I.K.U.*'s worlds. This inside/outside position does not just amplify the pleasur-
able "liveness" of the digital film. It implicates viewer-users in the conglomerate's
processes of extraction as interceptors of data transmitted between conglomerate and workers and, ultimately, as "secondary" consumers of digital imagery
simulating the work of producing simulated experience. In *UKI*, the new media
interface shifts from the multiple screens (theater, TV, computer, installation
surface) of *I.K.U.* to the embedded kinesthetic and viewing technologies of networked performance and gaming. Part 1 of *UKI* is a "live code live spam" performance featuring an off-site junkyard inhabited by post-*I.K.U.* trans genetic viral
mutants and electronic trash. Each permutation of this performance in different
locations centers around a video recording that seems to be feeding live from the
e-junkyard.[14] This video feed–recording is played onscreen while being patched
together with other audiovisual media objects (including DNA and virus imag-
ing) by on-site artists and programmers who work collaboratively to create, mix,
control, and show the performance as data flows. Each performance provides
a site-specific sensory experience of what appears to be "live" communication
from the trans genetic viral inhabitants of an e-wasteland off-the-grid.

Part 2 of *UKI* is a "viral coding viral orgasm" game with two levels. The first
level, "Infect the City," invites us (the public) to sign on as UKI viral agents
using a Google Maps API Geolocation interface that pinpoints our geographic
location using cell towers and WiFi nodes. Once we are geographically embedded, we can infect our city "gesturally" based on the relationship between our
bodily location and our surroundings. Zooming out from our city, we can view
red blots that signal the spreading virus across multiple cities on the world map.
After collecting enough points from spreading the UKI virus, we move to the
second level, "Enter the BioNet." This part of the *UKI* viral game allows the inner

biochemical worlds of UKI agent-players to infiltrate the microcomputing cells of the Genom Corporation's BioNet. Here, multiple UKI agent-players occupy a dark room together wearing biosensors that detect the skin's responses to internal emotion, thought, and motion. Sensory data based on skin responses is sent wirelessly from each agent-player to a computer, which uses the data to change the pattern, speed, and rhythm of moving red laser lights and the low bass pulsing of subwoofers in the room. When agent-players' biosensory data levels synchronize, one red laser beam in the likeness of one Genom microcomputing blood cell (representing one unit of millions of blood cells) goes out. The elimination of one laser beam or blood cell changes the level of self-sustaining orgasm produced by the engineered cell, which changes the pulsating rhythm of the subwoofers. Once all laser beams or cells are destroyed, the subwoofers cease also.

As the counterpart to *I.K.U.*'s world of embodied biological and media technologies, Cheang's *UKI* makes visible and "felt" the disembodied off-world sites that are the new frontiers colonized by transnational high-tech conglomerate states. The high-tech-initiated dematerialization of the human and human productivity (across biological, social, and political economic spheres of life) during the turn of the twenty-first century is further intensified by biomolecular and electromagnetic technologies that penetrate divisions between surface and depth, outside and inside, above and below, self and other, and subject and object. The Genom Corporation bypasses the use of human clones for mass sexual entertainment in order to capitalize directly on intracellular life through genetically engineered cells that self-reproduce orgasm. *UKI* Part 1 shows the fallout from this shift in the junked body parts that have been evicted from *I.K.U.*'s world. This electronic waste remains off-site and invisible in the transition to micro- and macro-scopic scales of technologically facilitated capitalism. Making the junkyard visible, *UKI*'s viral performance calls attention to the exploitative social ecologies produced by what is considered officially to be the clean and equalizing high-tech global economy. Electronic pollution in Ghana's global dumping grounds, cassiterite mining in the Congo, semiconductor sweatshops in Northeast and Southeast Asia, and undervalued creative labor in the global North highlight the new forms of extraction, exploitation, and labor that occupy the invisible edges of the networked transnational high-tech economy.[15] Instead of arguing for the inclusion of these off-sites into the formal political economy, *UKI* sees these wayward sites as sites of trans genesis, where rejected bodies reuse, revalue, reassemble, and transform refuse parts into trans genetic, species, and media forms.

Cheang's work ends where it begins, with the almost naturalized premise that the human never was pure or exempt from the exploitative operations of social institutions. In this way, Cheang's networked art focuses on the embodied perspectives of gender, racial, sexual, and class deviants pushed to edges of

Euro-American liberal political economies of the human, even as their/our bodies, cultures, and experiences are made objects of extraction. Without investment in late twentieth-/early twenty-first-century utopian or dystopian views on the human in relationship to technology, Cheang's work calls for a reclaiming of biological, communications, and media technologies from their control and management by transnational corporate states. By using the very high-tech networks created and used by dominant institutions, Cheang's *trans* media generates the possibility of autonomous, collaborative, and subversive play, pleasure, relation, and coordination.[16] In *UKI* and *I.K.U.* in particular, trans gender/sex/sexual, genetic, and species counter-humans create and transform the under- and off-sites of the twenty-first-century new global economy.

## CONCLUSION: TRANS MICRO-POLITICS

This chapter has focused on the interplay between the networked trans media art of Cheang Shu Lea and Ridley Scott's emblematic Hollywood film. In "reading" the differential representational politics of these cultural objects, I have used trans critical practices that build on—while also moving beyond—a *textual* politics of interpretation and meaning-making invested in exposing and countering ideologies that perpetuate heteronormative, racist white Euro-American social orders. Critical trans practices reconnect the politics of cultural interpretation, representation, and production to the technologies, political economies, and social histories that mediate culture, social identities, and political mobilization. They also question and reengage material relationships between culture, society, and political economy through everyday interactions at the micro scales of experience, embodiment, sensory perception, and biochemical processes. Counter to the psychologizing, individualizing, and privatizing of trans practices of bodily transformation and identification by medical, state, moral, and corporate institutions, critical *trans* practices are co-created in *situated* response to social conditions of racially binary gender/sex/sexual subjugation, policing, and control that penetrate and structure the biological, natural, and genetic, in excess of the paradigms through which we understand cultural "norms."[17]

Trans micro-practices emerge at a moment when social identities go beyond mere mediation by "secondary" cultural apparatuses legitimizing the unequal racial, gender, sexual, and class distribution of power, wealth, and value by liberal capitalist nation-states, led by the United States since the end of World War II.[18] They appear at the turn of the twenty-first century when digitally based transnational biocultural economies form the very infrastructure and adaptive motive force of political economies in the global North. Yet, trans practices and social identities do not represent a new avant-garde in relationship to a new postindustrial stage of liberal capitalism. As shown in the media art produced by a gender queer diasporic migrant wired to an island in North/Southeast Asia that never attained postcolonial nationhood amid Dutch, Japanese, Chinese, and American imperialisms, trans micro-politics draw from the critical experiences of trans people of color, low-income people, and diasporic migrants who have continued to navigate life at the edges of transnational imperial and liberal political economies in their past, present, and future incarnations.

## NOTES

1. I use the term *trans* broadly to include transgender, transsexual, genderqueer, bigender, third gender, mixed gender, gender f*uck, gender fluid, agender, genderless, MtF, FtM, Two Spirit, nonbinary, androgynous, feminine/masculine of center, and other non-*cisgender*/ *cis*sexual, gender-variant, and gender-nonconforming identities and expressions. Nevertheless, I use the term *trans* purposefully as a prefix delinked from gender to position *trans* as a potential intervention in the Western racially binary gender/sex/sexual system that continues not only to correlate gender with sex and sexuality but also to establish Western medical-political-economic conceptions of gender, sex, and sexuality (and their relationships to one another) as the hegemonic basis for understanding and valuing embodied experience, expression, and identification globally and universally. My use of *trans* as an intervening prefix is in conversation with the work of Janet Mock, Eva Hayward, and Mel Chen. See also the term "*trans**" as a way to include more diverse gender expressions and identities as the term *transgender* becomes more codified.
2. Thanks to Jennifer Terry for introducing me to Cheang's *I.K.U.* and *UKI*.
3. In addition to viewers' own suspicion about the authentic human status of Deckard, certain interviews with Ridley Scott have "confirmed" that Deckard himself is a Replicant. See *Blade Runner* (Four-Disc Collector's Edition).
4. On the relationship between analogy and analog, see Wendy Chun's work on digitalization.
5. For racial and gender analysis of Hollywood's archives of Orientalist imagery, see the work of Celine Parreñas Shimizu and Jack Shaheen.
6. In *The War of Desire and Technology at the Close of the Mechanical Age*, Allucquère Rosanne Stone interrupts scientifically driven narratives that represent communications technology in the virtual age as purely "prosthetic" tools that extend or replace human agency. Instead, she argues that computerized technologies are based in and help to create experiences of social interaction that transform the identities, boundaries, and relationships between technology and nature, human and machine, human and human, and human and self. For Stone, the gendered body itself is also a virtual "prosthesis" that provides zones of dynamic interaction, boundary shifting, and communicated meaning. This argument goes even further than displacing the social ordering of the body through the hierarchy of primary to secondary biological signs for sex. It displaces the body itself as the originary "home" and image for what is conceived of as the human spirit/soul/mind.
7. On the racially gendered and sexual figuring of Asian/American women through legal, public, and cinematic discourses, see the work of Laura Hyun Yi Kang and Celine Parreñas Shimizu.
8. This period of liberalization included the loosening and then lifting of Hollywood Production Codes by 1968. The codes censored not only the onscreen representation of homosexuality and other sexual or erotic practices deemed perverse but also erotic relationships between whites and nonwhites.

**9.** For Lev Manovich, new media is the "shift of all culture to computer-mediated forms of production, distribution, and communication" (2001, 19). The convergence of computing and media technologies, including film, has realized the potential for nonlinearity already present in cinema.

**10.** I would include the "unskilled" assembly work done by Third World women and girls in Export Processing Zones along the international chain of corporate production in this categorization of "secondary" intimate labor. Like work in service, leisure, entertainment, and sex industries, assembly work is not valued culturally or commercially within formal chains of productivity within the imaginary of global capital.

**11.** My claim builds on the work of Lisa Duggan and Dean Spade in appropriating the predominantly white Euro-American leftist critique of neoliberalism (and the material conditions the term describes) toward a focus on dispossessed racial, sexual, and gender social identities, cultures, and communities that remain illegible within paradigms of class and political economics, including trans women of color doing survival work.

**12.** On theories of autonomy under conditions of deindustrialization, see the work of Grace Lee Boggs. On the technological infrastructure that has facilitated deindustrialization while enabling unintended autonomous exploits, see the work of Alexander Galloway and Eugene Thacker.

**13.** In using the term *public sphere*, I am referring to Jürgen Habermas's intervention in conventional political theories of civil society by emphasizing the mediating role of print culture in facilitating popular participation in a bourgeois public sphere constituted as a rational sphere of action and decision making, independent from the authority of the state and family.

**14.** *UKI* Part 1's original performance was located at the Hangar Studio, Barcelona, where the junkyard set was built.

**15.** For more elaboration on the structural impact of high-tech digital economy on countries and local communities in southern Africa, refer to Sokari Ekine's work.

**16.** For further elaboration on my use of the term *trans media*, see my essay on "transmedia" co-written with Lissette Olivares in the *Transgender Studies Quarterly*.

**17.** Janet Mock's memoires in *Redefining Realness* give such close attention to these situated moments of negotiating survival, self-discovery, and self-transformation across different geopolitical locations and social institutions.

**18.** In using the description "secondary" cultural apparatuses, I am referencing Louis Althusser's "Ideology and Ideological State Apparatuses: Notes towards an Investigation" (Althusser 2001, 85–126).

## REFERENCES

Althusser, Louis. 2001. *Lenin and Philosophy and Other Essays.* New York: Monthly Review Press.

Anzaldúa, Gloria. 2012. *Borderlands/La Frontera: The New Mestiza.* San Francisco: Aunt Lute Books.

*Blade Runner* (Four-Disc Collector's Edition). Directed by Ridley Scott. 1982. Burbank, CA: Warner Home Studio, 2007. DVD.

Boggs, Grace Lee. 2012. *The Next American Revolution: Sustainable Activism for the Twenty-First Century.* Berkeley: University of California Press.

Chen, Jian, and Lissette Olivares. 2014. "Transmedia." *Transgender Studies Quarterly* 1.1: 245–248.

Chen, Mel Y. 2012. *Animacies: Biopolitics, Racial Mattering, and Queer Affect.* Durham, NC: Duke University Press.

Chun, Wendy Hui Kyong. 2013. *Programmed Visions: Software and Memory*. Cambridge, MA: MIT Press.

Duggan, Lisa. 2003. *The Twilight of Equality? Neoliberalism, Cultural Politics, and the Attack on Democracy*. Boston: Beacon Press.

Ekine, Sokari. 2010. *SMS Uprising: Mobile Activism in Africa*. Oxford: Pambazuka Press.

Everett, Karen. 1996. *I Shall Not Be Removed: The Life of Marlon Riggs*. Directed/performed by Karen Everett, Barbara Christian, Deborah Hoffman, Brian Freeman, and Vivian Kleiman. San Francisco: California Newsreel. Video.

Ferguson, Roderick. 2003. *Aberrations in Black: Toward a Queer of Color Critique*. Minneapolis: University of Minnesota Press.

Fiol-Matta, Licia. 2002. *Queer Mother for the Nation: The State and Gabriela Mistral*. Minneapolis: University of Minnesota Press.

Galloway, Alexander, and Eugene Thacker. 2007. *The Exploit: A Theory of Networks*. Minneapolis: University of Minnesota Press.

Habermas, Jürgen. 1991. *The Structural Transformation of the Public Sphere: An Inquiry into a Category of Bourgeois Society*. Cambridge, MA: MIT Press.

Harris, Keith. 2006. *Boys, Boyz, Bois: The Ethics of Black Masculinity in Film and Popular Media*. New York: Routledge.

Harvey, David. 1990. *The Condition of Postmodernity: An Enquiry into the Origins of Cultural Change*. Malden, MA: Blackwell Publishers.

Hayward, Eva. 2008. "More Lessons from a Starfish: Prefixial Flesh and Transspeciated Selves." *Women's Studies Quarterly* 36.3–4 (Fall/Winter): 64–85.

Hunter, Nan D. 2006. "Contextualizing the Sexuality Debates: A Chronology 1966–2005." In *Sex Wars: Sexual Dissent and Political Culture*, edited by Lisa Duggan and Nan D. Hunter, 15–28. New York: Routledge.

*I.K.U.* Directed by Cheang Shu Lea. 2000. Tokyo, Japan: Uplink Co., 2000. DVD.

Kang, Laura Hyun Yi. 2002. *Compositional Subjects: Enfiguring Asian/American Women*. Durham, NC: Duke University Press.

Keeling, Kara. 2007. *The Witch's Flight: The Cinematic, the Black Femme, and the Image of Common Sense*. Durham, NC: Duke University Press.

Manovich, Lev. 2001. *The Language of New Media*. Cambridge, MA: MIT Press.

Mercer, Kobena. 1994. *Welcome to the Jungle: New Positions in Black Cultural Studies*. New York: Routledge.

Mock, Janet. 2014. *Redefining Realness: My Path to Womanhood, Identity, Love & So Much More*. New York: Atria Books.

Nama, Adilifu. 2008. *Black Space: Imagining Race in Science Fiction Film*. Austin: University of Texas Press.

*Reel Bad Arabs: How Hollywood Vilifies a People*. 2007 Directed by Jeremy Earp and Sut Jhally. 2007. Northampton, MA: Media Education Fund. DVD.

Rubin, Gayle. 2011. *Deviations: A Gayle Rubin Reader*. Durham, NC: Duke University Press.

Shaheen, Jack. 2001. *Reel Bad Arabs: How Hollywood Vilifies a People*. Northampton, MA: Olive Branch Press.

Shigematsu, Setsu, and Keith L. Camacho. 2010. "Introduction: Militarized Currents, Decolonizing Futures." In *Militarized Currents: Toward a Decolonized Future in Asia and the Pacific*, edited by Setsu Shigematsu and Keith L. Camacho, 15–41. Minneapolis: University of Minnesota Press.

Shimizu, Celine Parreñas. 2007. *The Hypersexuality of Race: Performing Asian/American Women on Screen and Scene*. Durham, NC: Duke University Press.

————. 2012. *Straitjacket Sexualities: Unbinding Asian American Manhoods in the Movies.* Stanford, CA: Stanford University Press.

Sobchack, Vivian. 2001. *Screening Space: The American Science Fiction Film.* New Brunswick, NJ: Rutgers University Press.

Spade, Dean. 2011. *Normal Life: Administrative Violence, Critical Trans Politics and the Limits of Law.* New York: South End Press.

Stone, Allucquère Rosanne. 1996. *The War of Desire and Technology at the Close of the Mechanical Age.* Cambridge, MA: MIT Press.

*UKI.* Conceived by Cheang Shu Lea. 2009–2012. http://www.u-k-i.co/index.html.

# PART III CROSSING BORDERS/ CROSSING GENDER

# 6 · WHEN THINGS DON'T ADD UP

## Transgender Bodies and the Mobile Borders of Biometrics

TOBY BEAUCHAMP

In November 2001, the U.S. Congress held a hearing on "Biometric Identifiers and the Modern Face of Terror," in which Senator Diane Feinstein claimed that the individuals who carried out the airline hijackings of September 11, 2001 were able to do so because "we could not identify them" (U.S. Congress 2001, 36). Throughout the hearing, legislators and industry experts alike singled out biometrics as a crucial tool in identifying terrorists as well as in regulating immigration. Unlike identification documents that might be falsified or exchanged between different bodies, biometrics link identity to unique aspects of the individual physical body—such as fingerprints, facial features and bone structure, or irises—that are thought to be immutable and therefore objectively analyzed. Once such physical features are cataloged, they can then be used as comparative data to verify identity as bodies move through various types of security checks. Because it relies on data recorded directly from the physical body, biometric identification may appear to be—as the congressional hearing suggests—a more objective, accurate, and dependable method of identification.[1]

In this chapter I use the critical lens of Transgender Studies to examine recent biometric surveillance practices, a task that requires somewhat of a sideways approach since, with only very rare exceptions, biometric identification has not specifically addressed the category of transgender. In fact, gender and other identity categories may seem quite distant from biometrics: scientists, legislators, and police emphasize the ability of these technologies to analyze the body's immutable physical data empirically, thereby escaping the subjective character-istics of ID cards or self-reporting. Yet considering biometric surveillance in the context of transgender politics—even when very few cases explicitly concern transgender-identified people—offers a useful entry point for critically assess-ing biometrics' reliance on and (re)production of normative understandings of gendered and racialized bodies, particularly when used in efforts to identify the figures of the terrorist and the immigrant.

With this in mind, the chapter is divided into three major parts. In the first section I examine the notion that biometric surveillance avoids gender and racial bias by focusing only on objective data extracted from (and later matched to) individual bodies, and I clarify how normative ideals of gender and race underwrite this form of surveillance. In the second section I focus on biomet-ric technologies' purported ability to fix individual bodies in place and track their movements by hinging identity to unique, stable physical characteristics. I demonstrate how the persistent metaphors of mobility and deception attached to gender-nonconforming bodies work alongside state anxieties about national and gendered borders. The final section concerns new biometrics research that takes up "transgender" as a special object of study. I consider how such work might reinforce gendered boundaries and how nonconforming bodies become a contrast against which normative gender appears naturally stable, such that surveillance may seem harmless or nonexistent for normative bodies. I suggest that we might more usefully understand the difficulty with which surveillance technologies struggle to accurately identify noncompliant bodies as indicative of fundamental problems with rigid classification.

## CREATING CATEGORIES

Although post–9/11 state and public discourse often casts biometric surveil-lance as a newly emergent tool for national security, current biometric prac-tices rest on a long history of bodily classification. For instance, fingerprinting techniques forwarded by Francis Galton in late nineteenth-century England fundamentally relied on the physical body as an object to be studied, classified, and ranked. These programs worked alongside Alphonse Bertillon's nineteenth-century introduction of anthropometrics as a tool for distinguishing among individuals based on a detailed system of bodily measurements. Primarily used to track and identify criminals, early anthropometry both prefigures post–9/11 biometric surveillance and aligns with eugenics programs of the late nineteenth and early twentieth centuries. All of these efforts rely on visual scrutiny and sci-entific measurement of the physical body in order to justify classifying certain populations as unhealthy, dangerous, or degenerate. Drawing on the supposedly unambiguous truths of both the physical body and the photographic image, and backed by Western science's claim to a neutral gaze, biometric technologies have long been a site at which numerous investments in truth converge.

Yet while biometric programs may appear to classify the body ever more precisely, transforming it into objective, unalterable, and unambiguous data points, other technologies hinder these classification efforts by transforming bodies' appearances or movements. For instance, prosthetics alter or constrain the body's movements; surgeries add, remove, or reshape not only internal organs but also the body's visual surface; and synthetic hormones and other drugs augment or alter the body's chemical makeup. Moreover, even without obvious biomedical interventions, bodies push against and disrupt the calculating gaze of surveillance technologies. This is because, as I show below, such technologies interpret bodies through regulatory norms of race, class, sexuality, and gender—a lens through which various nonconforming bodies appear troubling or even illegible. Thus while biometric efforts such as fingerprinting and iris recognition may seem removed from cultural biases by merely recording individual bodily features, they are founded on the desire to distinguish scientifically between safe and threatening bodies, categories already shaped by gendered and racialized viewing practices.

Fingerprinting practices exemplify the ways that biometric classification relies on gender and race even while disavowing those categories' influence. Arguing against the common assumption that "individuality as expressed by the fingerprint inherently undermined racial categorization," Simon Cole demonstrates that Galton's groundbreaking work on fingerprint identification relied heavily on group categorization, by classifying samples according to the subjects' race and gender in an effort to determine group patterns (Cole 2009, 230). These early fingerprinting efforts sought to separate different groups neatly into clear hierarchies, and bodies deemed inconsistent or ambiguous helped justify eugenic logic, rationalizing the need to identify and eliminate impure subjects. Yet those same bodies confounded eugenic classification schemes: Cole notes that Galton repeatedly failed to classify prints according to predefined types, "because he kept coming across 'transitional' patterns that could be construed as belonging to more than one type," which he referred to as "mulatto," discursively linking mixed-race bodies with mixed-type prints (2009, 233). Although racial difference profoundly informed Galton's motivations and interpretations, fingerprinting could nevertheless appear removed from cultural bias—in ways that anthropometry's scrutiny of facial features often did not—because it used a less overtly racially charged bodily characteristic through which to push forward the classification of different racialized "types."

More recently, multiple research studies have sought to categorize fingerprint samples by gender, pointing out patterned differences used by researchers to distinguish between male and female prints. One study notes that gender classification through fingerprints could "minimize the suspects search list and give a likelihood probability value of the gender of a suspect" in criminal investigations (Badawi et al. 2006, 46). Other researchers propose even broader uses for reading gender through fingerprints, given "large scale adoption of fingerprint recognition for civilian applications" (Frick et al. 2008, 721). Because these studies themselves presume fixed and universally applicable definitions of "male" and "female," bodies and identities that do not conform to such definitions may disrupt the apparent precision upon which biometric surveillance relies. Moreover, the subjective conceptions of male and female bodies used by researchers to guide such studies help produce and shape the gendered categories that they take as unquestioned fact.

In their analysis of post–9/11 airport screening policies, Paisley Currah and Tara Mulqueen (2011) argue that, although gender in itself does not denote a unique individual identity, gender markers such as $M$ or $F$ nonetheless function as biometric identifiers: they are used to help verify identity based on physical characteristics assumed to be permanent and readily apparent. Currah and Mulqueen show how these assumptions may then situate gender-nonconforming bodies as threatening anomalies. Thus, while biometric surveillance may seem to define identity in ways that move beyond racial and gendered characteristics, it remains fundamentally tied to them. This is not only because "the machines must rely on the unpredictable technology of human perception" but also because categories of race and gender structure the very development of biometric research, data collection, and screening practices (Bohling 2012).

## SHIFTING BORDERS

Given this context, we might think more carefully about recent state investments in biometric surveillance programs. The reference to the "modern face of terror" in the 2001 congressional hearing invokes a desire for innovative ways of identifying terrorist figures who stealthily weaken the nation and stymie U.S. security measures. Kelly Gates explains that the state's repeated concept of the face of terror offers "a caricatured version of 'the enemy,' while at the same time suggesting the existence of a terrorist facial type" (2011, 106). Because the hearings focus on the face in this way, their primary goal seems to be determining appropriate strategies for classifying such a face, not just in terms of identity but through careful measurement and scrutiny of the body itself. In this context, the phrase "the face of terror" might imply that there is a particular bodily characteristic representative of the terrorist. The identification of such a characteristic would then promise to bring order—not through overt discipline but through observation and classification of the physical body—to a figure otherwise understood as chaotic and untraceable.

Just two weeks after 9/11 and almost two months before the congressional hearings on the modern face of terror, a major corporate developer of facial recognition and fingerprint matching programs, Visionics, released its own report, titled "Protecting Civilization from the Faces of Terror." Asserting that "our best defenses lie squarely with the ability to properly identify those who pose a threat to our national security and on that basis deny them free movement," the report offers Visionics' facial recognition technology as "the shield" that protects American citizens (presumably the "civilization" referenced in the report's title) from threatening, deceptive outsiders (Visionics 2001, 2, 5). Visionics is quick to assure us (twice within the space of an eight-page report) that "terrorism is not faceless and is not without identity" (5). Yet the very marker of "terrorist" is premised on such a figure being unknowable and unmanageable. This is a central contradiction for both Visionics and the entire project of biometric identification: although biometric technologies claim that bodies are inherently stable and identifiable, that promise is based on the fear and possibility that bodies can change and hide.

When Visionics CEO and chairman Joseph Atick spoke at the congressional hearings, his statement reiterated the notion that "terror is not faceless," but it also spoke to the ways that biometric surveillance sorts bodies and identities into safe/unsafe classifications that themselves appear predetermined (U.S. Congress 2001, 38). For instance, in explaining that biometric programs would not impinge on the privacy accorded to citizen bodies, Atick explains, "This is not a national ID system. It does not identify you or me. It is simply a criminal and terrorist alarm" (37). Such reassurances assume a clear and unwavering delineation between the terrorist and "you or me," suggesting that certain bodies are inherently fraudulent or dangerous and thus subject to biometric scrutiny while others are legible as good citizens as a matter of course. Atick also insists on the permanence and singularity of bodily identification, explaining that Visionics' facial recognition program takes a "faceprint" that is "identity-specific": "it does not change with aging and it is not affected by viewing conditions and also not affected by superficial disguises" (2001, 37). Biometric programs thus purport to identify and track those bodies that are, seemingly by definition, unknowable. As surveillance studies scholar Katja Aas explains, "now, with the help of technology, bodies are seen as a source of unprecedented accuracy and precision. The coded body does not need to be disciplined, because its natural patterns are in themselves a source of order" (Aas 2006, 153).

Senator Orrin Hatch (R-UT) praised biometrics as a safeguard against terrorism for just this reason, claiming that, "while individuals may be able to disguise their appearance sufficiently to fool the human eye, the technology [of] today can thwart the most sophisticated criminal mind" (U.S. Congress 2001, 9). Hatch went on to argue that, with the increased use of biometrics as part of

border security, "impersonation would be dramatically curtailed, if not elimi-
nated all together" (9). This stance is aligned with a statement from the U.S.
Department of Defense's research project on biometric surveillance, which contends that "terrorists are able to move freely throughout the world, [and] to hide
when necessary" (Defense 2003, 313). Meanwhile, Senator Strom Thurmond
(R-SC) called for biometric identifiers for all noncitizens entering the United
States and for a return to the annual registration of all immigrants and aliens, a
practice that was formally discontinued in 1981 (U.S. Congress 2001, 72). These
comments portray the threatening body as a foreign one that crosses national
borders undetected, its menacing mobility made possible by this body's inherent ability to hide or falsify its identity. In response to this threat, state actors
turn to biometric surveillance as that which would, by exposing the body's true
and singular identity, fix it in place and curtail its movement.

These remarks also further indicate why biometric surveillance may be of
concern for transgender and gender-nonconforming persons. Shoshana Magnet suggests that "most at risk from having their race, sex, and gender identities
biometrically codified are those who refuse neat categorizations as well as those
whose bodies the state believes to be a threat" (Magnet 2011, 48). The threat
that gender-nonconforming bodies appear to pose often stems from the association of gender transgression with inherent dishonesty: these identities "may be
misjudged as 'disguises'" or other forms of deception (Bohling 2012). Accusa-
tions of impersonation and deceptive identity regularly adhere to transgender
people in a number of cultural and political contexts. For instance, in 2012 an
Oklahoma judge refused to grant legal name changes to two transgender women,
writing in an order that "they are nothing more than an imitation of the opposite
sex" (Clay 2012). He claimed that "to grant a name change in this case would be
to assist that which is fraudulent." This discourse of fraudulence echoes across
popular culture sites such as daytime talk shows, police and medical dramas, and
reality television. Notably, the judge denying name changes cited DNA as evidence that one's sex and gender can never really change. Aligned with the most
basic logic upon which biometric identification rests, the judge's rationale insists
that identity is permanently and immutably located in the supposedly original
constitution of the body.[2]

This desire to hinge identity to the seemingly unchanging body is especially
clear in the context of antiterrorism efforts and the policing of national borders,
making biometric surveillance a particular concern for gender-nonconforming
people who are vulnerable to arrest, detention, or deportation. In a 2006 report
jointly released by the organizations Human Rights Watch and Immigration
Equality, a transgender woman from the Bahamas describes her experience as
an immigrant in the United States. Detained and awaiting deportation, she spent
several weeks in a men's housing unit before being transferred to a jail, where

her location in solitary confinement and the fact that the institution registered her under various names both hindered her ability to meet with the immigration officers assigned to her case. When she did see an officer, his explanation of her treatment succinctly linked her gender-nonconforming body with border control anxieties in the context of the war on terror. "He told me, 'These are scary times, what with terrorism, we need to know who we're letting into the country. When things don't add up'—me transitioning—'that's a problem,'" she recounts (Human Rights Watch 2006, 87). The officer's statement suggests that questions of citizenship and belonging depend upon both physical space and physical bodies. Likewise, the deceptive mobility that Hatch and Thurmond reference appears here as the transgression of two different but related boundaries—those drawn around gender and those drawn around citizenship—that link gender nonconformity to unregulated immigration practices.

The notion that physical bodies serve as the absolute, unchanging truth of identity attaches to the figure of the transgender person across multiple arenas, discursively and materially linking gender nonconformity to fears of deception that fuel many anti-immigrant and anti-terrorist measures. Magnet notes that, because studies and programs using biometrics "assume neat bifurcations of gender into the mutually exclusive categories of male and female, the transsexual and transgendered community in particular faces significant risks from biometric identification," including potentially dangerous public identification as transgender or vulnerability to "the prying eyes of the state" (Magnet 2011, 49). The body's noncompliance with gendered categories presumed to be stable and easily legible does not only disrupt the borders that the state relies on to clearly mark out citizenship and national security; it also throws into relief the normative assumptions—and thus, in Magnet's terms, the failures—built into biometric surveillance practices.

## NOVEL CHALLENGES

In response to the disruptions that gender-nonconforming bodies provoke in state surveillance practices, some of the most recent research in biometrics specifically addresses data collection and technological interpretation of transgender-identified bodies. For instance, researchers studying facial recognition technology contend that sex hormones used as part of medical transition change facial shape and texture in ways that present a "novel challenge" to biometric surveillance: "preliminary results indicate that HRT [hormone replacement therapy] significantly impacts match scores, necessitating the development of new algorithmic techniques to deal with this emerging challenge" (Ricanek 2013, 96). As part of their work on this topic, these researchers have compiled a database of face images of transgender-identified people who have taken hormones for at least one year and are developing new biometric recognition frameworks based on this data set to improve "recognition accuracy" (Ricanek 2013, 96).

At first glance, this research may appear beneficial: it names transgender as a category often misread by biometric practices and aims to interpret transgender people's biometric data accurately by specifically studying the bodies within that category. Such studies would seem to alleviate the problems that current biometric programs pose for transgender people. Yet they also have concerning effects. By defining "transgender" in particular ways (such as length of hormone use), the studies reinforce certain boundaries around this category, echoing the boundaries already in place around "male" and "female" bodies in biometric data collection and interpretation. As a result, this work produces new nonconforming bodies that are not compliant with these measures of transgender status. And although this research may appear to break down the universalized and normative male/female logic upon which biometric technology typically rests, positioning transgender bodies as a separate and unique "challenge" actually fortifies the boundaries around male and female as normative, legibly sexed bodies and fails to contest gendered categories in any significant way.

Additionally, while it may be unfair to expect otherwise from a research program clearly designed and funded to improve the efficacy of biometric technologies, the work undertaken here is troubling in that it supports a broader culture of surveillance by explicitly incorporating transgender bodies as new objects of study in state surveillance practices and policies. For those transgender people already scrutinized on the basis of race, nationality, or citizenship status, the amassing of databases for new transgender-specific biometric surveillance may increase vulnerability by improving the state's ability to identify and track them. Just as refining biometric technologies to include transgender bodies creates new forms of deviant illegibility (those bodies not recognized as transgender yet also not compliant with standardized male/female categories), it also creates new methods for the biopolitical regulation of transgender people as a population.

Rather than viewing transgender and gender-nonconforming bodies as problems that biometric technologies must adapt to account for, we might more usefully understand the problems as being built into biometric surveillance itself. The difficulties with which surveillance programs and technologies encounter nonconforming bodies also provokes confusion and anxiety in normative bodies, as when even the most privileged feel a seemingly unnecessary fear that their ID card will be misinterpreted, that their driver's license is out of date, that their body may set off the metal detector. In this broader context, we can productively understand the concept of bodily incongruences not as anomalous threats or as fixed markers of deviance but, rather, as constructed and shifting qualities—and in this way, indicative of how fragile the state's grasp on bodily norms might be. As Magnet contends, "biometric technologies cannot be counted on effectively and definitively to identify *any* bodies" (2011, 50). To refuse this conclusion—to remain invested in biometric data as the truth of gendered and racialized bodies—highlights the continued need for bodies marked as nonconforming or troublingly mobile to serve as contrasts against which normative gender and movement can be secured as both natural and stable.

The increased scrutiny or "challenge" of nonconforming bodies suggests biometrics' difficulty in categorizing what appears disorderly and indicates ruptures in scientific, gender, and racial systems so often assumed to be airtight. Katja Aas suggests that new biometric technologies work on a binary language that "radically reduces the possibilities for negotiation and therefore also resistance" (Aas 2006, 150). Yet this dependence on binary logic is necessarily undone by physical bodies' refusal to adhere to such classifications. Western science and the U.S. state have long touted biometrics as that which uncovers the fraudulent identity precisely because the body cannot lie. But this technology—and the interpretative work it produces—relies on rigid binary classifications of citizenship, race, risk, and sex/gender that are themselves pretenses. In this light, the duplicitous, dangerously mobile body is not tamed or uncovered by biometrics; rather, it reflects back biometric technologies' own falsehoods.

## NOTES

1. Although there are some similarities, biometric surveillance differs from other bodily identification practices such as genetic testing in part because biometric matches are meant to occur instantaneously and, in some cases, without any bodily information voluntarily or knowingly provided by the individual (as when facial recognition programs rely on photographs).

2. Like biometric programs, some LGBT advocates suggest that gender and sexuality are innate and tied to the body, such that one is "born" with a particular gender or sexual identity, as a response to anti-LGBT arguments that non-normative gender and sexuality are choices (and thus can and should be reformed). In turn, this strategy has come under critical analysis within queer studies (see for example Terry 1997). Currah and Mulqueen explain that in the specific context of biometrics, conceptions of gender as "an unchanging biometric characteristic" fail to account for the ways that gender is "not a singular entity" but includes "individual gender identity, state classification decisions (as M or F), a body that may or may not have been modified to some degree, and presentation through dress and behavior of the 'cultural insignia' of gender" (Currah and Mulqueen 2011, 571).

## REFERENCES

Aas, Katja Franko. 2006. "The Body Does Not Lie: Identity, Risk, and Trust in Technoculture." *Crime, Media, Culture* 2.2: 143–158.

Badawi, Ahmed, Mohamed Mahfouz, Rimon Tadross, and Richard Jantz. 2006. "Fingerprint-Based Gender Classification." In *Proceedings of the 2006 International Conference on*

*Image Processing, Computer Vision, and Pattern Recognition,* edited by Hamid R. Arabnia, 1:41–46. Las Vegas: CSREA Press.

Bohling, Alissa. 2012. "Transgender, Gender Non-Conforming People among First, Most Affected by War on Terror's Biometrics Craze." *Truthout,* April 16.

Clay, Nolan. 2012. "Oklahoma Judge Refuses to Let Men Planning Sex-Change Operations Have Feminine Names." *The Oklahoman,* September 16.

Cole, Simon A. 2009. "Twins, Twain, Galton, and Gilman: Fingerprinting, Individualization, Brotherhood, and Race in *Pudd'nhead Wilson.*" *Configurations* 15: 227–265.

Currah, Paisley, and Tara Mulqueen. 2011. "Securitizing Gender: Identity, Biometrics, and Transgender Bodies at the Airport." *Social Research* 78(2): 557–582.

Defense Advanced Research Projects Agency (DARPA). 2003. "Fiscal Year (FY) 2004/FY 2005 Biennial Budget Estimates." February.

Frick, Michael D., Shimon K. Modi, Stephen J. Elliott, and Eric P. Kukula. 2008. "Impact of Gender on Fingerprint Recognition Systems." In *Proceedings of the Fifth International Conference on Information Technology and Applications,* edited by David Tien and Manolya Kavakli, 717–721. Bathurst, NSW: Macquarie Scientific Publishing.

Gates, Kelly A. 2011. *Our Biometric Future: Facial Recognition Technology and the Culture of Surveillance.* New York: New York University Press.

Human Rights Watch and Immigration Equality. 2006. *Family Unvalued: Discrimination, Denial, and the Fate of Binational Same-Sex Couples under U.S. Law.* http://www.hrw.org/reports/2006/us0506/index.htm.

Magnet, Shoshana Amielle. 2011. *When Biometrics Fail: Gender, Race, and the Technology of Identity.* Durham, NC: Duke University Press.

Ricanek, Karl. 2013. "The Next Biometric Challenge: Medical Alterations." *Computer* 46.9: 94–96.

Terry, Jennifer. 1997. "The Seductive Power of Science in the Making of Deviant Subjectivities." In *Science and Homosexualities,* edited by Vernon A. Rosario, 271–296. New York: Routledge.

U.S. Congress. Senate Committee on the Judiciary, Subcommittee on Technology, Terrorism, and Government Information. 2001. "Biometric Identifiers and the Modern Face of Terror: New Technologies in the Global War on Terrorism." Washington, DC: U.S. Government Printing Office.

Visionics. 2001. "Protecting Civilization from the Faces of Terror: A Primer on the Role Facial Recognition Technology Can Play in Enhancing Airport Security." Jersey City, NJ: Visionics Corporation.

# 7 · CONNECTING THE DOTS

## National Security, the Crime-Migration Nexus, and Trans Women's Survival

NORA BUTLER BURKE

        In late January 2012, news rapidly spread through social media and among trans activists in Canada claiming that a recent amendment to federal flight regulations would ban all trans people from boarding a plane within Canada if they did not have identification documents that corresponded to their gender appearance, or if there were major discrepancies between different IDs (Gollom and Engelhardt 2012; Raj 2012). Article 5.2 (1) of the Identity Screening Regulations specified that "An air carrier shall not transport a passenger if . . . the passenger does not appear to be of the gender indicated on the identification he or she presents" (*Canada* 2007). Trans activists circulated petitions, spoke out in the media, and lobbied the federal government, denouncing the regulation as a violation of personal privacy and calling for its repeal. There was significant national media attention and social media outrage. Discussion of the regulations reached the Canadian Parliament's Transport Committee, and a member of Parliament motioned, albeit unsuccessfully, for the removal of article 5.2 (1) (Peesker 2012).

        If put into practice, this regulation would potentially impact many trans people's ability to travel in Canada, and as such, it is reasonable to suggest that this issue is deserving of attention. Access to transitional medical care and modification of legal name and sex designation remain limited for many trans people, and identity documents are a common source of discrimination. Furthermore, freedom of movement is commonly understood to be a fundamental human right, and such a bold denial of this right came as a shock to many. However, equally deserving of attention are the ways in which activists and the media addressed the flight regulations. Common refrains during this momentary upheaval included a public statement from a prominent activist that "Transgender people are completely banned from boarding airplanes in Canada" and a newspaper headline claiming, "Transgendered [sic] Community Effectively Banned from Flying" (Milloy 2012; Raj 2012). While the strategic use of this language successfully drew attention to broader restrictive administrative policies facing trans people, it is also imperative to interrogate the framing of these regulations and to consider their original intent.

## PROTECTING PASSENGERS, SECURING THE NATION

The article that trans activists and allies denounced in early 2012 had been adopted more than six months prior, when it was added to the Identity Screening Regulations of the Canadian Aeronautics Act. These regulations were first implemented in 2007, as a part of the "Passenger Protect Program." According to the Passenger Protect website, this program "identifies individuals who may pose a threat to aviation security and disrupts their ability to cause harm or threaten aviation by taking action, such as preventing them from boarding an aircraft" (Public Safety Canada 2014). Along with creating standardized regulations, Passenger Protect was also responsible for the creation of a Canadian no-fly list. Comparable to the no-fly list introduced in the United States by the FBI's "Terrorist Screening Center" following September 11, 2001, Canada's no-fly list contains individuals who are automatically banned from flying. This list has grown to over twenty-one thousand names in the United States; the Canadian government has continually refused to disclose the number of people on the list (ACLU n.d.; Bronskill 2014).

When the Passenger Protect program was introduced, it was condemned by a coalition of Canadian civil liberties, Muslim, and migrant rights organizations (Barrett 2007). The program was denounced as violating privacy rights and as ushering in a series of extreme and invasive national security measures. Many critics of the Canadian national security apparatus called out these regulations as being part of the domestic front of the "War on Terror," dedicated to surveillance and restriction of the freedom of movement both within Canada and across national borders.

Despite this important backdrop and the all but cursory evidence of trans people being banned from flying in practice, there was a stark silence about the source of these regulations during the 2012 outcry. In seeking reference to the origins of the gender-specific portion of the regulations, an article in *Now Toronto* offered clarification: "According to Maryse Durette, a senior adviser at Transport Canada, no trans people have been barred from boarding planes since the regulations went into effect in July. New regulations, she says, were introduced in response to a YouTube video showing veiled women boarding a plane without being required to show their faces" (Peesker 2012). This statement is illuminating on two counts. First, it confirms that while these regulations may inadvertently restrict the freedom of movement of trans Canadian citizens, they were implemented to legitimate long-standing practices of racial profiling and restriction of movement of people of color, particularly racialized Muslims, within and across Canada's borders. Second, it lays bare the limitations of activism that is rooted in an exclusionary framework of individual rights and citizenship. From this standpoint, the infrastructure and practices of state surveillance, racialized policing, and border imperialism that constitute contemporary practices of Canadian citizenship remain uncontested (Walia 2013).

## BEYOND FLIGHT REGULATIONS: UNCOVERING THE CRIME-MIGRATION NEXUS

Rather than taking an either/or approach to thinking about this brief historical moment (with a narrowly defined trans rights movement on the one hand and the underlying violence of racial profiling, state surveillance, and the War on Terror on the other hand), it may be beneficial to consider what is left unexamined in this conversation about trans people, migration, and criminalization. In this spirit, for the remainder of this chapter I will discuss some of the harmful, and at times deadly, legal regimes that migrant trans women in Canada, and Québec in particular, are subjected to.

As for many trans people, a central concern for migrant trans women in Canada is access to legal documentation. Noncitizens living in Québec face particular barriers to accessing identity documents that reflect their sex and/or name. According to the Québec Civil Code, people without citizenship, such as permanent residents, can never change their legal name and/or sex on their documents, regardless of surgical status, until they attain Canadian citizenship (Québec 1991). Access to legal Canadian citizenship itself is becoming increasingly restrictive and expensive and requires upward of ten years of residence in Canada before one can apply for consideration (Canada 2001). For people with a criminal record this process becomes all the more tedious as they are obliged to undergo a lengthy (minimum waiting period of five to ten years without additional criminal charges before applying) and costly ($631 per application) process of getting a "record suspension," otherwise known as a pardon (Canada 1985). Under these conditions, an increasing number of trans migrants, most notably migrant sex workers living in Québec, are practically undocumented—unable to change their legal name or sex for upward of twenty years after arrival in Canada, if not indefinitely. As exclusion from citizenship is increasingly defined in terms of "criminality," migrant trans people face potentially long-lasting consequences for engaging in precarious and criminalized forms of labor. When advocating for greater access to legal documents for trans people, it is critical to attend to the underlying frameworks of citizenship upon which demands for reform are commonly based. Failure to do so can reinforce the erasure of social groups who exist beyond the reach of a citizen-bound logic of human rights.

The highly selective nature of citizenship is mirrored by a broader politics of regressive immigration reform. Over the past nine years, the Conservative government has dramatically restricted access to refugee status and permanent residency, while increasing the precarity and disposability of migrant workers. Mexican migrants have been specifically targeted through strict visa requirements, a rapid decrease in the acceptance of inland refugee claims, workplace raids on undocumented workers, and a spike in deportations. Despite clearly documented threats to their lives, several Mexican migrants have been deported from Canada and subsequently murdered. In a lesser-known case, Rosa, a young Mexican trans woman living with HIV, was deported from Canada.[1] Rosa lived in Montréal for several years until her refugee claim was refused, despite having been raped by Mexican police officers and subsequently subjected to death threats. In 2009 she was deported on the grounds that she could relocate to safety internally within her home country. In December 2012, Rosa's friends in Montréal told me she had been shot dead outside her home. Rosa's murder came less than one year following the outcry over Transport Canada's flight regulations, yet it was met with no public acknowledgment. This deep divide between self-identified trans activists and sex-working Latina trans women in Montréal is not unique, but it clearly exemplifies a pronounced silence within trans rights movements about the violent practices involved in protecting citizenship. Like Rosa, trans women engaged in sex work have long been marginalized within dominant Canadian and U.S. transgender and queer political priorities—despite being without question the most heavily surveilled and criminalized group of trans people.

The combined effects of urban gentrification and displacement, neoliberal economic and political regimes, and targeted policing practices have resulted in a rapid deterioration in the working conditions of street- and bar-based trans women sex workers in many North American cities. In Montréal, members of the police's "morality squad" commonly pose as clients in order to arrest street-based sex workers on charges of solicitation. In addition to incarceration, conditions following conviction often include what is known as a *quadrilatère*, or red zoning (Stella n.d.). Effectively, this involves being banned from a multiple block zone. Commonly, this zone includes one's apartment—meaning that somebody who has been red zoned can only go to and from their home within that designated zone. For trans women, the sole trans sex worker bar was often included within this zone. This bar, which provided a sense of community and security for many sex workers, has recently been forced to close, only to be replaced by an upscale snack bar. Nonetheless, trans women with few, if any, alternative employment options frequently disregard these conditions in order to meet clients, risking retaliation from police and judges alike.

While working as a street outreach worker for a local trans health project in Montréal, I found it not uncommon to hear stories of police harassment and violence. Police would often call out the legal names of sex workers over their car loudspeaker, a tactic of intimidation and humiliation, as if to say, "we know who you *really* are." Stories of being verbally berated and threatened, pepper sprayed, beaten, and subsequently charged with assaulting an officer were regular occurrences for many women. One woman recounted her experience of being detained overnight for violating her bail conditions. While detained, an officer exclaimed that if she did not succeed in hanging herself in her cell, she would die of AIDS soon enough.[2]

Several decades of mobilization for sex workers' rights recently culminated in the Supreme Court of Canada striking down sections of the Criminal Code that criminalized several aspects of sex work in Canada (MacCharles 2013). In spite of this unanimous ruling, one year later, the Conservative government unveiled its "made-in-Canada" approach to sex work via the Protection of Communities and Exploited Persons Act, which introduced a series of amendments to the Criminal Code (Canada 2014). This bill not only reproduced conditions similar to the previous law but furthermore introduced the criminalization of sex workers' clients. Under this revamped criminalization regime, it is expected that street-based sex workers—predominantly poor, trans, Indigenous, racialized, and/or drug-using women—will continue to bear the brunt of state violence and will be forced into increasingly isolated and unsafe working conditions.

Beyond the countless acts of criminalization at the hands of the police and the criminal justice system, criminalized migrant sex workers face further penalization by Citizenship and Immigration Canada (CIC). According to the Immigration and Refugee Protection Act, permanent residents and refugees with a criminal record may be deemed as "inadmissible on grounds of serious criminality" (Canada 2001). Following amendments made under the Faster Removal of Foreign Criminals Act in 2013, this means that any non-citizen who has been punished for a criminal conviction with a prison sentence of six months or more could be subject to deportation (Canada 2013). This process of "double punishment" is part of a broader crime-migration nexus, wherein criminal and immigration laws are becoming increasingly intertwined within the logics of risk, security, and penality (Hagan et al. 2008). In one recent occurrence, a trans woman who came to Canada over twenty years ago as a refugee claimant from Latin America was investigated by the CIC on account of criminal convictions related to sex work and theft. The immigration judge ordered her deportation, claiming that she exposed people to a "lethal degree of risk," in part due to her failure to disclose her HIV status to her clients. In a rare turn of events, she successfully appealed this ruling and was able to remain in Canada (citation withheld). Despite this outcome, countless other migrants, including many trans women, are commonly subjected to various forms of immigration penality. A criminal conviction for HIV nondisclosure is but one of many criminal charges that can result in the incarceration and deportation of non-citizens. For migrant trans women, a disproportionately high number of whom are living with HIV, the possibility of being charged with HIV nondisclosure (frequently ruled by judges to be a form of aggravated assault) poses a significant danger to their safety (AIDS Action Now 2011).

## CONCLUSION

Two years following the outcry over the so-called flight ban, a related story flashed across social media and mainstream news outlets. In February 2014 the Canadian Border Services Agency (CBSA) detained Avery Edison, a young white trans woman traveling from the United Kingdom, due to a previously overstayed visa (Jones 2014). When Edison was transferred from detention at Toronto's Pearson airport to the Maplehurst Correctional Complex, a men's provincial prison, supporters and sympathetic media rushed to denounce Edison's situation. Despite being legally female, Edison had not undergone bottom surgery, and thus, according to both provincial and federal correctional regulations, she was to be held in a male prison. Following widespread public pressure and criticism, Edison was transferred to the adjacent Vanier Centre for Women, where she was held briefly before returning to London. The international outpouring of support in Edison's case over a period of four days was noteworthy and helped build momentum toward broader prison reform for incarcerated trans people in Ontario. In January 2015, in part due to human rights complaints filed by Edison, the provincial government announced that new admission and placement policy for trans inmates would be based on identification rather than anatomy (Strapagiel 2015). While clearly an important step in improving the conditions of incarcerated trans people, it has done little to draw into question the underlying reasons many trans people, trans women in particular, are likely to be incarcerated and, in some instances, deported.

Two months after news of Edison's detention subsided, I received a call from a young Mexican woman I had gotten to know as an outreach worker. She told me that she was being held at the Immigration Prevention Centre in Laval, north of Montréal. The police had come to her apartment in response to a neighbor's noise complaints, and upon realizing that she was undocumented and had a criminal record they arrested her and immediately transferred her to immigration detention. Maria was held for over a month in solitary confinement, and was faced with potential deportation. While she was ultimately successful in winning a last-chance application to remain in Canada, Maria's case was not the subject of national media coverage or popular mobilization. Rather, Maria's arrest and detention were merely routine practices of the Canadian criminal justice and immigration systems and unlikely to garner the attention of those outside her immediate social network. Unlike Edison's experience of detention and deportation, Maria's experience mirrors that of approximately five hundred thousand undocumented people living across Canada, and upward of ten thousand migrants detained every year, often held indefinitely, separated from friends and family, and faced with imminent deportation (End Immigration Detention Network 2014).

My goal in contrasting these two distinct narratives is not to discount the importance of rapid mobilization in response to Edison's detention, or even the so-called transphobic flight regulations, and the role that such high-profile cases can play in advancing necessary reforms. Rather, I want to encourage a critical reflection on the limits, and possible harms, of the framework within which these types of actions are commonly inscribed. Activism that selectively centers individual identity-based rights as the site of political change not only prioritizes certain lives over others (specifically, the lives of those who can access state-bound rights versus those to whom they are denied), it also commonly fails to appreciate the material conditions that underline the most harmful forms of violence—particularly state violence. Social movements that are not grounded in the knowledge and leadership of those most directly affected by violence risk reinforcing deep rifts that are drawn along preexisting racial, class, linguistic, and colonial border lines. In highlighting the knowledge and experiences of migrant, sex-working, Indigenous, and HIV+ trans women, among others, and considering the broader linkages to issues such as national security measures, colonization, migration, and criminal law, we can bolster an expansive methodological approach to critical thinking and political action that is grounded in the material everyday life.[3]

As I finish writing this piece, Canadian Prime Minister Stephen Harper has introduced Bill C-51, the Anti-Terrorism Act. In the likely event of its adoption, this new legislation will drastically expand policing powers in the name of deterring terrorism. Notably it will also expand the Passenger Protect no-fly list and grant greater discretion to deny people preemptively from boarding flights (Canadian Press 2015). While the Identity Screening Regulations that were so hotly contested by trans activists in 2012 remain a part of Passenger Protect's protocols, the short-term collective memory of social media–driven trans activism has seemingly long since forgotten and moved on to countless other flashpoints. As transgender rights increasingly enter mainstream political discourse and law, however, it is vital that we transform these flashpoints—such as the flight regulations—into opportunities for deepening our political analysis, broadening the scope of social action and alliance-building, and expanding our creative imaginations towards greater collective emancipation.

## NOTES

1. All names in this chapter have been changed to protect confidentiality of the individuals, both living and deceased, and in the case of Rosa, her friends and family.

2. Details from in-person conversation. Given the highly public nature of legal cases dealing with HIV nondisclosure, such as this one, and the use of the legal name of this individual, it is a political and ethical decision to refuse to provide identifying information.

3. While Two Spirit and trans Indigenous women are not directly discussed in this piece, their voices, experiences, and leadership need to be a central part of the conversation and action. For more insights, check out work by Aiyyana Maracle, Mirha-Soleil Ross, Monica Forrester, Jamie Lee Hamilton, and Sandra Laframboise, all of whom have a long history of ground-breaking community organizing and cultural production on issues including sex workers rights, Indigenous sovereignty, gender, and transsexuality.

## REFERENCES

AIDS Action Now. 2011. "HIV Criminalization." *AIDS Action Now: Action=Life*. Accessed January 5, 2015. http://www.aidsactionnow.org/?page_id=49.

American Civil Liberties Union (ACLU). N.d. "Factsheet: The ACLU's Challenge to the U.S. Government's No Fly List." Accessed February 22, 2014. http://www.aclu.org/national -security/factsheet-aclus-challenge-us-governments-no-fly-list. Unfortunately, this link is no longer accessible.

Barrett, Tom. 2007. "Grounding the No-Fly List: Rights Groups Seek to Block 'Illegitimate' Security Plan." *The Tyee*, January 18. Accessed February 13, 2015. http://thetyee.ca/ News/2007/06/18/No-Fly.

Bronskill, Jim. 2014. "Canadian No-Fly List Numbers Must Stay Secret: Government." *CBC News*, September 3. Accessed February 13, 2015. http://www.cbc.ca/news/politics/ canadian-no-fly-list-numbers-must-stay-secret-government-1.2754743.

Canada. 1985. Criminal Records Act, RSC, c C-47.

———. 2001 Immigration and Refugee Protection Act, SC, c 27. http://laws-lois.justice.gc .ca/eng/acts/I-2.5.

———. 2007. Identity Screening Regulations, SOR/2007-82. http://laws-lois.justice.gc.ca/ eng/regulations/SOR-2007-82/FullText.html.

———. 2013. Bill C-43. Faster Removal of Foreign Criminals Act, S.C. c. 16. http://laws-lois .justice.gc.ca/eng/annualstatutes/2013_16/page-1.html.

———. 2014. Protection of Communities and Exploited Persons Act, SC, c 25. http://laws -lois.justice.gc.ca/eng/annualstatutes/2014_25/FullText.html.

Canadian Press. 2015. "Anti-Terror Bill to Expand No-Fly Regime, Detention Provisions." *Huffington Post*, January 23. Accessed February 13, 2015. http://www.huffingtonpost.ca/2015/01/23/anti-terror-bill-no-fly-detention-steven-blaney_n_6534732.html.

End Immigration Detention Network. 2014. *Indefinite, Arbitrary and Unfair: The Truth about Immigration Detention in Canada*. Accessed January 5, 2015. http://www.truthabout detention.com/report.

Gollom, Mark, and Joseph Engelhardt. 2012. "Are Transgender Canadians Being Banned from Boarding Flights?" *CBC News*, February 2. Accessed January 5, 2015. http://www.cbc.ca/news/canada/are-transgender-canadians-being-banned-from-boarding-flights-1.1293810.

Hagan, John, Ron Levi, and Ronit Dinovitzer. 2008. "The Symbolic Violence of the Crime-Immigration Nexus: Migrant Mythologies in the Americas." *Criminology and Public Policy* 7.1: 95. doi: 10.1111/j.1745–9133.2008.00493.x.

Jones, Allison. 2014. "Transgender Woman Arrested at Pearson Moved from Men's Jail to Women's Facility." *Globe and Mail*, February 11. Accessed February 13, 2015. http://www.theglobeandmail.com/news/national/transgender-woman-moved-from-mens-jail-to-womens-facility-officials-say/article16818114.

MacCharles, Tonda. 2013. "Supreme Court of Canada Strikes Down Federal Prostitution Laws." *Toronto Star*, December 20. Accessed February 13, 2015. www.thestar.com/news/canada/2013/12/20/supreme_court_of_canada_strikes_down_federal_criminal_prostitution_laws.html.

Milloy, Christin Scarlett. 2012. "Transgender People Are Completely Banned from Boarding Airplanes in Canada." *Christin Milloy: Rise Up and Seize Equality*, January 30. Accessed January 5, 2015. http://chrismilloy.ca/2012/01/transgender-people-are-completely-banned-from-boarding-airplanes-in-canada.

Peesker, Saira. 2012. "Flying Fix: Trans People Fear New Rule That Gender on Passport Must Match Appearance." *Now Toronto*, February 9. Accessed January 5, 2015. https://nowtoronto.com/news/flying-fix/.

Public Safety Canada. 2014. "Safeguarding Canadians with Passenger Protect." Accessed February 13, 2015. http://www.publicsafety.gc.ca/cnt/ntnl-scrt/cntr-trrrsm/pssngr-prtct/index-eng.aspx.

Québec. Civil Code of Québec, CQLR c C-1991.

Raj, Althia. 2012. "Canada Identity Screening Regulations: Transgendered Community Effectively Banned from Flying." *Huffington Post*, January 31. Accessed January 5, 2015. http://www.huffingtonpost.ca/2012/01/31/canada-air-travel-transgendered-community_n_1245598.html.

Stella. N.d. "Accusée de sollicitation sur la rue? Travailleuses du sexe, informons-nous!" *Stella: Vivre et Travailler en Sécurité et Avec Dignité*. Accessed February 13, 2015. http://chezstella.org/stella/sollicitation.

Strapagiel, Lauren. 2015. "Ontario Will Now Assess Transgender Inmates Based on Identity, Not Anatomy." *National Post*, January 26. Accessed February 13, 2015. http://news.nationalpost.com/2015/01/26/ontario-will-now-assess-transgender-inmates-based-on-identity-not-anatomy.

Walia, Harsha. 2013. *Undoing Border Imperialism*. Oakland, CA: AK Press.

# 8 · AFFECTIVE VULNERABILITY AND TRANSGENDER EXCEPTIONALISM

## Norma Ureiro in *Transgression*

AREN Z. AIZURA

In December 2012 the Obama administration released a memo called "US Leadership to Advance Equality for LGBT People Abroad." The memo offers practical strategies to build on Secretary of State Hillary Clinton's notorious speech on LGBT rights at the United Nations in 2011; she verbally admonished nations in which homosexuality is a crime and framed the United States as at the forefront of efforts to combat homophobia. Clinton's speech coincided with a new U.S. government strategy "dedicated to combating LGBT human rights abuses abroad." The memo itself detailed a range of initiatives, including foreign aid targeted at LGBT communities internationally. Domestically, the memo claimed, the Department of Homeland Security had begun expediting the refugee applications of "particularly vulnerable" claimants, including LGBT refugees (Power 2012). This accompanied new field regulations in U.S. Citizenship and Immigration Services (USCIS) governing the treatment of LGBT refugee and asylum claims (USCIS 2011). Additionally, in 2011 Immigration and Customs Enforcement (ICE) and USCIS began to incorporate awareness training on LGBT issues into education for immigration enforcement officers.[1] ICE officers are now encouraged to consider whether a candidate for immigration detention has a long-standing same-sex partnership with a U.S. citizen in using prosecutorial discretion to defer deportations.[2] In a familiar exceptionalist narrative, Clinton's speech and the accompanying policy shifts frame the United

States as a beacon of liberal freedom where sexual and gender minorities can find better acceptance than in other parts of the world. These shifts also signal a new period of greater collaboration between the federal government and nonprofit organizations who advocate for LGBT immigrants.

In particular, trans and gender-nonconforming people have gained increased public awareness both from governmental agencies and in popular media. This has resulted in what appears to be a sea change in immigration and foreign policy from 2003, when the Department of Homeland Security issued an advisory that warned security personnel about cross-dressing terrorists (Beauchamp 2009). For example, the new USCIS regulations define transgender in detailed terms and point out the range of possible relationships between appearance, embodiment, and body modification: "Some transgender people dress in the clothes of the opposite gender; others undergo medical treatment, which may include taking hormones and/or having surgery to alter their gender characteristics" (USCIS 2011, 13).

This new atmosphere of acceptance of gender diversity within the federal government has also facilitated a new collaboration between LGBT nonprofits and government, in which trans and gender-nonconforming concerns play a key role. The Chicago-based nonprofit Heartland Alliance recently received funding from the U.S. Office of Refugee Resettlement to start the Rainbow Welcome Initiative, a resettlement program for LGBT refugees and asylum seekers that matches asylum seekers with resettlement service providers in Chicago, San Diego, and Philadelphia. Gender-nonconforming refugees have featured prominently in publicity for the program.[3] Immigration Equality, which ran a long campaign to include lesbians and gay men in family reunification visa categories, has more recently campaigned against placing transgender immigration detainees in solitary confinement or in administrative segregation. The plight of transgender people in U.S. immigration detention is the topic of a short documentary film, *Transgression*, made in 2012 by an Immigration Equality intern. *Transgression* tells the story of Norma Ureiro, one of Immigration Equality's clients and a trans immigrant to the United States whose story of surviving U.S. immigration detention forms the main narrative of the film. It is distributed via Youtube and Vimeo and is reportedly shown in ICE LGBT awareness training sessions.

Within international human rights regimes, transgender has thus become administratively visible as something that renders subjects particularly vulnerable, and which also requires governmental and bureaucratic literacy. Just as the cultural shift toward transgender visibility in the United States is rife with contradictions, so is this administrative shift. The forms of bureaucratic visibility tend to conform to conservative medico-legal definitions of what defines transsexuality even as those medico-legal definitions are being rewritten. As much as trans and gender-nonconforming immigrants have value internationally as subjects of human rights within the U.S. geopolitical imaginary, once their value in this imaginary has been exhausted, materially trans and gender-nonconforming immigrants appear to have little worth as bodies in need of housing, income, health care, and sociality. Indeed, this imaginary may still define such "rescuable" subjects as part of a geopolitical racial and terrorist threat that must also be extinguished in the logic of the "War on Terror." Thus, they are represented as both imbued with and stripped of rights at the same time, a predicament Sima Shakhsari calls the politics of rightful killing (Shakhsari 2014).

However, the question of which transgender and gender-nonconforming subjects can be said to be "vulnerable," requiring the nation's assistance, and which count as threats to the nation is subject to constant rearrangement and thus needs to be interrogated. In this chapter I argue that vulnerability is a biopolitical category: it accrues from the on-camera tears of transgender immigrant subjects encouraged to testify to their own traumatic histories of family abuse and to the U.S. nation's freedom and tolerance of diversity. Through a reading of *Transgression*, I argue that Ureiro's visual and affective vulnerability as an undocumented immigrant is cinematically produced through its contrast with the redemptive white nonprofit expert and advocate, who stands in for the progressive American nation. Vulnerability here becomes a method to extract value in the form of spectatorial sympathy. This extraction of value serves to conceal the reality, which is that, just as the U.S. government is assisting some transgender subjects to gain asylum and refugee status, other (or the same) transgender and gender-nonconforming bodies are rendered disposable by an immigration reform agenda that seeks to detain and deport "criminals."

Documentary film has become a particularly important form for the production and circulation of knowledge and affective imaginaries about gender-nonconforming people both in the United States and in the global South. If we can group these documentaries as a genre, the generic conventions pivot on an affective axis in which the triumph of hope over despair forms the most significant narrative arc. Documentary films about gender-nonconforming subjects tend to mobilize the conventions of ethnographic realism (Nichols 1994, 73), which work to exoticize documentary subjects as outsiders while simultaneously rendering them recognizable for a "mainstream" audience (Aizura 2014). Thus, it is important to interrogate the terms of representation under which they appear as vulnerable "Third World" victims, positioning the act of watching as an exercise in gaining familiarity and sympathy. *Transgression* is no exception; indeed, it draws on such cinematic conventions to form its narrative. Similar to other trans-themed documentaries such as *Paper Dolls* (2006) and *Les travestis pleurent aussi* (2008), *Transgression*'s spectatorial gaze is assumed to be that of (white, cisgendered) others who, in as far as they do not inhabit the world of the protagonists, must have it translated for them (Aizura 2009; 2014). Thus, documentary in this genre is ideologically structured to produce indignation in the spectator at the trans subject's helplessness, simultaneously reproducing the terms of a liberal humanist ethnographic gaze that displaces racialized trans subjects' agency onto "us," the viewers, who are incited to "do something."[4]

Particularly in documentaries featuring racialized, gender-nonconforming subjects, such generic conventions cast the protagonists as bodies whose vulnerability to violence and displacement makes them candidates for increased protection. This protection inevitably takes the form of a homonationalist desire to save LGBT people from the global South from the putative "barbarism" of their own cultural backgrounds (Puar 2007, 15–16). For example, *Paper Dolls* represents the country of origin of its protagonists, the Philippines, as very conservative and religious despite the presence of a large and visible gender-nonconforming, as well as *gay*, population in Manila, Quezon City, and other metropolises (Benedicto 2008; Garcia 2009). The pattern is so ubiquitous as to seem clichéd.

In relation to the current project, it is also important to note how documentaries circulate. Like other documentaries in this genre, *Transgression* is distributed online through the free video playback websites Youtube and Vimeo. This not only enables its circulation as a pedagogical tool in an increasing number of queer- or Transgender-Studies-themed college classes in the United States. It also enables its use for multiple training scenarios (including for ICE itself). The documentary does not address whether Ureiro herself was consulted about this form of distribution—which might be particularly pertinent given the traumatic and intimate details Ureiro provides about her life.

## INTERROGATING TRANSGENDER EXCEPTIONALISM

That transgender bodies are at the forefront of neoliberal state attempts to distinguish between vulnerable, disposable, and threatening populations is not a new insight. Toby Beauchamp's observation that "gendered and racialized bodies are central both to perceptions of safety and security" (2009, 365) gains even more relevance when we examine how transgender and American nationalism have played off each other in U.S. public discourse over the last two years, in a manner that provides an important background to *Transgression* but also intersects with it. In August 2013, Chelsea Manning (previously known as Bradley Manning) was sentenced to thirty-five years in prison for leaking classified documents. Immediately following sentencing, Manning requested that media refer to her using female pronouns and the name Chelsea. Despite some evidence that Manning had identified as trans all along, this seemed to shock mainstream America, and a veritable volcano of media coverage erupted. Claims that Manning's identification as transgender was an attempt to be placed in a women's prison competed with speculation that Manning released the files because she was transgender and thus already pathologically "sick." Meanwhile many media outlets flatly refused to honor Manning's request. Even some transgender commentators joined the fray. Blogger Autumn Sandeen described Manning's actions in releasing classified documents and her coming out as trans as similarly self-serving and without honor (Sandeen 2013, n.p.). Writer Jennifer Finney Boylan wrote a column in the *Atlantic* criticizing Manning for having disobeyed a military order. But Boylan thought that Chelsea Manning could redeem herself by serving the remainder of her sentence in a dignified way: "By comporting herself with dignity and accepting responsibility for her actions, she can show that a trans woman is a human being capable of reinvention and redemption" (Boylan 2013).

These perspectives on Manning demonstrate the strength of nationalist transgender discourses that assume recognition can only be won through supporting a fantasy of U.S. global imperialism. The performance of honor and dignity called for by Sandeen and Boylan echo the nationalist military exceptionalism that positions the United States as the global enforcer of freedom and equality (especially for "minorities"). I call these discourses "transgender exceptionalism." The term *transgender exceptionalism* tracks the nationalist logic in which the U.S. nation fantasizes its own superiority, tolerance, and exceptionality in relation to transgender life, pitted against other nations and "cultures" deemed intolerant, barbaric, transphobic, or homophobic. As Puar recounts in *Terrorist Assemblages*, homonationalism traced how the United States temporarily suspended its "heteronormative imagined community to consolidate national sentiment and consensus through the recognition of some, though not all or most, homosexual subjects" (Puar 2007, 3). Puar refers to exceptionalism here as "a process whereby a population comes to believe in its own superiority and its own singularity" (2007, 5). By 2014, however, it is clear that the subjects recognized in order to sustain the fantasy of a cohesive national imaginary are not just "homosexual," but all shades of queer—and in particular, transgendered.

At the Homonationalism and Pinkwashing conference in New York in April 2013, Jasbir Puar referred to such moves as a new iteration of homonationalism: "transgender homonationalism."[5] While it is rhetorically useful, this formulation inadvertently asserts a temporal narrative that is central to the structure of exceptionalism more generally, wherein transgender follows queer, always designated as coming after the lesbian and gay movement—which in turn is assumed to inherit the black civil rights project. In fact, currents of transgender exceptionalism have been tracked, critiqued, and resisted by many people both in grassroots organizing and in the academy for many years now (Aizura 2006; Beauchamp 2009; Gehi 2009; Haritaworn 2012; Namaste 2005; Shakhsari 2014; Spade and Willse 2014).

Additionally, it is important to be clear on why there is a need to distinguish between homonationalism and transgender exceptionalism. This is not to assert a categorical difference between sexuality and gender and thus between homo and trans (indeed, this distinction itself is specific to a Euro-American homonationalist imaginary). Rather, it means tracing how "transgender" and other categories to catalogue gender-nonconforming practices have always attached differently to rights discourses and affective modalities than the category of "lesbian and gay" does, and to acknowledge their different institutional and historical lives. Within the assemblages of transgender exceptionalism, strategic value is attached to gender-nonconforming bodies as the repositories of future rights and future privileges in their status as mascots for the newly homo-friendly liberal democracies of the global North. Affective vulnerability becomes a form of currency through which trans of color bodies become recuperable for the exceptionalist project. This will become particularly clear in my reading of *Transgression*.

## VICTIMHOOD AND VULNERABILITY IN *TRANSGRESSION*

Directed by Daniel Rotman, *Transgression* is a short documentary film that focuses on transgender immigrants and their experiences in the U.S. immigration system as they seek asylum. The film was made after Rotman spent a summer fellowship interning at the New York–based nonprofit Immigration Equality. On returning to studies at Harvard the next year, he entered a documentary-making competition sponsored by the Harvard Law School. *Transgression*'s main protagonist is Norma Ureiro, one of Immigration Equality's clients and a trans immigrant to the United States whose story of surviving U.S. immigration detention forms the main narrative of the film. Through subtitles, *Transgression* relates what it deems the most important details of Ureiro's life. Originally from Mexico (we are not told where), she crossed into the United States in the early 2000s. In 2006 she was detained by immigration authorities and eventually deported. Soon after, she crossed the border again. Once in the United States, she was arrested and placed again in immigration detention. During this second round of detention, the film informs us by subtitle, Immigration Equality took on her case. At the end of the film it is still not clear whether Ureiro has been granted refugee status or if she won legal status in some other way.

On the face of it, *Transgression* is about the indignities of immigration detention for transgender detainees. An enduring indignity for trans people who get incarcerated is being placed in gender-segregated detention according to birth-assigned gender; very few, if any, prisons actively allow trans women to be housed with women, or trans men with men. *Transgression*, however, focuses on how trans immigration detainees in the United States are often put in solitary confinement, euphemistically called administrative segregation. Ostensibly administrative segregation is intended to protect trans or gender-nonconforming detainees from other detainees, but it means they have to endure worse treatment than the general detention center population. This might include a single hour of exercise per day (the remaining twenty-three hours are spent in a cell), and extremely limited access to visitors and legal counsel. Like other nodes of the prison industrial complex, immigration detention centers tend to see trans inmates as "disruptive," refusing them access to hormones or gender-appropriate clothing and responding punitively when inmates request such privileges (Gehi 2012, 374; Spade 2011, 147). Additionally, older forms of silencing and othering women of color in general can be seen in full force here. Thus my reading draws on and extends woman of color feminist critiques of the constitution of "Third World women" in America feminist theory, such as Aihwa Ong's observation that non-Western women are "wrenched out of the context of [their] society and inscribed within the concerns of Western feminist scholars" (1988). I also benefit from Chandra Mohanty's incisive critique of how "Third World women" are represented as the victims of particular socioeconomic systems' Western feminist discourse, which renders them powerless and elides an understanding of non-Western women as historical agents (1991, 56–57). While *Transgression* presents a slightly different case, it reproduces a similar ideological economy of representation in which U.S.-based lesbian and gay human rights discourse objectifies racialized gender-nonconforming subjects in the service of the LGBT movement.

This form of objectification is evident from the opening of the film. The first frame shows Ureiro's face in deep close-up. The background behind her is dark. She is silent, but her eyes are red and she has tears on her face; it is clear she has been crying. Framed in the same deep close-up, Ureiro says in Spanish, "They put me back again. Alone in a dark cell, it's like a segregation they use to punish people for fighting or other things. They put me in that box." Off camera, an interviewer asks in Spanish, "From the first day? And how long were you there for?" Consistent with this opening, in which the spectator first encounters Ureiro as the tearful and traumatized brown victim, *Transgression* renders Ureiro's role to be the object of spectatorial pity (or at best, sympathy). Other white experts—staffers from Immigration Equality—take on the roles of explaining and interpreting Ureiro for an audience assumed to have no solidarity with, or experience of, the events that befall trans undocumented immigrants or trans people of color.

Following the first minute in which Ureiro tells her story, for example, we hear a brief explanation of Immigration Equality's interest in transgender immigration detention from Victoria Neilson (who was then the legal director at Immigration Equality). Senior staff attorney Aaron C. Morris explains administrative segregation. In contrast to the darkened and anonymous room in which Ureiro is filmed, Morris and Neilson are both interviewed in crisp light rooms. Morris is filmed at a desk, presumably his own office. "They're very vulnerable, very vulnerable to sexual assault. They're very vulnerable generally." The content of what Morris is filmed saying can be taken as informative and instructive, not to mention politically sensitive. However, his words also perform the epistemological violence of U.S. neoliberal multiculturalism. Transgender immigrants are a population, a "they," a new intersectional identity among others about whom the arbiters of diversity must be educated and informed in order to develop policy that "includes" them in the national polity. Indeed, the first fact viewers hear about transgender immigrants is a generalized vulnerability that renders them irrevocably other, unknowable except through their vulnerability.

Morris continues, "They're placed with the other population, sometimes they're placed with the *criminal* population, sometimes they're actually placed with *sex offenders*. . . . So DHS [Department of Homeland Security], in an attempt to make it safe for the trans person, will often pull them out of the general population and isolate them." Here Morris paints transgender immigrants as the innocent victims of a harsh immigration system—but also, crucially, what he calls the "criminal population." This is undoubtedly true. However, it is important to interrogate Morris's performance of a discursive division between innocent trans detainees and "criminals." When Morris cautions that transgender immigrants might be placed in detention with sex offenders, he neglects to mention that trans detainees are likely to be understood by the law as criminals and, given the number of states that count sex work as a sex offense, as sex offenders.[6]

By distinguishing transgender immigrants from criminal populations, Morris misses a crucial opportunity to point out that trans women of color, including many immigrants, are profiled and criminalized by the police as sex workers. My argument here depends on a more nuanced reading of the conditions of immigration detention than Morris offers in the film. Although doing so risks my becoming the white interlocutor who argues over the facts with another white interlocutor, erasing trans immigrants' subject position once again, nonetheless it is important to offer some statistical and scholarly evidence here to shift focus to the criminal justice system's own criminalization of transgender people of color.

The large majority of arrests that result in immigration detention happen through police profiling and brutality. Gender-nonconforming people are more likely to be targeted by the police as criminals, whether they are engaged in criminalized activity or not. Pooja Gehi points out that wearing tight clothes or "too much" makeup is seen as reasonable cause for a solicitation arrest (2012, 370). The case of Monica Jones in Phoenix illustrates how a black trans woman asking for a ride from a stranger resulted in a wrongful charge of manifestation of prostitution (Ludwig 2014). While another expert from Immigration Equality mentions later in *Transgression* that prison guards are responsible for some of the worst offenses, Morris's words here downplay how the carceral state itself poses a threat to the lives of gender-nonconforming immigrants in the form of violence perpetrated by prison guards, wardens, prosecutors, immigration judges, and the entire apparatus of immigration regulation itself. By framing Ureiro as vulnerable from the detention center population itself rather than from the guards, Morris depicts the Department of Homeland Security as a neutral party attempting to "make it safe for the trans person" by placing them in "administrative segregation" rather than making the institution responsible for housing trans women with the male prison population.

It is easy to understand these moments of elision as unintentional or perhaps strategic. However, the epistemological and ontological violence made by such elisions is real. Morris's statement about trans women immigrants being vulnerable from the "general population," sex offenders, and criminals asserts an implicit distinction between the civilized and tolerant Morris (and by proxy, the entire LGBT nonprofit industrial complex) and the ignorant, barbaric, and trans/homophobic undocumented immigrants who make up the "general population" in a detention center. This has two effects. First, it invokes a racist fantasy of detention centers as filled with violent and *macho* Latino men who pose a threat to Ureiro herself (and, by implication, the nation).[7] Second, it not only erases the possibility of solidarity between immigration detainees in an abstract sense but also conceals the history of solidarity and common goals between queer and trans immigrant organizing and the broader movement against immigration regulation in the United States and internationally. Many ongoing grassroots campaigns against deportation and detention by immigrant justice groups in the United States work with queer, trans, and gender-nonconforming immigrants or have organized LGBTQ-focused campaigns for immigration reform.[8] These networks include significant numbers of organizers who work inside detention centers.

## BEACONS OF HOPE: EXCEPTIONALIST MYTH

*Transgression* also offers a subtext to the criticism of solitary confinement in U.S. detention centers by presenting the United States as a liberal place in which Ureiro finally feels free and safe. This subtext is ambivalent. On one hand, the United States looks punitive because of its abuse of transgender detainees; on the other hand, the United States is presented as a bastion of democratic tolerance.

The middle part of the film focuses on Ureiro's retelling of how her family regarded her sexual and gender non-normativity. Once again, Ureiro's statements are given "context" and made legible by Morris, who states at the beginning of the section, "For our clients who come from very repressive environments, very conservative, very often religious environments, it's very common that a transgender person is disowned by their family." The film cuts back to Ureiro offering a lengthy testimony of violent abuse, ending with her statement, "There are no human rights there . . . to them we don't exist." The film immediately cuts to a shot of the Statue of Liberty, with the subtitle "Norma crossed into the U.S." The subtext is pretty clear: the United States was a logical destination for Ureiro because of the values of democracy, freedom, and tolerance symbolized by the statue. (Indeed, almost every film about immigration in the United States depicts the Statue of Liberty as a symbol of hope for immigrants.) In particular, the directors encourage us to imagine that, in the United States, attitudes toward trans people are not as discriminatory and phobic as in Mexico. Ureiro can be thus excused by more conservative viewers for crossing the border illegally because of the implication that she could not survive in Mexico. Again, the cinematic tone is central here: Morris is filmed with bright light in his office while Ureiro is filmed here in extreme close-up in a dark room—in fact, it is reasonable to assume that the film's opening shots of Ureiro crying are taken from this segment of her interview. The silent, bright shot of the Statue of Liberty in an expanse of blue sky opens up the frame and provides a moment of respite for viewers after they hear Ureiro's story, symbolically underscoring the exceptionalist myth of the United States as more tolerant than elsewhere.

When the film returns to the subject of violence in immigration detention, however, a similar subtext is present. Ureiro tells the story of her deportation, subsequent recrossing and rearrest, cut with disturbing music and a number of shots of prison bars, which fade to unsettling black. The film eventually arrives at the moment in the story when Immigration Equality takes on her case. Ureiro is now filmed sitting on a park bench in New York with her small dog: it is as if Immigration Equality's decision to step in representationally delivers her from the dark room, tears, and vulnerability into everyday life (and the symbolic freedom of the banal everyday that every American is assumed to desire: walking the dog). Morris explains in voiceover that Ureiro's case is not isolated, and that "trans women are regularly abused." Viewers are soon shown who is responsible for this abuse through a close-up shot of a highlighted newspaper article, "Transgender People Murdered as World Resists Change" (Curtis 2011). A line from the article is highlighted and enlarged: "Their research indicates there have been at least 681 reports of murders in 50 countries since 2008." The clear implication here, given the plotting of the narrative of Ureiro's move to the United States, is that transphobic violence is most prevalent in "backward" nations that are resistant to progressive (that is, liberal democratic) change. The point is made again as the film cuts to another newspaper headline, "Hate Crimes against Gay,

Transgender People on the Rise." While the headline is shown for only a couple of seconds, not enough time to read the entire article or place it, the inclusion of this particular newspaper headline undercuts the exceptionalist narrative: it is a 2011 article from the *Los Angeles Times*, which explains how transphobic and homophobic violence in the United States—not the rest of the world—is increasing (Romney 2011). When this headline fades to black, the film takes a beat and then brightens into a shot of another American emblem of free enterprise and liberalism, the Empire State Building. Ureiro explains in voiceover that, "The U.S. was another world to me, something totally different. I could feel the difference. I could feel free."

It is not to question the personal truth of Ureiro's words here that I make this critique. Rather, it is to point out the discursive economy of exceptionalist representation that constructs how Ureiro's story can be told and how it can be received. The transgender person of color whose experience forms the relatable "human" side of this documentary is only present to provide her experience. She is not asked about the politics of immigration or transgender politics; nor is she asked to talk about her thoughts on how the immigration detention system should be changed practically for trans detainees. Indeed, by the end of the film, the narrative about inhumane immigration detention has fallen to the wayside and spectators are left with the narrative of Ureiro being saved by Immigration Equality. For Immigration Equality, this narrative is, of course, strategic: it is designed both to elicit sympathy for Ureiro and to position Immigration Equality itself as a nonprofit organization that is truly committed to transgender immigrants.

On further investigation, even this seemingly clear fact requires questioning. A subtitle toward the end of the film reads, "After immigration authorities detained her again, Immigration Equality took on her case." *Transgression* glosses over the process of Ureiro's legal representation during her detention and release, so it is never concretely clear how Immigration Equality assisted her. The impression the film gives is that the Immigration Equality legal team worked with Ureiro to get her out of detention and then later on fighting for legal status. However, the reality may have been very different. According to people close to the case, when Ureiro was in immigration detention, Immigration Equality claimed it did not have the resources to assist her in getting released. Immigration Equality took on Ureiro's case only after she had been released. The labor of helping Ureiro get out of detention and caring for her while she was inside fell to community activists, friends, and individual volunteer attorneys rather than Immigration Equality. Since *Transgression* has been released, Ureiro has not spoken at screenings of the film. Given numerous critiques of the LGBT nonprofit world (INCITE! Women of Color Against Violence 2009; Manzanala and Spade 2008), this is hardly surprising. But it might also direct us to look toward trans/queer abolitionist and grassroots political models in which getting all trans immigrants who are criminalized or locked up out of incarceration is prioritized above policy directives that understand individuals only as cases whose political mileage is more important than their material consequences. Further, it should warn us to think of trans immigrants and trans people of color more generally as political agents who need to be involved, consulted with, and paid for representational projects that are made about them.

## CONCLUSION

*Transgression* offers a pertinent illustration of the symbolic burden placed on trans women of color, many of whom are also immigrants, to represent consistently as victims of the most heinous crimes of transphobic violence. Trans women of color are indeed overrepresented in statistics counting violent crime toward trans people, as well as rates of arrest and incarceration. (Admittedly, the recent emergence of hate crimes as a juridical category has ushered in a new biopolitical era when such statistics became countable.) However, the way Ureiro is presented in *Transgression* as a mere victim, rather than as the agent of her own political power, is hardly unfamiliar. The Transgender Day of Remembrance (TDOR), which tallies a global list of transgender people murdered each year and commemorates their deaths with vigils and memorial services annually on November 21, offers another salutary example. Implicitly or explicitly, the statistics quoted on each nation-state imprint a shocking transnational sensibility on proceedings (nothing exemplifies this more ironically than watching mainly white midwestern college students at a 2009 TDOR vigil in Indiana struggle to pronounce the "foreign" names of those on the list). Yet TDOR vigils often end in calls for nation-bound legislative recompense such as national hate crimes laws, which would not help most of the people on the list of dead—not to mention that many seem to be vulnerable as sex workers or undocumented immigrants who are also subject to criminalizing anti-sex-work laws or the violence of numerous security agencies (Lamble 2008; Namaste and Soleil-Ross 2005, 90–91). A similar effect can be seen in writing on the global feminization of labor. As Neferti Tadiar (2009) puts it, writing on feminist critiques of globalization, "immigrant female domestic and/or sex workers . . . come to embody the material consequences of the gendered, racialized, and sexualized aspects of the normative logics of the capitalist economy."

In order to sustain the critique I make in this chapter beyond a cinematic analysis, it is necessary to think through the positionality of those who represent and are represented within the assemblages of transgender exceptionalism—and this includes academic research and, unavoidably, this current work. In my own capacity as a transgender immigrant to the United

States who escapes the worst regulation and criminalization through whiteness and economic privilege, it is essential to question the investment of
many Trans Studies scholars in a rights-and-respectability model that relies
on U.S. exceptionalism. Immigration is not about distributing rights among
the most worthy, responsible, or deserving. Rather, it is a complex of regimes
that deploy contradictory mechanisms to optimize labor flows, filter particular
populations into and out of territories, secure those populations, and manage
popular political discourses around protecting nation-states from, or opening
up nation-states to, immigration. Positionality and representation are always
close at hand here: in these contradictory systems, immigrants must comply
with various exhortations to "be visible" or to "represent" themselves within
particular discourses in order to gain access through the next doorway and
in particular to gain legal status. The symbolic and material debt incurred in
such an exchange ensures the pliability and self-surveillance of the immigrant
herself. Globally, trans and queer racialized immigrants are continually asked
to "tell their stories" in order to put a "human face" on an "abstract problem," to
solicit donations for various nonprofit groups, and most often to negotiate
the border in the form of immigration regulations, asylum processes, and
refugee claims. Immigrants themselves must be perfectly aware that this is
an exchange; it is in their interests to calculate accordingly the value, and the
copiousness, of their tears. The abstraction of trans people of color into subjects of suffering and vulnerability also prevents the formation of a political
model that might understand how the privileges and freedoms of those who
are documented—or not sex workers, or not transgender—are cosubstantial
with and intimately connected to those who are exhorted to speak.

NOTES

1. These initiatives include a training module on LGBT refugee and asylum claims, which
the "US Leadership" memo claims is now taught in basic training for all new officers who
adjudicate asylum cases.
2. The term *prosecutorial discretion* refers to the process by which an ICE agent can now
decide if an immigration detainee receives deferred action (or, not deporting someone) rather
than being deported, on the basis of having family relationships or belonging to a vulnerable
category of personhood. Prosecutorial discretion is used in a small number of cases, but the
number of cases closed via prosecutorial discretion appears to be rising. See "Rebound Seen
in New ICE Prosecutorial Discretion Closures," Transactional Records Access Clearinghouse, http://trac.syr.edu/immigration/reports/308/#pd, accessed October 4, 2013.
3. A transgender man called Aren who came to the United States from Iran via Turkey was
interviewed about his participation in the resettlement program in Philadelphia for a press
release by the Nationalities Service Center, the host organization in Philadelphia. The same
person took part in panels about transgender refugee resettlement at the Philadelphia Trans
Health Conference in 2012, a measure partially used to publicize this new program and the

U.S. government's change of policy about transgender immigrants. See Nationalities Service Center 2012: "Rainbow Welcome Initiative Caters to LGBT Refugees," http://www.nscphila .org/rainbow-welcome-initiative-caters-to-lgbt-refugees. Accessed June 16, 2013.

4. For this line of thinking I am indebted to an essay published anonymously, "No Way Home: Immigration, Ideology, and Agency in the film *Which Way Home*," http://nomajesty .tumblr.com/post/26742378271. Accessed June 20, 2012.

5. Jasbir Puar, Keynote, Homonationalism and Pinkwashing conference, New York, April 2013.

6. Several states require adults convicted of prostitution-related offenses to be listed on sex offender registries. Until 2012, Louisiana required people convicted of "crimes against nature by solicitation" to be listed on sex offender registries. In California, the passing of Prop 35 in 2012 means that people convicted of sex work and trafficking offenses (often sex workers themselves) are now listed on California's sex offender registries. See Gira Grant 2012.

7. This is consistent with Lionel Cantú's observation that in the "Western queer imaginary Mexico and its men are locked in a spatio-temporal warp of macho desire": this fantasy is both threatening and desired. See Cantú 2009, 114.

8. For example, the National Day Laborer Organizing Network, which is responsible for the #Not1More anti-deportation campaign, co-organized over fifty national LGBTQ organizations to "come out" against Secure Communities (an information sharing program between state and federal law enforcement and ICE) in 2011. http://www.ndlon.org/es/pressroom/ press-releases/item/176-lesbian-gay-bisexual-transgender-and-queer-lgbtq-organizations -come-out-against-ices-secure-communities-deportation-program. Accessed March 3, 2014.

## REFERENCES

Anonymous. 2013. "Rebound Seen in New ICE Prosecutorial Discretion Closures," Transactional Records Access Clearinghouse. Accessed October 4, 2013. http://trac.syr.edu/ immigration/reports/308/#pd.

Aizura, Aren Z. 2006. "Of Borders and Homes: The Imaginary Community of Transsexual Citizenship." *Inter-Asia Cultural Studies* 7.2: 289–309.

———. 2009. "'Travellers across the Boundaries of Sex': Travel, Transnationality and Trans Subjectivities." PhD diss., University of Melbourne.

———. 2014. "Trans Feminine Value, Racialized Others, and the Limits of Necropolitics." In *Queer Necropolitics*, edited by Jin Haritaworn, Adi Kuntsman, and Silvia Posocco, 129–148. New York: Routledge.

Beauchamp, Toby. 2009. "Artful Concealment and Strategic Visibility: Transgender Bodies and State Surveillance after 9/11." *Surveillance and Society* 6.4: 356–366.

Benedicto, Bobby. 2008. "The Haunting of Gay Manila: Global Space-Time and the Specter of Kabaklaan." *GLQ: A Journal of Lesbian and Gay Studies* 14.2: 317–338.

Boylan, Jennifer Finney. 2013. "Longing for the Day When Chelsea Manning and I Both Seem Boring." *The Atlantic*, August 22. Accessed August 30, 2013. http://www.washington post.com/lifestyle/style/longing-for-the-day-when-chelsea-manning-and-i-both-seem -boring/2013/08/22/7bf52c42-0b5d-11e3-b87c-476db8ac34cd_story.html.

Cantú, Lionel. 2009. *The Sexuality of Migration: Border Crossings and Mexican Immigrant Men.* Edited by Salvador Vidal-Ortiz and Nancy A. Naples. New York: NYU Press.

Curtis, Rebekah. 2011. "Transgender People Murdered as World Resists Change." Reuters, November 11. Accessed July 13, 2013. http://www.reuters.com/article/2011/11/16/us -transgender-idUSTRE7AF1UA20111116.

Garcia, J. Neil. 2009. *Philippine Gay Culture: Binabae to Bakla, Silahis to MSM*. Hong Kong University Press.

Gehi, Pooja. 2009. "Struggles from the Margins: Anti-Immigrant Legislation and the Impact on Low-Income Transgender People of Color." *Women's Rights Law Report* 30: 315–329.

———. 2012. "Gendered (In)security: Migration and Criminalization in the Security State." *Harvard Journal of Law and Gender* 35: 357–398.

Gira Grant, Melissa. 2012. "California's Prop 35: A Misguided Ballot Initiative Targeting the Wrong People for the Wrong Reasons." *RH Reality Check*, November 1. Accessed July 23, 2013. http://rhrealitycheck.org/article/2012/11/01/prop-35.

Haritaworn, Jin. 2012. "Colorful Bodies in the Multikulti Metropolis: Vitality, Victimology, and Transgressive Citizenship in Berlin." In *Transgender Migrations: The Bodies, Borders, and Politics of Transition*, edited by Trystan Cotton, 11–31. New York: Routledge.

INCITE! Women of Color Against Violence. 2009. *The Revolution Will Not Be Funded: Beyond the Non-Profit Industrial Complex*. Boston: South End Press.

Lamble, Sarah. 2008. "Retelling Racialized Violence, Remaking White Innocence: The Politics of Interlocking Oppressions in Transgender Day of Remembrance." *Sexuality Research & Social Policy* 5.1: 24–42.

Ludwig, Mike. 2014. "Sex Work Wars: Project ROSE, Monica Jones, and the Fight for Human Rights." *Truth Out*, March 13. Accessed March 15, 2014. http://truth-out.org/news/item/22422-sex-work-wars-project-rose-monica-jones-and-the-fight-for-human-rights.

Mananzala, Rickke, and Dean Spade. 2008. "The Nonprofit Industrial Complex and Trans Resistance." *Sexuality Research and Social Policy* 5.1: 53–71.

Mohanty, Chandra Talpade. 1991. "Under Western Eyes: Feminist Scholarship and Colonial Discourses." In *Third World Women and the Politics of Feminism*, edited by Chandra Talpade Mohanty, Ann Russo, and Lourdes Torres, 51–80. Bloomington: Indiana University Press.

Namaste, Viviane. 2005. "Against Transgender Rights: Understanding the Imperialism of Contemporary Transgender Politics." In *Sex Change, Social Change*, 139–168. Toronto: Women's Press.

Namaste, Viviane, and Mirha Soleil-Ross. 2005. "Activist Can't Go On Forever Acting in the Abstract: Interview with Mirha Soleil-Ross." In *Sex Change, Social Change*, by Viviane Namaste, 117–138. Toronto: Women's Press.

Nationalities Service Center. 2012. "Rainbow Welcome Initiative Caters to LGBT Refugees." Accessed June 16, 2013. http://www.nscphila.org/rainbow-welcome-initiative-caters-to-lgbt-refugees.

Nichols, Bill. 1994. *Blurred Boundaries: Questions of Meaning in Contemporary Culture*. Bloomington: Indiana University Press.

Ong, Aihwa. 1988. "Colonialism and Modernity: Feminist Re-presentations of Women in Non-Western Societies." *Inscriptions* 3–4. Accessed March 5, 2014. http://culturalstudies.ucsc.edu/PUBS/Inscriptions/vol_3-4/aihwaong.html.

Power, Samantha. 2012. "US Leadership to Advance Equality for LGBT People Abroad." White House Memorandum, December 13. Accessed October 3, 2013. http://www.whitehouse.gov/blog/2012/12/13/us-leadership-advance-equality-lgbt-people-abroad.

Puar, Jasbir. 2007. *Terrorist Assemblages: Homonationalism in Queer Times*. Durham: Duke University Press.

Romney, Lee. 2011. "Hate Crimes against Gay, Transgender People Rise, Report Says." *Los Angeles Times*, July 31. Accessed July 13, 2013. http://articles.latimes.com/2011/jul/13/nation/la-na-lgbt-hate-crimes-20110713.

Sandeen, Autumn. 2013. "Thoughts on Chelsea Manning's Coming Out." *The Trans Advocate*, August 23. Accessed August 30, 2013. http://www.transadvocate.com/thoughts-on -chelsea-mannings-coming-out_n_10072.htm.

Shakhsari, Sima. 2014. "Killing Me Softly with Your Rights: Queer Death and the Politics of Rightful Killing." In *Queer Necropolitics*, edited by Jin Haritaworn, Adi Kuntsman, and Silvia Posocco, 93–110. New York: Routledge.

Spade, Dean. 2011. *Normal Life: Administrative Violence, Critical Trans Politics, and the Limits of Law.* New York: South End Press.

Spade, Dean, and Craig Willse. 2014. "Sex, Gender, and War in an Age of Multicultural Imperialism." *QED: A Journal in GLBTQ Worldmaking* 1.1: 5–29.

Tadiar, Neferti. 2009. "Toward a Vision of Sexual and Economic Justice." *Scholar & Feminist Online* 7.3. Accessed March 4, 2011. http://sfonline.barnard.edu/sexecon/tadiar_01.htm.

*Transgression.* Directed by TJ Barber, Toni Marzal, Morgan Hargrave, and Daniel Rotman. 2011. A10 Films, Harvard Law Documentary Studio, 2011. http://transgressionfilm.tumblr .com.

U.S. Citizenship and Immigration Services. 2011. "Guidance for Adjudicating Lesbian, Gay, Bisexual, Transgender, and Intersex (LGBTI) Refugee and Asylum Claims: Training Module." Accessed March 13, 2014. http://webcache.googleusercontent.com/ search?q=cache:mTXnkpCDebYJ:http://www.uscis.gov/sites/default/files/USCIS/ Humanitarian/Refugees%2520%2526%2520Asylum/Asylum/Asylum%2520Native %2520Documents%2520and%2520Static%2520Files/RAIO-Training-March-2012.pdf %2BGuidance+for+Adjudicating+Lesbian,+Gay,+Bisexual,+Transgender,+and+Intersex +%28LGBTI%29+Refugee+and+Asylum+Claims:+Training+Module&oe=utf-8&hl= en&&ct=clnk.

# PART IV  TRANS ACTIVISM AND POLICY

# 9 · THE *T* IN *LGBTQ*

## How Do Trans Activists Perceive Alliances within LGBT and Queer Movements in Québec (Canada)?

MICKAEL CHACHA ENRIQUEZ

In Québec, trans activists have recently won the ability to change their gender designation on identity documents without receiving sex reassignment surgery. It is largely by entering into alliances with other social movements that the trans movement obtained recognition from the provincial government, and this will hopefully succeed in reducing the control of medical and judicial institutions on trans bodies. The objective of the present chapter is to identify the dynamics of alliance building between trans activism and LGBQ activist movements in Québec, based on twelve qualitative interviews of trans militants. I will first briefly explore the literature on the subject and then present the methodology and the research participants. Thereafter, I will present the results of the research. I argue that LGBTQ alliances are marked by an ambivalence caused by contradictory forces. On the one hand, there are dynamics that arise from discourse and actions that strengthen connections within this community and are associated with trans inclusion. On the other hand, there are forces that act to drive trans activists and LGBQ activists apart, often resulting in trans exclusion.

## ALLIANCES AND SOCIAL MOVEMENTS

Building alliances remains an important process in social movements because it increases the number of people fighting against a specific oppression and consequently the chances of gaining social progress. Alliances must be seen as dynamic, diverging, and converging toward a greater movement. Indeed, alliance dynamics seem capable of redefining social movements. Inspired by the French sociologist Lilian Mathieu (2004), I consider that three forms of alliances exist within social movements:

1. Within a social movement where activists experience a common form of oppression. For instance, my research focuses primarily on the experiences of transphobia and cissexism. However, tensions exist between trans activists in regards to age, location (for example, urban Montréal versus rural regions), language, identity (transsexual, transgender, genderqueers, and so on), and socioeconomic status.
2. Between activists experiencing a common form of oppression and activists participating in the struggle, but not experiencing it. In particular, we can think of the role played by experts within the trans movement, such as psychologists, sexologists, researchers, or artists. They may hold positions of power that should be challenged.
3. Between different social movements. These alliances tend to emerge when activists are participating in several social movements or experiencing multiple forms of oppression. Lilian Mathieu refers to the *multipositionality* of such actors. For example, the trans movement allies itself mostly with other gender- and sexuality-related movements—sex workers, HIV-positive people, feminists, and the LGB (lesbian, gay, bisexual) and queer movement.

## THEORETICAL LINKS BETWEEN OPPRESSION EXPERIENCED BY LGBTQ PEOPLE

The LGBTQ category (lesbian, gay, bisexual, transgender, and queer) is often used as an umbrella term for people experiencing oppression because of their sexuality or their gender identity. Two main systems of oppression that affect LGBTQ people will be considered here: cissexism and heterosexism. *Cissexism* can be defined as the system that oppresses people who cross gender boundaries and that encourages people to maintain the gender they were assigned at birth. *Heterosexism* can be defined as the system that oppresses individuals whose sexual experiences do not happen exclusively with people of the *opposite sex* and persuades most people to restrict themselves to heterosexual sex.

While both systems are different, common links exist between cissexism and heterosexism as argued by different authors. Julia Serano (2007), an American trans activist and theorist, explains that cissexism arises from the idea that the gender identity of trans people is inferior to that of cisgender people. She holds that cissexism, transphobia, and homophobia originate from what she defines as *oppositional sexism*: the idea that sex is divided into two rigid and opposite categories, each possessing distinct attributes, aptitudes, abilities, and desires.

Another American trans author, Pat Califia (2003), considers that gender transgression is another cause of homophobia: "Straight culture reads much of the public expression of gay identity as gender transgression. To them, we're all part of the same garbage heap of sex-and-gender trash. It is practical points like this that can most easily draw queer and trans activists together" (256). He invites activists to forge links with each other based on the commonalities among different forms of oppression. The sense of belonging to a community is reinforced through what Gaëlle Krikorian calls an *insult community*, because cissexist and heterosexist behavior tends to overlap (Krikorian 2003). Furthermore, a recent study on homophobia in school environments by Line Chamberland et al. (2011) shows that effeminate men or masculine women experience discrimination more often than homosexual or bisexual people. The study suggests that homophobia primarily targets gender transgression as an indicator of non-heterosexual sexuality.

## CONCRETE LINKS BETWEEN LGBTQ ACTIVISTS

Researchers in Trans Studies have developed a strong understanding of the links between the oppressions experienced by trans people and those experienced by gay, lesbian, bisexual, and queer people. Scholars have shown that the first wave of LGBTQ alliances appeared during the late 1960s in France (Foerster 2006) and in the United States (Stryker 2008).[1] Susan Stryker explains that the emergence of the queer movement in the 1990s over issues related to HIV/AIDS rekindled this first wave of alliances between trans and LGB activists. Moreover, the rise of the broader LGBT movement during the 1990s and the 2000s in the Western world attests to the bonds between the diverse social movements. Indeed gay, lesbian, bisexual, and trans organizations are increasingly using the *LGBT* acronym to refer to a broader community. Kendal L. Broad (2002) argues that the addition of the *T* in *LGBT* can be viewed either as exclusionary identity politics or as a turn toward queer politics. The author takes into account the complexity and ambivalence within these relations by concluding that it is not necessarily one or the other, but instead, that the queer movement has had a profound influence on the evolution of the mainstream gay and lesbian movement toward a broader LGBT struggle.

In a 2009 study, Amy L. Stone argues that there are three reasons for allies to join another cause, or to use her terminology, three forms of "approximating experiences": "*borrowed approximations* or knowing a member of the marginalized group and being witness to their suffering; *overlapping approximations* or the analogy to some oppression they have suffered; and *global approximations* or a connection to their democratic or political orientations" (2009, 338).

Based on thirty-two interviews, she shows that gays and lesbians have different attitudes with respect to the inclusion of trans-identified people. Younger gay men holding positions of power within the LGBT movement tend to oppose the integration of new groups, while older gay activists, especially those who have fought for social justice, tend to operate through global approximations. Preoccupied with gender issues and power relations within the LGBT movement, lesbians include trans activists with greater ease. However, their feminist consciousness leads them to fear trans people's taking too much space within the movement and to be apprehensive of losing space to the benefit of trans people.

The LGBTQ alliance therefore appears to be ambivalent. Even if both theoretical and concrete links could be built between trans and LGBQ activists, there remain dissonances that could lead to the exclusion of trans people in the LGBTQ movement. To illustrate this point, in the next section of this chapter I will focus on my own research on the experiences and discourses of trans activists in Québec.

## METHODOLOGY AND PRESENTATION OF THE INTERVIEWEES

Twelve semi-structured interviews were conducted between April 2010 and February 2011 with trans activists from Québec who had been actively participating in trans activism for at least one year. During the interviews, three lines of inquiry were explored: (1) the dynamics of trans activism; (2) the meanings given to participation in trans activism; and (3) the links between trans activism and other social movements. After describing the participants, I will focus on the third line of inquiry.

I met with seven trans women and five trans men. Four of the participants identified as trans, four as transsexuals, one as genderqueer, one as transgender, one as queer and trans, and the last as trans and genderqueer. The participants self-identifying as queer or genderqueer were all trans men. Furthermore, their sexual orientation covered a wide spectrum as they identified as lesbians, bisexuals, queers, or heterosexuals. They were between twenty-two and sixty-six years old and their involvement as trans activists started between 1980 and 2009. Most of them were Francophone and only two of the twelve participants were Anglophone.[2] They were highly educated: four were PhD students, two were master's students, two obtained a bachelor's degree, one was a bachelor's student, another obtained a professional diploma. Two participants did not study at university.

Nine of the participants were members of at least one trans organization, and four of these individuals had worked in a paid job as a trans activist. Two of the twelve activists were not linked to any group, as they considered their involvement to be "personal" and "occasional." One participant became involved in trans activism only recently and perceived himself to be a sympathizer of one organization.

In the remainder of this chapter, I will discuss my research on the spaces conducive to alliances. Then, I will continue with the debates within trans activist groups regarding alliances with LGBQ activists, and carry on with the transphobia and cissexism in the LGBQ community. I will end by exploring some ideas to improve the inclusion of trans activists within the LGBTQ movement.

## Spaces Conducive to Alliances

Many participants in my study insisted on the importance of allying themselves with other groups in order to support a range of fights against oppression in addition to their main struggle against trans oppression. LGBTQ allies were considered particularly important, and the activists interviewed were quite loquacious about them. My analysis of the spaces in which links could be built between trans and LGBQ activists allows us to see on what basis alliances were built, as well as the resistance toward inclusion of trans people in these spaces. I argue that three particular environments have been conducive to the alliance among trans and LGBQ activists: HIV spaces, queer spaces, and LGBT spaces.

1. *HIV spaces.* The first space conducive to creating alliances was in communities fighting against HIV. This space linked trans women and gay men because the epidemic strongly affects these two groups. Research demonstrating that trans women are particularly struck by HIV (Herbst et al. 2008) opened the path toward obtaining public funds for trans organizations. In the 1990s, this had a major impact on the constitution of alliances related to health issues surrounding HIV/AIDS and sex work.

One HIV-positive activist spoke about her commitment to the fight against HIV in the 1990s. Although she had an important position within an HIV support group, she encountered a lot of resistance from certain gay men. Indeed, she named this organization a "gay-men-fortified castle" where she was able to find her place despite this transphobia. This alliance was ultimately built by HIV-positive trans women sex workers who fought to be included in the HIV movement. It reveals the importance of these women in the emergence of trans activism during the 1990s. Alliances with HIV activists have not evolved toward greater inclusion since this time. For example, the activists interviewed named many important HIV groups that still did not address the particularities of trans embodiment in their prevention campaigns.

2. *Queer spaces.* Alliances also occurred in English-speaking queer spaces aimed at students and young people. Queer activists wanted to link their movements to liberate both gender and sexuality by strategically focusing on feminists and those who are most marginalized in the LGBTQ movement. Such alliances left their mark through name changes to the McGill and Concordia Universities' Centers for Women during the first half of the 2000s. They became respectively known as the Center for Gender Advocacy and the Union for Gender Empowerment. In a sense, the name changes symbolized their broadened mandate to deal concurrently with feminist, queer, and trans issues. These changes were the source of much debate, illustrating once again the ambivalence with which the inclusion of trans people is met with in these spaces. Similarly, in the mid-2000s, Project 10 (a group reaching young Anglophones from sixteen to twenty-five years old) developed "Project Max," which aimed at including trans people. They released a guide for trans people explaining how to navigate the health system in order to change their gender, their name, and their sex designation.[3] Today, the high number of trans people associated with Project 10 attests to the success of their inclusion campaign. Indeed, each of these three organizations (Center for Gender Advocacy, Union for Gender Empowerment, and Project 10) implemented deep changes in order to include trans people. They have become trans-friendly organizations, welcoming trans people, delivering services, and participating in trans coalitions such as the Trans Health Network.

In comparison, queer Francophone spaces emerged only recently. In 2009 PolitiQ-Queers Solidaires (Queers in Solidarity) was formed and immediately started a trans committee. Julie, a Francophone participant, sees queer as being inclusive of trans people: "PolitiQ is not trans as such, but queer, that is larger and including trans." PolitiQ's committee launched a coalition to organize the first protest movement in public spaces in front of the Directeur de l'état civil, the institution that regulates name and sex designation changes.[4] Two hundred people were present at the protest, and sixty-four groups—including thirty-nine that were LGBTQ-identified—signed the declaration. The support of the LGBT and queer movements was significant as two-thirds of the signatures came from members of those movements. In a sense, the queer Francophone movement through its discourse and language contributed in bridging the gap between the queer Anglophone and the LGBT Francophone communities. Although these two communities rarely collaborate, the organization of the protest became a space where the Anglophone and Francophone activists could build a coalition.

3. *LGBT spaces.* The third type of alliance is located in the predominantly French-speaking LGBT movement, which started in the mid-2000s. The event responsible for the emergence of this alliance is the États Généraux des Communautés LGBT in 2004. It was an important forum for LGBT activists. Trans people were welcomed for the first time at the third iteration of this event. There were about a dozen trans people among the four hundred delegates present. The États Généraux was mandated to establish a common set of demands to negotiate with the government. Noticing that demands related to trans issues were not emerging from the workshops, trans activists insisted that a crosscutting principle be voted on during the plenary session, which was the case (TCLGQ 2004). Marie, one of the interviewees, explains that the États Généraux enabled significant changes within and outside of the LGBT communities:

> The gay community played an important role. Even though it wasn't always well done, even though not all issues were considered, they were able to spread the word "trans" in many communities where trans people did not have access. Spreading a word is significant. . . . Within the LGBT community, deep changes happened because some were willing to bridge the gap between the two and acknowledged that we needed to stop confining ourselves to our own "sheds." . . . The T are now an important actor in the LGBT community. (Marie)

From the mid-2000s, gay and lesbian groups evolved significantly to create the LGBT movement. The alliance has benefited social progress and critical bonds now exist between allies regarding the experience of oppression and common methods of action. However, trans inclusion is not ubiquitous and differs on a case-by-case basis, as certain organizations remain LG or LGB. Indeed, a trans contingent has been present within LGBT Pride Montréal parade only since 2009. These elements demonstrate the ambivalence with which the LGBT alliance is treated both by trans activists and by LGB activists. LGBT committees of French-speaking labor unions have similarly evolved toward increased inclusion of trans people. Since these committees hold significant roles within LGBT coalitions, they have been made aware of trans issues through their participation. Consequently, the LGBT alliance has facilitated the development of actions targeting transphobia at work. For instance, some unions have adopted motions about trans workers and recently the Canadian Labour Congress published a guide for workers in transition. Finally, the alliance has also resulted in the political recognition of trans activists. Many demands regarding trans people were brought forward during different rounds of negotiations with the government. Since 2005, after the États Généraux des Communautés LGBT, there has always been at least one trans person present during negotiations. This recognition has resulted in political gains, such as reduced waiting time for name changes.

### Debates within Trans Activist Groups Regarding
### the Alliance with LGBTQ Activisms

As demonstrated above, the creation of space for an LGBTQ alliance has always been accompanied by ambivalence, which is to say, discourses and practices of inclusion and exclusion. Each time trans activists had to fight, with the support of their allies, to create a broader understanding of struggle that includes trans people. However, these activists have encountered resistance to an LGBTQ alliance even among some trans activists. Indeed there are several conflicting perspectives within trans activist groups regarding alliance with LGBQ groups, as a discourse analysis of my interviews reveals. For instance, Bobby thinks that there are important links between these movements. "Trans identities belong to the LGBT movement and to the queer movement. . . . I believe that how trans people experience oppression is similar to how other people experience oppression with respect to gender and sexuality." For Johnny, the experiences of oppression have the same origin: "Even though our needs and [the] everyday life [of LGBTQ] differ in the details, the social discrimination we face, it comes from the same place. The public at large puts us in the same basket." Monique expresses the same idea: "For the average person, homosexuals, transsexuals, transgenders [sic], they're all mixed up in the same basket."

Another participant, Bruno, highlights that there are important parallels to be made between these two forms of oppression, but that they remain fundamentally different: "It's not the same thing. In one case, it's the orientation and in the other, it's the identity. Therefore, in my opinion, it's two different realities, two different sets of problems and therefore, two different sets of needs."

According to Monique, a longtime trans activist, the realities of trans and LG people differ to the point of being incompatible. Her heterosexuality has made her oppose an alliance with LG groups for a long time, but in the past few years, she has changed her mind: "It's very recent. Because the older transsexuals did not want [to make bonds with LG people], and also, a few younger people who had some power in the community preferred that transsexuals remain an autonomous group." This quote illustrates the divergence between trans heterosexual people, who generally feel less concerned about this alliance, and trans LGBQ people, who support it, as described by Marie: "Often it seems there is a problem in our community, you know? Because there are some who do not want to be associated with gay people because they are heterosexuals and on the contrary, those who are gay and lesbian. Well yeah, but they are our best allies and we should associate with them."

Finally, my research shows that it is primarily trans lesbian activists who support the alliance. The sexual orientation of trans activists seems to influence their propensity to make an alliance with LGBQ people. It confirms that the multipositionality of some activists helps build alliances.

## Transphobia and Cissexism in the LGBT Community

Although more and more groups use the acronyms *LGBT* or *LGBTQ* to describe themselves, there remains much transphobia and cissexism. Many groups marginalize and exclude trans people, mostly in an unconscious way. It manifests itself through the way that trans issues are ignored or put on the back burner, as expressed by François and Johnny:

Groups that claim to be LGBT are in fact gay and lesbian groups. (François)

The comment I keep hearing is: "The world isn't ready yet." Even in the LGBT community, bi and trans people keep getting told that. It's very frustrating because I believe in solidarity and nobody moves forward without everybody else moving forward. (Johnny)

Also on this theme, another participant explains that generally, when the *T* is added, the group still just deals with sexuality issues. He asks the following: "If it says LGBT or if it says LGBTQ, then often the question is: 'Well, that's great, but where is the T? Where is the trans stuff that is part of this panel, is part of this workshop, is part of this organization?'" (Mike). Moreover, according to Bobby, LGBQ activists never sufficiently question the power they hold:

Often trans people are mentioned but it isn't, really . . . You know, it's like oh LGBT, but the T is not really there, you know? In English, we speak of accountability. You know . . . We're mentioned because we want to be included but it's more tolerance than actual inclusion, really. . . . Being tolerant, it means that nothing changes, because it is the same people who hold the positions of power, and these people can say, "Well, I won't use my power against you, but I won't give you some, either." There's no actual exchange, there's no will to leave some space for trans people.

Another participant, Catherine, highlights the consequences of excluding trans issues in LGBTQ organizations: "They do actions for gays and lesbians, but not for trans people. If there's something for trans people, they rarely have the time to take care of it. Or because they don't know the cases well enough or because they don't have much experience with them, well when they do take care of it, they do it all wrong!" Clearly, many trans people have experienced transphobia and cissexism within organizations that claim to be LGBTQ. The banishment of trans issues to the backburner and the invisibility of gender issues within certain groups illustrates the ambivalence with which the inclusion of trans people within the LGBTQ movement is treated.

It is interesting to note that there are individual dynamics in each of the communities that comprise the LGBTQ umbrella and that are unique to each of them. Hélène considers that when LG people gained equal rights, it created space for trans issues to be brought forward:

> For a long time, gays were the enemies of lesbians. Maybe you're old enough to have witnessed this. Gay people were the enemies of transgendered people, lesbians were also enemies for transgender and transsexual people, whom they deemed false women.[5] So from the beginning, it wasn't easy; they were fighting for their own rights. But now that they gained equal rights, some became more open and looked at the issue of transgender and transsexual people as marginalized groups who need to be defended and protected.

It should be noted that important bonds have existed between lesbians and trans people. The activists interviewed repeatedly mentioned that they received support from lesbian activists but, paradoxically, faced resistance from lesbians regarding their inclusion in the LGBTQ alliance as lesbians were afraid of losing space and visibility to trans people. Thus, trans and cis lesbians are those who seem to be at the center of the dynamics in LGBTQ alliances, confronting certain mainstream gay activists who refuse to question gender norms.

## Some Strategies to Improve the Inclusion of Trans Activists within the LGBTQ Movements

Despite ongoing resistance and the many difficulties encountered, the trans activists interviewed considered the LGBTQ alliance to be very important and proposed several ideas to improve upon and perhaps resolve the ambivalence with which the inclusion of trans people is treated in the LGBTQ movement. Three strategies were identified by participants. The first strategy involves addressing the double standard used by LGBTQ activist groups on gender identity and sexual orientation issues. As Marie illustrates: "One thing that is hardly understood in trans groups is that if we really want to become LGBT, it means that while organizations who are gay- and lesbian-based need to open up to trans realities, that is trans identity, it also requires that trans groups open up to the sexual orientation of their members, which means that we are not only trans, but that we also have a sexual orientation." The inclusion of trans heterosexual people within LGBT organizations would be a key indicator of trans inclusion for Marie.

The second strategy relates to consciousness raising and facilitating dialogue. Johnny actively participates in a LGBT group at his workplace where he raises questions about trans issues in order to increase the awareness of his colleagues: "There could be more solidarity. And we also want to make people understand that within this large group comprising LGBT people, if only L and G move forward, then they only re-create the conditions for marginalizing people. And in a sense, that's a form of double marginalization. And how do you raise consciousness? Well, it's by keeping the dialogue open." Bobby, too, believes that consciousness raising and increasing dialogue remain the best strategies: "The concrete changes I would like to see in LGBT groups relate to how the people who work in those groups should learn how to make their services more inclusive. . . . If you're getting told that what you do is problematic, then it's learning to say, 'Okay, what can I do to solve this?' that is entering into a dialogue instead of being defensive about it." Bruno is also an advocate for consciousness raising. He explains that the inclusion of trans people within large LGBTQ groups will enable trans people to gain ground: "When we'll be able to reach large groups such as Gai Écoute, GRIS-Montréal on trans issues, well I think that it'll be a matter of time before we reach all the smaller groups for the T to really become integrated. To reach that goal, well it requires that trans people get out there, speak out and hold conferences."

The third strategy is to make trans organizations gain a leadership role in the LGBTQ movement, as Julie voices: "So, if an organization watches over their balcony toward the trans group right next to it and realizes that, 'Damn, there's stuff happening in the trans community,' well that's leadership. It's the power that others can grant to us. So, other communities will realize that we're believable, that we make stuff happen, that we're moving forward, that our cases are serious, and that we have real demands." These three strategies can be seen as tools to build a LGBTQ movement that really includes different communities.

## CONCLUSION

My research has contributed to the understanding of how alliances between trans and LGBQ activists emerged in Québec. It shows that alliances remain ambivalent. Indeed there are spaces, actions, and discourses that gather the different communities together, but they also separate them from each other. In order to create more inclusion, this ambivalence must be dealt with directly—by opening the channels of communication and creating awareness, which can help to deconstruct the doubts that alliances raise, and by clearly recognizing the contribution of trans people to the LGBTQ movement. It is important that LGBTQ activists take into account the different realities of each group so as not to erase their different needs and therefore to benefit the dominant group within the community, namely, cis gays and lesbians. By adopting the demands of different LGBTQ communities and by enabling trans people to acquire positions of leadership, LGBTQ organizations would create a public affirmation that would dispel many doubts surrounding alliances. We wish that all LGBTQ organizations would dare to put into place a campaign that showcases the demands of trans people and that grants them the importance they deserve.

## NOTES

Thanks to Jean-Philippe Ung, Jeremy Lane, Michael Hawrysh, and Danielle Beaulieu for their translation of this text.

1. From a historical perspective, Stryker (2008) explains, "In practice, the distinctions between what we now call 'transgender' and 'gay' or 'lesbian' were not always as meaningful back then as they have since become. Throughout the 2nd half of the 19th century and the 1st half of the 20th century, homosexual desire and gender variance were often closely associated" (34).
2. Québec is a province of Canada that is mainly French-speaking.
3. This document is no longer available, but it inspired ASTT(e)Q guide (Ezra 2012).
4. In English: Registrar of civil status of Québec.
5. In this quote, the interviewee considers just trans women when she talks about trans people.

## REFERENCES

Broad, Kendal L. 2002. "GLB+T? Gender/Sexuality Movements and Transgender Collective Identity (De)Constructions." *International Journal of Sexuality and Gender Studies* 7.4: 241–263.

Califia, Pat. 2003. *Sex Changes: The Politics of Transgenderism.* Berkeley, CA: Cleis Press.

Chamberland, Line, Gilbert Émond, Michaël Bernier, Gabrielle Richard, Marie-Pier Petit, Marilyne Chevrier, Bill Ryan, Joanne Otis, and Danielle Julien. 2011. *L'homophobie à l'école secondaire au Québec: Portrait de la situation, impacts et pistes de solution.* Montréal: Université du Québec à Montréal.

Ezra, Jackson. 2012. *Self-Referred: A Québec Trans-Health Survival Tool.* Montréal: ASTT(e)Q.

Foerster, Maxime. 2006. *Histoire des transsexuels en France.* Saint-Martin de Londres: H&O Éditions.

Herbst, Jeffrey H., Elizabeth D. Jacobs, Teresa J. Finlayson, Vel S. McKleroy, Mary Spink Neumann, and Nicole Crepaz. 2008. "Estimating HIV Prevalence and Risk Behaviors of Transgender Persons in the United States: A Systematic Review." *AIDS and Behavior* 12.1: 1–17.

Krikorian, Gaëlle. 2003. "Transphobie." In *Dictionnaire de l'homophobie,* edited by Louis-Georges Tin, 406–408. Paris: Presses Universitaires de France.

Mathieu, Lilian. 2004. *Comment lutter? Sociologie et mouvements sociaux.* Paris: La Discorde.

Serano, Julia. 2007. *Whipping Girl: A Transsexual Woman on Sexism and the Scapegoating of Femininity*. Berkeley, CA: Seal Press.

Stone, Amy L. 2009. "More than Adding a T: American Lesbian and Gay Activists' Attitudes towards Transgender Inclusion." *Sexualities* 12: 334–254.

Stryker, Susan. 2008. *Transgender History*. Berkeley, CA: Seal Press.

Table de concertation des lesbiennes et des gais du Québec (TCLGQ). 2004. *De l'égalité juridique à l'égalité sociale: Actes États Généraux 2004 des communautés LGBT du Québec*. www.cqgl.ca.

# 10 · TRANSLATINA IS ABOUT THE JOURNEY

## A Dialogue on Social Justice for Transgender Latinas in San Francisco

ALEXANDRA RODRÍGUEZ DE RUÍZ
AND MARCIA OCHOA

This chapter is a conversation between the authors held in July 2013 to memorialize the founding and first five years of El/La Para Translatinas, a social justice and HIV prevention program for transgender Latinas (*translatinas*) based in the Mission District of San Francisco. Alexandra worked as program coordinator at El/La from 2006 until 2011 and is currently an activist and educator in Mexico City. Marcia, currently a member of El/La's advisory board, served in the volunteer position as director of program and evaluation from 2006 through 2013 and before that time was a member of the advisory board of Proyecto ContraSIDA por Vida, the organization from which El/La emerged in 2006. Her experience working with translatinas in San Francisco began in 1994 when she was office manager of Proyecto.

As longtime collaborators, we took this opportunity to reflect on the process of change we have watched El/La go through. Though we mention several names of people who have worked with El/La, we want to be clear that we are representing only our own experiences of building the organization. Our perspectives are our own and, of course, give only part of the story of El/La. In this conversation, we talk about our motivations for working together, how El/La began, how we started using the term *translatina* to organize, what our core values are, how we developed programs at El/La, and some moments that were particularly traumatic, including the death of Ruby Ordeñana and our first defunding.

We conclude with some thoughts about migration and how Alexandra has continued her work beyond San Francisco. We hope this conversation is the beginning of a long-term process for both of us in learning from our experiences at El/La and continuing the work for social justice for translatinas everywhere.

## ABOUT EL/LA

El/La is a space where translatinas have come together to address individual and collective concerns in order to promote their survival and dreams. You can learn more about our programs or contact us through our website: www.ellaparatrans latinas.org. Our organizational vision and mission statements are:

> *Vision*: El/La Para Translatinas works to build a world where translatinas feel we deserve to protect, love, and develop ourselves. By building this base, we support translatinas in protecting ourselves against violence, abuse, and illness, and in fully realizing our dreams.

> *Mission*: El/La is an organization for translatinas that builds collective vision and action to promote our survival and improve our quality of life in the San Francisco Bay Area. Because we exist in a world that fears and hates transgender people, women, and immigrants, we fight for justice. We respond to those who see us as shameful, disposable, or less than human. We are here to reflect the style and grace of our survival, and to make new paths for ourselves.

## WHY WE DID THE WORK

MARCIA (SANTA CRUZ, CA): I want to have a conversation where we go over the history of El/La, we think about it, we talk about it, maybe we agree about some stuff, maybe we don't. We scream at each other and laugh and . . . [laughs]

ALEXANDRA (MEXICO CITY, DF): . . . and cry!

MARCIA: And cry! [laughs] Just tell the story of El/La and how El/La became what El/La is, what El/La was when you left, and what it is now. I have a few questions, but do you have any questions that you want to start out with?

ALEXANDRA: What came to my mind is why is it important for you to focus on helping translatinas to have a space like El/La?

MARCIA: I will always feel very indebted to translatinas in San Francisco who, when I first moved there, could be very loving with me and recognized my gender. I felt that was so important to me when I was twenty-three and just getting to San Francisco. Coming from the experience of not ever really being in a society where I would be recognized for who or what I was, I feel there's a level of legibility that I've been able to experience with translatinas in particular.

The other reason is because I saw that at Proyecto [Proyecto ContraSIDA por Vida] there was a group of us that were college educated, some of us were immigrants, some of us were raised in the States, but we had a kind of social mobility. There was a group of trans women who, no matter how smart they were or how able to survive they were, they were not getting the kind of social opportunities that we were getting. Those of us who were able to get some access to college, the arts, hold down a job, we were doing OK. The trans women were not doing so great. They were dying, depressed, not able to be employed . . . We had this idea of an egalitarian community, of a social movement where queer, LGBTQ, whatever, Latinos were all gonna kind of dream our way into fabulousness. That fabulousness only works in some ways for some people, not for everybody. So part of that was also my commitment to that community, and for all of us to be lifted up, as some individuals were.

In Venezuela I started to realize that unless and until the ways that transgender women were [treated were improved, then] we were all still going to be subject to different forms of gender violence. These women in Venezuela, the *transformistas* I worked with, were the ones that were catching the most shit. I got some violence or prejudice around my gender presentation, but it was nowhere near what the women, the effeminate gay men, and the women who were trans, the kind of heavy policing that they got. I felt that out of a commitment to that work, it was really important for me to keep doing this in San Francisco. Plus, it was my mental health plan for when I went to work at [UC] Santa Cruz. [laughs]

ALEXANDRA: Fabulous.

MARCIA: It kept me sane, girl!

ALEXANDRA: For me, it was a discovery, a wake-up call to be in a city like San Francisco and have the fabulous, tremendous opportunity that you gave me to work at El/La. It made me realize how fucking privileged I had been my entire life. Because, to begin with, I grew up with my family, I had [the] opportunity to go to school, to work, to feel loved, to be in therapy since I was six and a half years old. I was able to come to terms with my gender identity, with my sexuality, with who I wanted to become. That's something that, when I came to San Francisco and I started working with these girls, I realized that most of them didn't have. I felt obligated, but I also felt a responsibility to make sure that these women at least knew that they had a chance. Because, just by the fact that you put on some high heels and a dress, go out on the street and make yourself so visible in a society that points out anything that is different. . . . To see these girls having the guts to go out, stand on a corner, or to try to be who they wanted to be—I wanted to make sure that they knew just that alone makes them so strong and so powerful.

MARCIA: Can you tell the story that you told in Chicago about why you came to work for El/La?

ALEXANDRA: I was fed up of seeing, reading in newspapers about trans women, especially translatinas being always so stigmatized and stereotyped, and more than anything victimized. Whenever a translatina was murdered, it was always this "prostitute," "man dressed up as a woman," or "drug addict"—this horrible person, they did a favor taking out. Then a very dear friend of mine, Ana Fernández, who I had known my whole life, died in San Francisco. She was murdered and victimized. Not only was she a victim of domestic violence but she was also a victim of the system because she was tagged all along as a drug addict and a sex worker and all those stereotypes. When she died, it got to me. I was living in LA in my little bubble. Married, working at LAX, and having this fabulous life, living near the beach and . . . like, everything is beautiful, you know? When this thing happened, I tried to help Ana Fernández. I came to San Francisco in November to try to help her out, to help her go into rehab. I didn't know the city of San Francisco. I didn't know anybody. I didn't know . . . um . . . what's that place where the girls go? Walden House.

*Ah, sin saber qué era Walden House. So yo me puse en el internet a buscar y descubrí, le hablé a Ana, le dije, "mira, este lugar," tienen un programa y allá llamé, y me dijo "sí, sí, sí" y cuando fui a San Francisco, desgraciadamente a Ana Fernández le pegó el marido y andaba toda golpeada con los ojos morados. Se me escondió, no . . .*[1] She didn't want me to see her like that, so I couldn't help her. A month later, she was dead. How do you think I felt? I felt like I had failed her. I'm here living in my fucking bubble, in my lie that is so normative, so perfect when my friends, my sisters are still dying, and nobody is doing nothing about it. Nobody is out there saying she was a human being and she was doing something and she was trying.

I went into a depression from December till Pride Day in San Francisco. I was really depressed. My husband [at the time] was like, "What's wrong with you?" When we went to Pride in June, I saw how fabulous the community was there, and I told him, "I want to be part of this, I want some of this." That's when we started scouting San Francisco in September and October. [I quit my job of eleven-plus years and] we finally moved, and I applied for a job at Castro Health Center, *o como se llama*. Of course, I had no experience. I got rejected. That's when JoAnne Keatley [Alexandra's friend and a member of El/La's advisory board] told me, "You know what? El/La is looking for somebody and I think you'd be perfect for the job."

## THE BEGINNING

ALEXANDRA: I had no experience whatsoever working in social justice or community work, or with LGBTQ communities, but I had the desire to do something. You saw that drive and you gave me that opportunity and for that I'm so grateful to you because you believed in me.

MARCIA: Well, you were a godsend, girl! I had just been asked to supervise the program, as you remember. We were with [our first fiscal agent] Mobilization Against AIDS International, and Donna Rae [Palmer, the executive director of MAAI] didn't speak any Spanish! She was having to supervise [the staff] who were still on the transgender prevention contract after Proyecto [closed its doors].

They had moved the office in 2005 over to where we are now, from across the street. It was so sad in that office. First of all, nobody was ever in. We had an office that nobody ever opened. [The staff] were saying that they were working out of people's hotel rooms, and doing outreach, and I remember I got asked by Donna Rae to write the [annual] monitoring report in August, and I said, "Oh, well where are the files—the client files—so I can review them?" [A staff person said,] "Here's some boxes." There were rat turds in those boxes, her cell phone bills, random papers. It was just [a] shambles. I remember I was on the phone with my friend Juana María in the storage room, trying to dig through this box, trying to find these files and I was crying. . . . I was like, "Proyecto is *gone*. I'm digging through a box full of rat turds." You know? There's no community, there's no love here. I don't know what we can do here. I think for me it was that transition from Proyecto. I was one of the last people to stay attached to the vision of that organization and I was ready to let go of it. Because I said—and [the staff] were right about this—translatinas, transgender Latinas needed something on their own terms, that wasn't what Proyecto was to us, to my generation.

ALEXANDRA: Exactly.

MARCIA: So, [the staff] came up with that name [El/La] and, JoAnne and I never really liked it. . . . I tried to get you to change it, but it stuck. Then, I was only about a month or two into being the supervisor there as a volunteer and finishing my dissertation, I was living in San Francisco and I had just started [teaching] at UC Santa Cruz and then . . . my true love Alexandra comes along [laughs]. I was thinking we can't even imagine a room full of transgender Latinas talking to each other about *anything*, much less HIV prevention, right?

ALEXANDRA: Exactly.

MARCIA: So, can you tell me a little bit how you moved it from that nothing—no community, no dialogue, no safety in sitting down—to a room full of translatinas talking over each other and *cotorreando*[2] and then having serious conversations and talking seriously about the things that were going on in their lives? How did that happen?

ALEXANDRA: That is really important because I think that is the essence of what El/La is, and that you and I and Elissa [Vélez, the first office manager of El/La] built together. I'm not going to take all the credit, because if it wasn't for you, if it wasn't for Elissa, I would have never been able to do it. But, you said something really important and it was something that I learned there, that it was on their own terms, and it's something that probably nobody ever paid attention to.

Because remember when I came to work there, I came from corporate, I came from LAX, I came from Delta, I came from private companies, air cargo, so in my mind, I'm this . . . institutionalized (or whatever you want to call it) person that comes to work nine to five. [laughs]

MARCIA: Ahh-ha! That went out the window the first day!

ALEXANDRA: Monday through Friday [laughs] . . . eh, and it was like, of course, you know! Translatinas are waking up at three or four o'clock in the afternoon and . . . and they're like, "Oh, what am I going to do right now? I'm bored. I'm going to go walk the streets." I didn't know that, of course. So remember when I started opening El/La with [the outreach worker] and she was like, "Oh girl, nobody's going to come at that time." I [would insist], "No but we need to stay open, we need to open, we need to stay there." "Oh no, no, no, you don't need to stay here, just go to Tom Waddell [Transgender Health Clinic] and give condoms and that's the whole work for the week." I was like "No! We need to stay there and open the office, so people know that we're open and they come." Of course, I open at nine, nobody will come, I open at twelve, nobody will come.

So then I started going to Tom Waddell and finding out why the girls don't come. It's because, to begin with they say to me, "Well, we don't go to those places because they always give us condoms, they give us a plate of food, and all they talk about is HIV prevention. We already know all that. We want something different, we want a place where we can come in the afternoons and stay there and *echar cotorreo* and *checkar*³ our e-mails, or our Facebook or whatever . . ." So I started talking to the girls and I said, "Well, if we open late, are you going to come and tell *tus amiguitas*⁴ that they can come? We're going to have food and we're going to have coffee and you can talk about anything."

I think that was really important. To listen to them, because also, what triggered everything for these girls is that they started coming and said "Well, my boyfriend beats me up, I have no place to live, I don't have papers, I'm HIV positive, I need hormone treatment. . . . Who's going to help me? How can I get help?" I was like, "Oh, shit, how did I get myself into this!?" [laughs] I'm new to this city, I don't know nobody! That's when I remember telling you, "Well, we need to help these girls. We can't just listen to their needs and do nothing about it!"

That's when I started going around knocking on doors. I think Ramón [Ramírez, El/La volunteer] was really important in this as well. I give him a lot of credit because thanks to him I was able to learn that there were other groups where the girls can go and talk and meet people. It was really, really important to me also because I noticed that the translatinas were like, "Oh no, we don't go *con los jotos*, no, we're not gonna go with gay men. *No nosotras somos trans, ¿cómo vamos a ir con los jotos?*"⁵ I was like, "Why is that, you know?"

I mean, if we go out in the street and we're visible in society, why can't we go in a place full of gay men and make sure that they know that we are present, that we are a movement, that we are there. . . . We need to take up space. I always had privilege in my life to take up space, to go and apply for a job, to go to school, et cetera. That these girls knew they could go anywhere they please and take up space—that alone was really important. The girls knew that they had El/La as their space and it was for them. When they started coming, and they saw that they were . . . treated with respect—because that was also really important to me, that these girls get treated how I would like to be treated—be greeted at the door, and as soon as I get there, somebody offers me coffee, or a cookie or whatever was available, and says, "Hey, how are you doing? What's going on?"

MARCIA: *El trato humano.*[6]

ALEXANDRA: Yeah. Not that clinical, "Sit there, we're going to get to you in twenty minutes," and an hour goes by and nobody comes to talk to you, and you're there sitting, waiting for someone to pay attention to you, no. . . .

I wanted to ask you—and I think to me it's always been a curiosity—but what did you see in me when I came and applied? Because, to be honest with you, I didn't think I was going to get that job.

MARCIA: Well, I think what I saw in you was definitely a fierce sense of commitment to the work from the very beginning. You told me the story about Ana and that you had made this move and I got a sense that you really were serious about wanting to do this work. Also, what I really loved about you when I first met you was that you have a curiosity and an excitement about the world. When we start doing real kind of cynical triage work, where we're just making the next referral, going to pass out the condoms, whatever, we lose sight of the heart of the work. I saw that you were very much tapped in, that you were very much excited about doing the work, and I think that became very true as you continued. Even when things got hard you didn't lose that sense of wonder at bringing a group of translatinas together, advocating for social justice for translatinas, showing up at [the] Trans March with wedding dresses. I think we get, often, really jaded in this work, especially in HIV prevention, and you didn't bring that. You were definitely not about that.

ALEXANDRA: I'm glad you see that because, to be honest with you—and I think you remember because at some point you put me in check, and I know you and I have little disagreements and maybe differences—but I always learn from you because you have a sense of community outside of the box. Me, I was more like, "Why do these girls want to do sex work, damnit!? Why don't they want to take classes?? *Chingada madre!!* I did it!"

MARCIA: [Laughs] "Why can't they pull themselves up by their own bootstraps?!"

ALEXANDRA: Of course, I have my family that loved me, that told me, "You're worth it, you're a beautiful being, *tú vales mucho.*"[7] Some of these girls didn't have that. Now I understand that. When people tell you you're worthless, you're nothing, you're dirty, you're filthy, you're trash, well, that's how you feel. For you there's not going to be many opportunities in life because you're going to feel that the only thing you can do is work that is very stereotyped and stigmatized. Now I recognize that sex work itself is not easy, [but it] empowers these women. Not only translatinas, not only trans women, but also any kind of human being who does sex work. It's not just because it's the only option, it's a way of staying in control. To me it's really important to recognize and praise the people that do it because it's not an easy thing to decide, "Well, tonight I'm going to go and stand on a corner and try to make some money." I mean, not all of us can do it.

This was really shocking and at the same time a learning experience. I learned a lot working at El/La. I had to leave my prejudice, my sense of, "Well, why do people want to do this?" You taught me not to be like that. I realized I have to be more conscious of the needs of these girls. You cannot . . . make somebody change their behavior unless you help them to solve their needs. When I saw girls that would come to me and say, "Well, I have a boyfriend that beats me up, I don't have a place to live, I don't have papers, I'm HIV positive, I'm doing sex work, I mean, what are you going to do for me?"

It was this wake-up call that action needed to be taken to be able to really make a difference in the life of these girls. Period.

## ORIGINS OF *TRANSLATINA*

MARCIA: Can you talk a little bit about how the term *translatina* came into existence?

ALEXANDRA: Ah, great question! To me, it was difficult to refer to these girls as "transwomen" or "trans girls" or "*transgéneros*" o . . . et cetera. They were all from different places. They were from Cuba, El Salvador. There were some girls that came, I remember, from Argentina, there were some from Puerto Rico. At some point I said, well, maybe if I just call them "translatinas" I'm including all of them, because they're all Latinas, they all speak Spanish, and . . . that's how it came about.

MARCIA: So you came up with that word?

ALEXANDRA: Yeah, I didn't want to separate the girls. I learned from you . . . to be more conscious about being inclusive of people's backgrounds, of people's places of origin . . .

MARCIA: I remember when you started using that word, and I was like, "Oh, let me make sure I have that down right!" [laughs] Because I thought it was great. Then I started using it, and we started using it in the materials for El/La. I remember at some point people started answering the phone, "El/La Para Translatinas," remember that? It sounded so musical and sweet, and I didn't ask anyone, I just changed the name of the organization!

ALEXANDRA: I remember!

MARCIA: Because first we were "El/La Transgender Latina HIV Prevention Program." So, we started to use it, and then, I wonder if you saw it being used outside of San Francisco?

ALEXANDRA: No. To be honest with you I didn't see that used until the movie *Translatina* came out [in 2007], but that's after JoAnne Keatley had taken it to some conference. JoAnne told me, "I used the term *translatina* and everybody liked it." They even clapped.

MARCIA: So how does it feel to have invented a word?

ALEXANDRA: It's just like everyday business, going to work . . .

MARCIA: What do you think the term *translatina* did for the community-building project? What do you think the term *translatina* did for us at El/La, for transgender Latinas anywhere else? What work did you see that term doing?

ALEXANDRA: I think that the term *translatina* became a way of empowerment and a way of including and a way of giving visibility to a community that was always in the background. Because that's how I felt when I came to San Francisco about translatinas and I started working at El/La. I mean, there was no sense of community among us, the translatinas. Nobody cared about translatinas. I had to knock on so many doors. In a way I think that *translatina* the term kinda placed translatinas, made their presence felt.

MARCIA: Did you see the girls taking up that word too? Did that word have meaning for people at El/La?

ALEXANDRA: Definitely. I think more than anything because they knew they were part of something. In a way the fact that you're a translatina and that you are so visible in the city and that you are at City Hall, and that you are now going to events, and that translatinas are going to City College, and are going here and are going there, and they have a space—that is in a way getting some respect. I think that made the girls feel a sense of doing something positive, something good.

I myself knew that I was doing something, because to be honest with you, Marcia, I never expected to be recognized. . . . [For example,] I remember when I went to Chicago to the conference on "Sex, Race, and Gender." When I told the story, people said "Oh my God! We thought that you were always in this type of work." I never really expected to be recognized or anything because that wasn't my idea of the work I was doing. To me it was more like a responsibility and an obligation to my community, to these girls, and . . . to make sure that we have a safe space and that we are recognized for who we are as women that have so many walls to tear down, so many *retos*,[8] no? Not only language, not only culture, not only documentation, but so many things within our own LGB community.

## ATTAINING VISIBILITY

MARCIA: Let's talk a little bit about how the history of El/La evolved. We've talked about how we started El/La, we didn't talk so much about Tan Bella,[9] that first photo shoot that we did that got people into it. So, take us from 2006 to until you left in 2011. What happens next, what happens after we get the groups going and you start having girls come to the office and you're helping them out?

ALEXANDRA: This was important because, I say, "I'm doing this for you, no? I'm helping you, no? I'm helping you to get the hormones and helping you to get your papers, I'm helping you to get *vivienda*. But now I want to know what else needs to be done here so we can stay involved, so you can stay involved? I don't want you to just come here and tell me 'I need this, and I need and I need' and El/La give, give, give, give. I also want to make sure that we as a group of translatinas give visibility to what we're doing." What else can we do? How far can we take it? That's what it came to. I don't know if you remember that we had these groups [called] Viernes Social.[10] I let the girls talk about all their shit, and their ideas, and "Oh, *pues yo quiero que me hagan un taller de maquillaje, yo quiero que me hagan . . . yo quiero*."[11] No? Many times I was like "Oh, gosh!" *¡Ya cállate!*[12] [Laughs]

MARCIA: . . . and then you had Cinema Club.

ALEXANDRA: Yeah, that was important to me. The Cinema Club. Because it was a way to educate through film. At least so they could . . . see themselves reflected in film.

MARCIA: I just thought what was so important is that you recognized the amazing emotional intelligence that translatinas have and the conversation that they have about interpersonal issues, social questions. I feel nobody in San Francisco gave translatinas credit for engaging in the world the way you gave them credit through Cinema Club. People had different levels of access to education and literacy and all these things, and Cinema Club was such an important part of our intervention in that you really recognized that people had questions and answers, and that talking about film was one way to get to those . . . curiosities, you know?

ALEXANDRA: Exactly. We all come from different backgrounds, histories, cultures. . . . I wanted to see how one piece of film will contribute to, expand their minds. Many times the girls would get like, "Aaahh, I don't want to talk about it." "No. We're going to talk about it. We just saw a film, a great film, and I want to know what you think, what you felt, what impacted you? Why?" It was really important to see that these girls have critical thinking, and more than anything that they will catch things, they will learn, they will say, "Oh, I never thought about it, I never thought that . . ." For example, when I would show a film like *Boys Don't Cry*: Why do you think trans men are so invisible? Why do you think trans men are so ignored in our community? [Asking] things like that made these girls talk about it. It was really important to see where they come from and make them talk.

MARCIA: One of the things that I've always had questions about—and I showed you that article of mine "Perverse Citizenship"[13]—I think about citizenship as a kind of participation, right? One of the big parts of participation is being talked to as a participant! Like being hailed . . .

ALEXANDRA: *Yes!*

MARCIA: . . . as somebody who has something to say. You can see it when kids don't get called on in school. When certain classes of kids get ignored because people think they're stupid or they don't think they speak English well enough or whatever it is, those kids do worse in school because they're not being hailed as participants in that system. They're being excluded by being ignored, by not being given any credit. That Cinema Club, we did it—remember because we couldn't really get credit for doing it from [our] HIV prevention [contract], so we did it as an extra thing—and it was the glue that held all of our other programs together. People would come for that, there was no pressure, they weren't going to get a lecture, they were curious about the films and then they would get hooked and they'd keep coming back!

ALEXANDRA: Yeah, remember how I stayed away from the word *clients* or *patients*? We always said, "They're program participants." That's what I wanted them to be, I wanted all of them to be participants, I wanted all of them to be involved, included. The Cinema Club was this great tool, a way of . . . bringing in that sense of community. Remember when we screened the *Muxes*, that movie? We had that room with thirty people in there—the translatinas, the gay men, *las jotas*,[14]—everybody was there and I was just in amazement. I was like "Whoa!" This is possible.

I think listening to the girls, to what they wanted to be included in and what's important to them—makeup, clothes, looking good, feeling good . . . *ser presentes, llamar la atención, ser escandalosas.*[15] That gave place to *los talleres de maquillaje y todo eso, de modelaje, fotografía.*[16]

## *NUBES Y ANGELES* AND RUBY ORDEÑANA

MARCIA: I wanted you to talk a little bit about *Nubes y Angeles*,[17] because that was another thing we did just after the beginning of [El/La], and then I wanted to ask you about Ruby Ordeñana, because I think that's really the [moment] when El/La became the El/La we know now.[18]

ALEXANDRA: *Nubes y Angeles* was a great project. I'm very grateful to many people that helped me put it together because my idea was about giving visibility to transphobia more than anything—I always try to stay away from portraying translatinas as victims. More than that it was about these powerful beings with this resilience that no matter how you go about your daily life and where you are in your life, you still are this person that has culture, that has knowledge, that has empowerment. So *Nubes y Angeles* to me was a way of giving visibility to transphobia and to our history. If you remember I talked a lot about my experience as a teenager in Mexico City as a trans girl. I also wanted to make sure that we gave visibility to the community that we have in San Francisco, and go beyond that. When I started thinking, what else is beyond all that? There's always somebody behind a dead daughter or son, there's always another history.

Ruby Ordeñana was a wake-up call to reality. Even though I was in the United States, even though I was in a city like San Francisco, where *la diversidad sexual, o* sexual diversity is okay and is welcome and is not a big deal, translatinas are still being victimized and being murdered. It was shocking. I was like, how can this still be happening? I mean in the twenty-first century in a city of the first world, in the United States, a girl is being killed and treated like a piece of nothing for her gender identity. It was painful. It was really painful. I think that gave me a strength and gave me that rage, gave me enough adrenaline to say, "*No*. I'm not going to stay silenced." I'm not going to just say, "Oh, well, you know, that happens," like the newspapers would say, "Well, she was a drug addict, a prostitute, a transvestite . . ." No. No, no, no. I mean, I mobilized, you know?

MARCIA: You mobilized and you also represented translatinas in a way that nobody in San Francisco ever had before. Right? I mean, have you ever seen anything like that before? I would almost say in the country, no translatina had ever been that articulate, a spokesperson, had ever been able to give interviews that really expressed the rage and the analysis you had about that situation. Bilingually. On the English-language and the Spanish-language media.[19]

ALEXANDRA: Thank you. No, I never thought about it that way. I just thought, "Fuck it, I'm not going to stay silent. I'm not going to fucking let this go by quietly and just put it under the carpet and say oh well . . . another one." No. No.

MARCIA: I think the other good thing that came out of that was the connection we had with Communities United Against Violence (CUAV). [That connection] really solidified around the response to Ruby, and I think that's when they started to see that our group really had the ability to respond. They were great allies. Isa [Noyola, El/La cofounder] was very important in responding.

ALEXANDRA: Yeah, I remember when [that] happened and somebody, I think it was JoAnne [Keatley] called me and said, "You know what? They found the body of a trans girl." I go, "Well, what do you mean?" And they go, "It was one of our girls, she was a translatina." My first call was to CUAV. My first call was to Tina [D'elia].

"Hey, have you heard about this?" Tina was like, "No, can you get more info?" I started moving. Making phone calls and trying to get the story right. Pretty soon [an El/La participant] came and gave details, and I passed it on to Tina and we were like, "We gotta respond to this." I said, "Tina, we have a responsibility, it's a translatina."

MARCIA: You heard they got that guy, right?

ALEXANDRA: Yeah, of course!

MARCIA: Well, eventually. But they didn't test the DNA for a few years.

ALEXANDRA: Exactly, he had victimized other people. We got another girl that was victimized by him as well. That's how they caught him, remember? It was another girl, another translatina, and she came to El/La for help.

## GROWING PAINS

In 2009, El/La transitioned to a new fiscal agent. During this process, the contracts that supported our HIV prevention activities were put through a public bidding process, which resulted in the contracts being awarded to another organization in San Francisco. Although we appealed the decision and the process, we were unable to restore our funding through the Department of Public Health. We organized with several other allies and successfully advocated for the allocation of new funds from the city to continue supporting our programming. We were very fortunate that some anonymous donors stepped in to provide private funding that allowed us to keep our offices open. During the year we were without funding, we operated on a shoestring budget as an all-volunteer group.

MARCIA: How did you feel when we were first defunded?

ALEXANDRA: I got discouraged to some point. How is it possible that all the work that we're doing is not getting supported? But, I could see why. Of course, [there were] all these big fishes claiming to be doing the work for thirty years and we are a little agency that has been struggling all along. Although we've been very visible and we've been working our asses off. I mean, the translatinas, who cares? Who are they? That was the moment in my professional life when I had to like say, you know what? This cannot be happening. Because if I just say, "Oh well, they defunded us. Sorry," and turn around and tell the girls, "Sorry, we got defunded and that's it, this is the end." It was a moment of many sacrifices because remember, you and I both went without pay.

MARCIA: Well, I didn't get paid before anyway, but you didn't have any other way to make money! I was worried about you when that happened.

ALEXANDRA: Yeah, but it was all meant to be, Marcia, because we made it. We made it and it was all well worth it.

MARCIA: I think we surprised a lot of people after we got defunded, because people were not expecting that we would stay open.

ALEXANDRA: I know it. What really did it to me was the response that we got from the community. We got people [having] our backs.

MARCIA: Yeah, we found some major donors who were really able to pull it out . . . and let us keep our doors open for a year! Without [public] funding. Which is just amazing. That for me was all a lesson in how solidarity work gets done, and I learned a lot from you in that because of the ways that you had made connections with so many other people in the trans community across social movements. You had so much respect, and you were able to communicate what El/La was about and what it needed in ways that people really responded to. Not like "I'm going to raise money on this campaign right now," but just really honest, straight-up movement work. Straight up social justice work that is about meeting an urgent need in the community and doing the work not for the salary or the money or the rewards but because it's work that needs to be done. I learned a lot from watching you go through that time period and your connections with all these people who just had a *lot* of respect for you. It was really able to keep El/La open.

ALEXANDRA: I think also it was that visibility that we were able to create with El/La and the girls and the work that we were doing. If we didn't have that, if we didn't have these girls going and telling their stories and talking to people and saying, "You know what, if it wasn't for El/La we wouldn't have this, or I wouldn't have been able to do this," people wouldn't have believed in us. But people believed because we have fruits to show. It wasn't ever my intention to be that way, but I'm glad because in a way that's what made El/La so believable and it built that reputation of El/La being a place that *really* fought for social justice for translatinas.

MARCIA: It was amazing. So talk to me a little bit about what happened with the volunteers after we got defunded. How you felt about it then, how you see it now.

ALEXANDRA: Well, you know how I fought because I believed in helping them out, in trying to make them see that whatever they were doing, it was worth it. That's why it was important to have this group of volunteers in whom I believed. Because I truly believed. I mean for me to walk out of El/La for what, a month, a month and a half, and leave it in the hands of these volunteers, I believed in them, I never expected it to be the way it turned out. . . . But of course, you learn from your mistakes because, of course, they didn't have the same experience that I had, they didn't have the same training that I had. They didn't have the same uprooting that I have, per se. They were babies, it was as if I leave my teenage daughter for a month at home by herself and say, "You take over." Of course! She's going to be making parties every weekend. So, I learned a lot from that.

MARCIA: Yeah, I think we both learned.

*Note:* In December 2009, as part of our response to the defunding, we began to include several trusted volunteers who had worked with Alexandra at the organization in the day-to-day operations. Unfortunately, this resulted in a breach of trust around the use of the El/La space while Alexandra, who was at El/La every day without pay, took some much-needed time off during the holidays. The breach of trust resulted in the dismissal of the volunteers and created a deep conflict in the community of El/La around the direction of the organization.

Alexandra and Marcia discuss the impact of that conflict and the lessons we learned through it.

ALEXANDRA: I learned more than anything not to give so much trust to people and also [to] have this sense of ... *valorar*[20] ... your work. Because in a way I said, "Here, *toma todo, y aquí está en tus manos.*[21] Bye."

MARCIA: Well, I think I learned a lot about ... how to slowly put opportunities for leadership in front of people but not to do it all at once. To do it in a way that allowed people to develop as leaders in a way that protected the organization. There were so many misuses of the space I literally had nightmare visions about getting a phone call that somebody was dead in the office. . . .

Asking people to be accountable in ways that they were not ready to be accountable, and expecting that others would have the same values that we had was just not ... I learned that lesson. It's not that I don't trust those people but that I can be more realistic about what expectations I can have of people.

ALEXANDRA: Exactly. Because I expected it to be like if I was coming. Of course that's impossible.

MARCIA: So, I know that it felt like a big betrayal at the time, and out of that experience another group was created, and they had their own life. It was a big lesson. . . .

I was writing the conclusion to my book at one point and I wrote about *fracaso*, and the heartbreak that you feel sometimes when you're doing organizing, right? I was thinking of that disappointment. So I wanted to ask you, what lessons did you learn and have you used those lessons in your work now? Is it something that you've taken away from your work at El/La?

ALEXANDRA: Well, it might sound really frivolous or ... um, I don't know, cynical. I learned that you cannot, you cannot throw pearls to the pigs. [Laughs]

MARCIA: [Laughs] Pearls to swine! That's what you meant by "valuing your work more"?

## CRUCÉ LA FRONTERA EN TACONES

ALEXANDRA: I think it's really, really important to know your position. I wish I had the opportunity right now to have a chance like I did at El/La. If you're put in a place like that it's for something, it's because you're doing something right, or because you know something. I don't think I had wisdom to recognize that before. Now I do, of course. Although I haven't done that kind of work here in Mexico.

MARCIA: I don't know if the word *translatina* really works in Mexico. I wonder if it could?

ALEXANDRA: No, and I have used it a couple of times. I've given a conference at UNAM [Universidad Nacional Autónoma de México]. Someone came and asked me, "What is a translatina? Why do you use that?" I just explained it like I told you, just to be inclusive of all the trans women that come from all over Latin America.

MARCIA: Well, *translatina* is also about the trip, the journey. I mean, I think in Mexico, too, you're talking about rural to urban migration, migration from Central America, migration to the States and back. All these different journeys that are marked. I think the trick is to find the language for the thing that is a special, unique form of honoring the lives of those folks, those people who are the most excluded from social movements. As I say in "Ciudadanía Perversa," those people who are inventing gender on their own terms with whatever they have access to, and who aren't marked by the middle-class, First World discourse, NGO discourse of lesbian, gay, bisexual identity, even trans now, identity. But who are . . . ¡autóctonos! ¡autóctonas! (Ochoa 2004).[22]

ALEXANDRA: *Autóctonas.* Yeah, and I think that's really important because, interestingly, I created a presentation called *Crucé la frontera en tacones.*[23] I did it at UNAM and people were like, "Big deal, she was a trans immigrant, and she went to the U.S. and she confronted new identities, but so what?" But then I did that piece at the Human Rights Commission here in Mexico City as well, and people were like, "Whoa!" you know? Like, "She's talking about trans immigration, she's talking about intersecting identities . . . not only as a trans but then as an undocumented . . . et cetera, et cetera, et cetera." People were taken away. Same thing in Spain, you know? I did *Crucé la frontera en tacones* in Spain and people were amazed. They were like, "How is that possible?"

MARCIA: Well, when you do it in Mexico City in particular, but when you do it in Mexico, crossing the border is a privilege! [Laughs] You know what I mean? So they don't read it in the same way as everybody in Spain—that's the "oppressed" experience, right? *Crucé la frontera en tacones* is a marker of relative privilege. But at the same time, I think part of it is just how difficult it is for Mexican culture to admit how shaped it is by migration.

ALEXANDRA: Yeah. When I did a presentation at the Human Rights Commission, and I'm talking about crossing the border undocumented, somebody, and I hate to say this but some *elitista*[24] was talking about "Oh, I went to Canada with my visa . . ." I was like, why do you even have to talk about that? Why do you even have to even bother telling me! *Que yo crucé la frontera a los quice años indocumentada, huyendo de la persecución que había aquí en el DF, en todo Mexico por decir. . . . Y tú estás hablando de que "Ay, me fui a Canadá con mi visa y llegué allá y pedí asilo y . . ." No.*[25]

MARCIA: What I know from Venezuela, the middle-class movement, [the] LGBT movement was so unable to assimilate the experiences of people who were completely socially marginalized and in poverty, especially trans women because they just would not take those experiences seriously. This is what my critique was, that the movement needed to start to find ways to talk to and listen to folks from that experience, because that's who determines whether or not the politics are actually effective. That's whose lives are in the balance. They're the ones who are the most affected by the policies that we're talking about. So it's not about gay marriage or health benefits, or being able to adopt kids. It's about being able to be a kid and stay in your family, or get a job, or be free of violence from the police. If the LGBT movement agenda *en nuestros países*[26] doesn't pay attention to that then it's . . . not doing the work.

ALEXANDRA: Exactly. Also, I always thought . . . Oh my God, poor me, I had to leave my house, I had to leave my education, I had to leave my comfortable life here in the city because of persecution, and I had to cross the border in high heels *y sin documentación y afortunadamente yo fui la única que no corrí so, a mí no me agarró la migra. Y yo decía, ay, qué miedo, y pobrecita y . . .*[27] and when I heard the stories of a poor girl from Guatemala, *cruzando en tren y violada y golpeada y robada y no llega a la frontera y todavía la meten en una cajuela . . . digo puta madre, no?*[28] That was why for me it was so important to do *Crucé la frontera en tacones.*

Because there's no way. There's no way that our stories are just going to be hidden or silenced . . . no. It's important that people know that it's not because we go after the so-called American Dream. What American Dream? To me it's like, no, it wasn't an American Dream, and for most translatinas it's trying to survive, trying to stay alive.

## NOTES

1. Passages in Spanish will be translated into English in the endnotes to reflect the bilingual nature of the conversation. Translation: "Ah, without knowing what Walden House was. So I got on the Internet to search and found out, I talked to Ana and told her 'look, this place' they have a program there and I called them, and she told me, 'yes, yes, yes,' and when I went to San Francisco, tragically, Ana Fernández had been beaten by her partner and was walking around all beat up with black eyes. She hid from me, no . . ." All translations by Marcia Ochoa.
2. Translation: chit-chatting, gossiping (like parrots, or *cotorros*).
3. Translation: gossip and chit-chat, check e-mails.
4. Translation: your girlfriends.
5. Translation: "No, we're trans, how are we going to go with the gay boys?"
6. Translation: dignified, decent treatment.
7. Translation: You are worth a lot.
8. Translation: challenges.
9. Tan Bella was a modeling and self-esteem workshop for translatinas that included a professional quality makeup session and photo shoot, first held in 2006, and repeated in 2007 (Más Bella) and 2009 (Siempre Bella).
10. Social Fridays.
11. Translation: "Oh, well I want you to put on a makeup workshop for me, I want you to . . . I want."
12. Translation: "OK, be quiet!"

13. "Perverse Citizenship," an essay Marcia published in Spanish in 2004 and in a revised and expanded version in English in 2008 (Ochoa 2004; 2008).
14. Translation: the lesbians.
15. Translation: being present, calling attention to themselves, being scandalous.
16. Translation: the makeup workshops and all that, modeling, photography.
17. *Clouds and Angels*, a play written by Alexandra and several program participants, staged in the fall of 2007 in a theater in the building where El/La has offices.
18. Ruby Ordeñana was a young Nicaraguan transgender woman who had participated in Proyecto's ESL class, which Marcia taught along with Isa Noyola. She had participated in some of El/La's programming as well but was found murdered in March 2007, her naked body dumped in an industrial area of San Francisco.
19. Interview available at Lee 2007.
20. Translation: valuing.
21. Translation: "Take everything, and it's in your hands now."
22. Translation: autochthonous. This is a term used in Latin America to describe something that is unique to the context in which it develops, whether that is a person, a social organization, or a form of expression. It can have connotations of "folkloric" or "quaint" but also includes a sense of sovereignty and uniqueness.
23. Translation: "I Crossed the Border in High Heels." A performance Alexandra developed to describe her experience as an undocumented translatina immigrant to the United States.
24. Translation: an elitist.
25. Translation: "I crossed the border when I was fifteen years old undocumented and running away from the persecution there was here in Mexico City, in all of Mexico actually. . . . And you're talking about 'Ay, I went to Canada on my visa and got there and requested asylum and . . .' No."
26. Translation: in our countries.
27. Translation: and without papers and fortunately I was the only one who didn't run so the Migra didn't catch me. And I would say ay, how scary, poor girl and . . .
28. Translation: crossing on a train and raped and beaten and robbed and she's still not at the border and they stick her in a trunk . . . I say God damn, no?

## REFERENCES

Lee, Vic. 2007. "Series of Unsolved Transgender Murders." KGO-TV *ABC 7 News*, March 23. http://www.truecrimereport.com/2009/11/transgender_rapist_and_murder.php.

Ochoa, Marcia. 2004. "Ciudadanía perversa: Divas, marginación y participación en la 'localización.'" In *Políticas de Ciudadanía y Sociedad Civil en Tiempos de Globalización*, edited by Daniel Mato, 239–256. Caracas: Facultad de Ciencias Económicas y Sociales, Universidad Central de Venezuela. Available online at http://www.globalcult.org.ve/pub/Rocky/Libro2/Ochoa.pdf.

———. 2008. "Perverse Citizenship: Divas, Marginality, and Participation in 'Loca-Lization.'" *Women's Studies Quarterly* 36(3–4): 146–169.

Rodríguez de Ruíz, Alexandra. 2007. *Crucé la frontera en tacones*. Performance. Queer Latino/a Arts Festival, Galería de La Raza in San Francisco.

# 11 · *LGB* WITHIN THE *T*

## Sexual Orientation in the National Transgender Discrimination Survey and Implications for Public Policy

JODY L. HERMAN

The National Transgender Discrimination Survey (NTDS) revealed that trans people face alarming levels of discrimination and experience a host of negative outcomes, such as in health and well-being (Grant et al. 2011). The NTDS focused on discrimination based on anti-trans bias, which is bias against a person or group of people based on gender identity, gender expression, or trans status. Yet, some trans people may experience discrimination based on sexual orientation as well. As one NTDS respondent noted, "It is hard for me to distinguish between when I was discriminated against for being gay and when I was discriminated against for being gender nonconforming." Trans people who are also LGB stand at a unique intersection in the larger LGBT community, placing them at risk for experiencing discrimination across multiple sites of oppression. Because of this, one may expect an increased risk of experiencing discrimination among LGB trans people as compared to trans people who are heterosexual or "straight." As this study will show, each group may have particular areas where they are vulnerable in regard to discrimination and negative outcomes.

This study engages the following questions: How do trans people identify their sexual orientation? Are there differences in trans people's experiences based on sexual orientation? What are the implications for the laws, regulations, and practices that comprise public policy and public administration in the United States? To begin to address these questions, in this study I outline the various ways in which respondents to the NTDS identified their sexual orientation and explore the differences among the experiences of trans people based on sexual orientation. I will first describe the various self-reported sexual orientations that NTDS respondents used to identify themselves and how these sexual orientation identity groups differ (or not) based on demographic variables such as age, race, and gender. I will then analyze how NTDS respondents' experiences of discrimination and outcomes differ based on sexual orientation. Findings from this study will shed new light on the division, inseparability, and overlap of sexual orientation and gender identity, which may impact how these concepts are understood and discussed in the movement for LGBT rights and how they are reflected in public policy and public administration.

## METHODS

This study utilizes data from the National Transgender Discrimination Survey (NTDS), conducted by the National Gay and Lesbian Task Force and the National Center for Transgender Equality. This seventy-item survey was distributed in cooperation with over nine hundred organizations across the United States and was also announced through listservs and online communities. It was made available both online and on paper in English and in Spanish. The survey was open to participants for over six months, beginning in fall 2008, and it resulted in 6,546 valid responses, which is the largest sample of trans and gender-nonconforming people in the United States to date (Grant et al. 2011). Survey respondents answered questions about a broad array of topics, including demographics, gender identity and transition, and experiences with employment, education, health care, housing, family, identity documents, police and incarceration, and public accommodations. The result is a rich dataset that allows us to examine how respondents' experiences may differ based on their self-reported sexual orientation.

The NTDS asked respondents about their sexual orientation in the following question:

69. What is your sexual orientation?
    ☐ Gay/Lesbian/Same-gender attraction
    ☐ Bisexual
    ☐ Queer
    ☐ Heterosexual
    ☐ Asexual
    ☐ Other, please specify _____

Of NTDS respondents, 6,368 (97%) completed this question and 698 of these respondents (11%) selected the "other" category to write in their own response to the question. The write-in responses were also analyzed for this study, and a total of 194 were recoded into the existing categories of gay/lesbian/same-gender attraction, bisexual, queer, heterosexual, or asexual. After this recoding process, 8 percent of the sample remained in the "other" category. These 194 respondents had either written in an existing category or given more information about the existing category. For example, one trans woman who selected "other" entered, "Heterosexual female (prefer men)." This respondent was recoded as "heterosexual." In addition, those who described themselves as "straight" and/or attracted only to a different gender identity were recoded as "heterosexual." For instance, one trans man wrote in, "Straight. I'm a man and I'm attracted to women." A trans woman wrote in, "Straight, I'm MTF and partner is male." The remaining 504 respondents who selected the "other" category are described in table 11.1. To examine the differences between respondents of different sexual orientations, this study employs Pearson's chi-square tests of independence and t-tests for difference in means.[1] Findings from statistical tests are noted in tables 11.2 through 11.4.[2]

## DEMOGRAPHICS AND GENDER- AND TRANSITION-RELATED MEASURES

### Self-Identified Sexual Orientation

Twenty percent of respondents reported being bisexual. An equal percentage of respondents (22%) reported being gay, lesbian, or having same-gender attraction only and being heterosexual, straight, or having exclusively different-gender attraction. Twenty percent identified as queer. Smaller groups of respondents identified as "other" (8%) and asexual (4%).

As described in table 11.1, nearly a quarter of the respondents that selected "other" identified as pansexual, about 16 percent identified as transgender, transsexual, or another gender identity, and 11 percent reported being unsure or questioning. The identities in table 11.1 are listed as they were written by the respondents in most cases. Those who entered a gender identity only, other than transgender or transsexual, included responses such as "I am now all female," "male," "feminized male," "cross dresser," "M2F/female intersexed," and "gender nonconforming." Forty-eight respondents did not provide enough information to categorize their sexual orientation, such as in the following responses: "Don't care," "It's complicated," "none," "I don't know how to categorize," "committed monogamous relationship," "me," "open-minded," "very complicated," and "freed male." Those listed here as having a stable attraction, but their gender changes, included responses such as the following: "attracted to women, however my gender appears at the time" and "heterosexual as man, lesbian as woman." Seventeen respondents entered in their own unique identity that did not correspond with

**TABLE 11.1**     Write-in Response of NTDS Respondents Who
Selected "Other" for Sexual Orientation (n=504)

| | Frequency | Percentage of "other" | Percentage of sample |
|---|---|---|---|
| Pansexual | 116 | 23.0 | 1.8 |
| Transgender/transsexual/ provided a gender identity only | 80 | 15.9 | 1.3 |
| Unsure/questioning | 55 | 10.9 | 0.9 |
| Did not provide enough information to categorize | 48 | 9.5 | 0.8 |
| Entered multiple sexual identities | 39 | 7.7 | 0.5 |
| Attraction stable, but respondent's gender changes | 27 | 5.4 | 0.4 |
| Celibate/not currently sexual | 19 | 3.8 | 0.3 |
| Attracted to anyone/everyone gender doesn't matter | 17 | 3.4 | 0.3 |
| Entered own unique identity | 17 | 3.4 | 0.3 |
| No labels/does not identify with a label | 16 | 3.2 | 0.3 |
| Heteroflexible/primarily different-gender attracted | 13 | 2.6 | 0.2 |
| It depends/it varies | 12 | 2.4 | 0.2 |
| Heteroqueer/queer hetero | 12 | 2.4 | 0.2 |
| Omnisexual | 9 | 1.8 | 0.1 |
| Commented on the question only | 7 | 1.4 | 0.1 |
| Bi-curious | 7 | 1.4 | 0.1 |
| Two-Spirit | 4 | 0.8 | 0.1 |
| Intersex | 4 | 0.8 | 0.1 |
| Polysexual | 2 | 0.4 | 0.1 |

existing categories. Examples of these responses include, "ambisexual," "pomosexual (postmodern)," "fluid," and "flexitarian." Finally, seven respondents commented on the question itself and gave responses such as the following: "This question does not make sense in this context," "This makes no sense to me," "This should be a 'check all that apply,'" and "Is this a trick question?"

## Race, Age, Income, and Educational Attainment

Some notable differences emerge when looking at race, age, income, and educational attainment by sexual orientation in the NTDS, but those differences are more pronounced when looking at the lesbian, gay, bisexual, queer, asexual, and other (LGBQAO) groups separately. LGBQAO respondents overall were more likely to report being multiracial than heterosexual respondents (13% versus 8%). When looking at the sexual orientation groups individually, bisexual respondents were more likely than all other groups to report being white (81%). Those identifying as "other" were the least likely to report being white (66%)

and the most likely to report being multiracial (18%). Lesbian and gay respondents were more likely than all other groups to report being black or African American (6%). Respondents selecting "other" were more likely than all other groups to report being Latino/a (8%).

LGBQAO respondents overall were younger than heterosexual respondents, with 72 percent under age forty-five compared to 65 percent of heterosexual respondents under age forty-five. Queer respondents overall were much younger than all other groups, with 95 percent under age forty-five. Asexual respondents were older than other groups, with only 51 percent under age forty-five.

LGBQAO respondents overall reported less annual household income than heterosexual respondents, with 39 percent reporting $50,000 or above versus 47 percent among heterosexual respondents. Among LGBQAO respondents, bisexual respondents reported the highest income, with 46 percent reporting $50,000 or above. Queer respondents and respondents selecting "other" reported the lowest incomes of all groups, ranging from 32 to 33 percent with annual household incomes of $50,000 or above. It should be noted that the percentage of each group with less than $10,000 in annual household income is much higher than the percentage of the U.S. general population with that level of income at the time of the survey (4%).[3]

There is no significant difference in the educational attainment of LGBQAO and heterosexual respondents. However, differences emerge when considering the various sexual orientation groups separately. Notably, queer respondents reported the highest educational attainment of all groups, with 61 percent having earned a college degree or higher. In contrast, 47 percent of the full sample reported having a college degree or higher. Those selecting "other" had the lowest educational attainment, with 38 percent having a college degree or higher.

### Gender- and Transition-Related Measures

The NTDS asked several questions regarding respondents' gender identity and certain aspects of gender transition. Table 11.2 presents gender, transition status, the age a person began living full-time in a gender different from the one assigned at birth (hereinafter referred to as "living full-time"), whether others can tell if the respondent is transgender or gender nonconforming without verbally disclosing their transgender status or gender nonconformity, and whether the respondent is generally "out" to others about being transgender or gender nonconforming. Findings for heterosexual respondents and the combined LGBQAO respondents are shown, as well as the findings for the individual groups within the LGBQAO sample.

LGBQAO respondents overall were more likely than heterosexual respondents to identify as genderqueer or gender nonconforming assigned female at birth (12% versus 1%). Heterosexual respondents were more likely than

TABLE 11.2 Gender- and Transition-Related Measures by Sexual Orientation, Column Percentages

| Gender- and transition-related variables | Hetero-sexual or straight | LGBQAO respondents | | | | | | Full sample |
|---|---|---|---|---|---|---|---|---|
| | | All LGBQAO | Lesbian or gay | Bisexual | Queer | Asexual | Other | |
| **Gender**** | | | | | | | | |
| Trans women (MTF) | 46 | 46 | 59 | 59 | 11 | 70 | 49 | 47 |
| Trans men (FTM) | 30 | 27 | 16 | 15 | 57 | 12 | 25 | 28 |
| Cross-dresser (male assigned) | 21 | 8 | 4 | 17 | 1 | 8 | 10 | 11 |
| Cross-dresser (female assigned) | 0 | 4 | 4 | 2 | 7 | 2 | 3 | 3 |
| Genderqueer/GNC (male assigned) | 2 | 3 | 4 | 2 | 2 | 3 | 3 | 3 |
| Genderqueer/GNC (female assigned) | 1 | 12 | 13 | 4 | 22 | 6 | 10 | 9 |
| **Transition status*** | | | | | | | | |
| Currently live full-time | 60 | 53 | 56 | 51 | 53 | 56 | 54 | 55 |
| Do not yet live full-time, but want to | 24 | 28 | 23 | 35 | 22 | 35 | 30 | 27 |
| Do not want to live full-time | 16 | 19 | 21 | 14 | 25 | 9 | 16 | 18 |
| **Age began living full-time^** Younger than 18 | 9 | 5 | 5 | 3 | 6 | 2 | 10 | 6 |
| 18 to 24 | 28 | 29 | 19 | 18 | 56 | 15 | 35 | 29 |
| 25 to 44 | 43 | 40 | 39 | 48 | 34 | 36 | 32 | 40 |
| 45 to 54 | 15 | 18 | 25 | 24 | 3 | 27 | 18 | 17 |
| 55 or older | 6 | 7 | 12 | 7 | 1 | 20 | 5 | 7 |
| **People can tell I am trans/GNC even if I don't tell them*** Always | 4 | 7 | 9 | 4 | 9 | 4 | 8 | 6 |
| Most of the time | 9 | 18 | 19 | 12 | 25 | 20 | 17 | 16 |
| Sometimes | 21 | 29 | 27 | 30 | 29 | 30 | 29 | 27 |
| Occasionally | 31 | 29 | 31 | 31 | 24 | 31 | 31 | 29 |
| Never | 36 | 17 | 15 | 23 | 14 | 15 | 15 | 21 |
| **Outness*** | | | | | | | | |
| Generally out | 45 | 63 | 63 | 52 | 77 | 57 | 63 | 59 |
| Generally not out | 55 | 37 | 37 | 48 | 23 | 43 | 37 | 40 |

NOTE: Columns in this and subsequent tables may not add to 100 due to rounding.
*All tests indicated statistical significance (p <.05).
^No t-test performed.

all LGBQAO respondents to identify as cross-dressers assigned male at birth (21% versus 8%). It should also be noted that nearly all cross-dressers assigned female at birth reported an LGBQAO identity. Among the individual LGBQAO groups, those selecting "other" are similar in terms of gender to all LGBQAO respondents, but other groups have some notable differences. The vast majority of asexual respondents identified as trans women (70%). Lesbian or gay and bisexual respondents also have relatively large percentages of self-identified trans women compared to other groups (59% each). Most queer respondents identified as trans men (57%) and genderqueer or gender nonconforming assigned female at birth (22%).

Differences emerge between heterosexual and LGBQAO respondents in regard to transition-related measures in the NTDS. Heterosexual respondents are slightly more likely to have reported currently living full-time (60%) than LGBQAO respondents overall (53%) and all groups separately (51–56%). This could be due to the fact that heterosexual respondents were older overall than LGBQAO respondents. However, heterosexual respondents also are slightly more likely to have begun living full-time at a young age than the combined group of all LGBQAO respondents, with 37 percent living full-time at twenty-four years of age or younger versus 34 percent of all LGBQAO respondents. However, queer respondents and respondents selecting "other" began living full-time at younger ages than all other individual groups.

The most notable differences in regard to transition-related measures arise in regard to two categories: first, whether others can tell if the respondent is transgender or gender nonconforming without verbally disclosing their transgender status or gender nonconformity; and second, in regard to being "out" to others as transgender or gender nonconforming. Heterosexual respondents were more likely to report that others can never tell that they are transgender or gender nonconforming, with 35 percent of heterosexual respondents reporting this versus 17 percent of LGBQAO respondents. Heterosexual respondents were also more likely to report they are not "out" to others about being transgender or gender nonconforming. Fifty-five percent of heterosexual respondents were not "out" while 37 percent of LGBQAO respondents were not "out." Bisexual respondents were most likely among LGBQAO respondents to have reported not being "out" (48%). Queer respondents are the most likely among LGBQAO respondents to have reported being "out" (77%).

## OUTCOMES AND DISCRIMINATION EXPERIENCES IN THE NTDS BY SEXUAL ORIENTATION

Employment

NTDS respondents, regardless of sexual orientation, reported experiencing discrimination in all areas of employment covered in the survey. The rate of unemployment among NTDS respondents was 14 percent, which is double the U.S. unemployment rate at the time of the survey (Grant et al. 2011). No significant difference was found between heterosexual respondents and LGBQAO respondents overall in unemployment. However, those who selected "other" as their sexual orientation had the highest reported unemployment rate (20%) out of all listed groups.

In regard to experiences of discrimination in employment (see table 11.3), LGBQAO respondents overall experienced a significantly higher rate of reporting harassment on the job (51%) and having worked in the underground economy (17%). Looking at the sexual orientation groups separately, asexual respondents reported losing a job due to anti-trans bias at a relatively high rate of 35 percent versus 25 percent of LGBQAO respondents overall. Asexual respondents also reported not being hired due to bias (54%) and being harassed on the job (60%) at relatively high rates. Queer respondents and those selecting "other" were the most likely to have worked for income in the underground economy (19% and 21%, respectively).

Education

The vast majority of all NTDS respondents who attended school as transgender or gender nonconforming reported being harassed in K–12 by teachers and/or other students (78%). As shown in table 11.3, LGBQAO respondents overall reported a significantly higher rate of experiencing harassment at school than heterosexual respondents (80% versus 71%). Heterosexual respondents were more likely than all LGBQAO respondents to report having to leave school because the harassment was so bad (17% versus 12%). Nineteen percent of asexual respondents left school because of harassment, which is the highest percentage of all listed groups.

Health

Various aspects of health—including HIV, suicide, access to health care, and experiences with health care providers—were explored in the NTDS. Table 11.3 presents selected findings related to health in the NTDS by sexual orientation. The prevalence of HIV among NTDS respondents was over four times that of the U.S. general population (2.64% versus 0.60%) (World Health Organization n.d.).[4] LGBQAO respondents overall had a lower prevalence of HIV

TABLE 11.3. Discrimination/Outcomes by Sexual Orientation, Column Percentages

| Discrimination/outcome variables | Hetero-sexual or straight | LGBQAO respondents | | | | | | Full sample |
|---|---|---|---|---|---|---|---|---|
| | | All LGBQAO | Lesbian or gay | Bisexual | Queer | Asexual | Other | |
| **Employment** | | | | | | | | |
| Lost job due to anti-trans bias* | 27 | 25 | 30 | 28 | 15 | 35 | 28 | 26 |
| Not hired due to anti-trans bias* | 42 | 45 | 49 | 44 | 39 | 54 | 49 | 44 |
| Harassed by someone at work due to anti-trans bias† | 46 | 51 | 54 | 49 | 48 | 60 | 51 | 50 |
| Ever engaged in sex work, drug sales, or other underground economic activities for income† | 14 | 17 | 14 | 17 | 19 | 12 | 21 | 16 |
| **Education** | | | | | | | | |
| Harassed by anyone in K-12 due to anti-trans bias† | 71 | 80 | 74 | 77 | 85 | 79 | 83 | 78 |
| Had to leave school because anti-trans harassment was so bad† | 17 | 12 | 12 | 12 | 9 | 19 | 16 | 13 |
| **Health** | | | | | | | | |
| HIV status[r,s]  Negative | 88 | 89 | 90 | 90 | 90 | 88 | 83 | 89 |
| Positive | 4.03 | 2.16 | 3.06 | 1.77 | 0.86 | 1.14 | 4.66 | 2.64 |
| Don't know | 8 | 9 | 7 | 9 | 9 | 11 | 12 | 8 |
| Ever attempted suicide† | 36 | 42 | 40 | 40 | 43 | 45 | 47 | 41 |
| No health insurance† | 15 | 20 | 19 | 19 | 20 | 23 | 22 | 19 |
| Doctor refused to treat due to anti-trans bias* | 20 | 18 | 19 | 19 | 15 | 29 | 20 | 19 |
| Ever postponed getting medical care when sick/injured due to provider discrimination† | 25 | 29 | 26 | 22 | 40 | 28 | 27 | 28 |

*Only the chi-square test including all Q69 identities indicated statistical significance ($p < 0.05$).

†All tests indicated statistical significance ($p < 0.05$).

‡T-test only performed for those who reported being HIV positive.

than the overall sample (2.16%). The prevalence of HIV among heterosexual respondents, on the other hand, was significantly higher (4.03%). Respondents identifying as lesbian or gay and respondents selecting "other" as their sexual orientation also had elevated prevalence of HIV, at 3.06 percent and 4.66 percent, respectively.

Forty-one percent of NTDS respondents overall reported having attempted suicide. The prevalence of suicide among NTDS respondents vastly exceeds the prevalence of suicide attempts in the U.S. population (4.6%) and among lesbian, gay, and bisexual adults (10–20%) (Kessler, Borges, and Walters 1999; Nock and Kessler 2006; Paul et al. 2002). LGBQAO respondents overall had higher prevalence of suicide attempts (42%) than heterosexual respondents (36%), with prevalence of suicide attempts ranging from 40 to 47 percent among the various LGBQAO sexual orientation groups. LGBQAO respondents overall were more likely than heterosexual respondents to be without health insurance (20% versus 15%) and to have postponed getting needed medical care due to discrimination from doctors or other health care providers (29% versus 25%). Notably, 40 percent of queer respondents reported postponing needed medical care due to discrimination, which is the highest incidence among all listed groups. No significant difference was found between heterosexual respondents (20%) and all LGBQAO respondents (18%) in regard to doctor refusal to provide care due to anti-trans bias, though 29 percent of asexual respondents reported this, which is the highest prevalence for all listed groups.

## Family Rejection
The NTDS asked respondents about their families, including parents, significant others, and children, and if their relationships with their families had been impacted after disclosing that they are transgender or gender nonconforming. Fifty-seven percent of NTDS respondents overall reported experiencing rejection by their families. Table 11.4 shows that LGBQAO respondents overall experienced family rejection at a significantly higher rate than heterosexual respondents (59% versus 53%). Queer respondents reported the lowest rate of family rejection (50%) and respondents selecting "other" reported the highest (67%).

## Housing
Table 11.4 provides findings related to housing in the NTDS by sexual orientation. Heterosexual respondents were more likely to have reported being homeowners than LGBQAO respondents (42% versus 30%). Queer respondents were much less likely than all other groups to have reported being homeowners (14%). NTDS respondents overall reported experiencing homelessness (19%) and being evicted due to bias (11%). No significant differences were found

TABLE 11.4  Discrimination/Outcomes by Sexual Orientation, Column Percentages

| Discrimination/outcome variables | | Hetero-sexual or straight | LGBQAO respondents | | | | | | Full sample |
| --- | --- | --- | --- | --- | --- | --- | --- | --- | --- |
| | | | All LGBQAO | Lesbian or gay | Bisexual | Queer | Asexual | Other | |
| Family rejection | Experienced family rejection due to anti-trans bias† | 53 | 59 | 60 | 61 | 50 | 63 | 67 | 57 |
| Housing | Homeowner† | 42 | 30 | 34 | 37 | 14 | 42 | 27 | 32 |
| | Ever experienced homelessness* | 19 | 18 | 19 | 17 | 15 | 27 | 22 | 19 |
| | Ever evicted due to anti-trans bias* | 12 | 11 | 12 | 11 | 6 | 16 | 17 | 11 |
| Public accommodations | Ever denied equal treatment in public accommodations due to anti-trans bias† | 38 | 44 | 43 | 39 | 53 | 40 | 43 | 43 |
| | Ever verbally harassed in public accommodations due to anti-trans bias† | 44 | 55 | 52 | 48 | 68 | 49 | 51 | 52 |
| | Ever survived physical assault in public accommodations due to anti-trans bias† | 6 | 7 | 7 | 6 | 9 | 9 | 8 | 7 |
| Police and incarceration | Ever arrested for being trans or gender nonconforming† | 9 | 6 | 9 | 6 | 3 | 6 | 10 | 7 |
| | Ever sent to jail or prison for any reason† | 17 | 15 | 17 | 15 | 10 | 19 | 21 | 16 |

*Only the chi-square test including all Q69 identities indicated statistical significance ($p < 0.05$).

†All tests indicated statistical significance ($p < 0.05$).

between heterosexual and LGBQAO respondents for these experiences, and their reported experiences are quite similar in prevalence to the survey sample as a whole. However, there are some notable findings regarding housing when we look at the individual sexual orientation groups. Asexual respondents had a higher prevalence than other groups of experiencing homelessness (27%). Asexual respondents and those selecting "other" were more likely than others to have been evicted due to bias (16% and 17%, respectively).

## Public Accommodations

The NTDS asked respondents about their experiences in fifteen specific places of public accommodation, such as restaurants, retail stores, hotels, public transportation, government agencies, emergency rooms, and the court system. Respondents were asked whether they had experienced harassment, physical assault, or being denied equal treatment in these spaces. For the purposes of this study, these experiences were aggregated over all the areas of public accommodation covered in the NTDS, and the findings by sexual orientation are presented in table 11.4. Significantly higher percentages of LGBQAO respondents overall reported having these negative experiences in places of public accommodation as compared to heterosexual respondents. Queer respondents seem particularly vulnerable to these negative experiences, having reported the highest prevalence of these problems of all listed groups: 53 percent reported being denied equal treatment, 68 percent reported being verbally harassed, and 9 percent reported being physically assaulted in places of public accommodation. Nine percent of asexual respondents also reported being physically assaulted in places of public accommodation.

## Police and Incarceration

Both differences and similarities exist between heterosexual and LGBQAO respondents in the NTDS in regard to interactions with police and incarceration. No significant differences emerged between heterosexual and LGBQAO respondents in reported experiences with police. About a third of the NTDS sample as a whole reported one or more negative experiences with police, including unequal treatment (16%), verbal harassment (27%), and physical assault (4%). Similar percentages of heterosexual and LGBQAO respondents reported these negative experiences. However, there are significant differences between heterosexual and LGBQAO respondents in terms of arrest and incarceration. Nine percent of heterosexual respondents had been arrested for being transgender or gender nonconforming, whereas 6 percent of LGBQAO respondents overall reported such arrests. Reports of arrest among LGBQAO groups ranged from 3 percent of queer respondents on the low end to 10 percent of those selecting "other" on the high end. Heterosexual respondents were also significantly more likely than LGBQAO respondents overall to report being sent to jail or prison for any reason, though the difference is small (17% versus 15%). Among LGBQAO groups, the pattern is similar to arrests in that percentages ranged from 10 percent of queer respondents on the low end to 21 percent for those selecting "other" on the high end.

## DISCUSSION

Although it is not clear how well the NTDS sample represents the trans population of the United States as a whole, this study, based on a large U.S. sample, provides evidence that most trans people do not identify as heterosexual or straight. Only 22 percent of NTDS respondents identified that way. About half of respondents who did not identify with the categories listed in Question 69 of the survey identified their sexual orientation as pansexual, transgender, or transsexual, or they were unsure or questioning. In regard to the demographics of sexual orientation groups, large differences do not emerge between heterosexual respondents and all LGBQAO respondents, though heterosexual respondents overall were slightly older and with higher annual household incomes. In this analysis of demographic patterns, one must look at the individual LGBAO groups to find substantial differences, such as in regard to age where queer respondents were markedly younger than other groups.

Differences are more striking between heterosexual respondents and all LGBQAO respondents in terms of gender identity, transition, recognition by others that they are transgender or gender nonconforming, and being "out" to others about being transgender or gender nonconforming. For instance, male-assigned cross-dressers made up a relatively large portion of those who identified as straight or bisexual. Heterosexual respondents were less likely to be "out" as transgender or gender nonconforming and were less likely to report that others can tell they are transgender or gender nonconforming. It is beyond the scope of this study to explain why this is the case, but it should be noted that there is a significant relationship between being "out" and recognition by others as being transgender or gender nonconforming.[5] One possible implication of this relationship is that because some people are *unable* to *not be* recognized by others as being transgender or gender nonconforming they are more likely to "come out." Since heterosexual respondents overall were generally older and also transitioned at younger ages, this may explain, at least in part, why they were less likely to be recognized as transgender and gender nonconforming and also less likely to be "out."

NTDS respondents overall reported experiencing an alarming level of discrimination and violence due to anti-trans bias. Yet, LGBQAO respondents seem to have experienced higher rates of harassment. Except for harassment by police, a significantly higher percentage of LGBQAO respondents reported experiencing harassment in all instances analyzed in this study than heterosexual respondents. Analyses conducted for this study do not allow us to draw conclusions as to why this is the case, but it could be related to the fact that LGBQAO respondents were more likely to be "out" and recognized by others as being transgender or gender nonconforming. Being "out" and being recognized by others could also be a factor in explaining why LGBQAO respondents had elevated levels of discrimination and assault in places of public accommodation as compared to heterosexual respondents. However, a significantly higher percentage of heterosexual respondents reported leaving school because the harassment they experienced was so bad. Although they reported less harassment in school than LGBQAO respondents, this may speak to the severity of the harassment they experienced in the school context.

Although heterosexual respondents seem to have fared the same as—or in some cases better than—LGBQAO respondents on most measures included in this study, it is particularly notable that heterosexual respondents had a prevalence of HIV that was nearly double that of LGBQAO respondents (4.03% versus 2.16%). Only those who selected "other" as their sexual orientation had a higher percentage of respondents who are HIV positive (4.66%) among all sexual orientation groups. According to UNAIDS and the World Health Organization, 0.6 percent of adults in the United States were HIV positive as of 2006, just two years before the NTDS data collection began (World Health Organization n.d.). Prevalence of HIV among heterosexual respondents is nearly seven times higher than among the U.S. population, and it is nearly eight times higher among those selecting "other" as their sexual orientation. This suggests that heterosexual trans people and those selecting "other" may have particular risk factors regarding HIV that are different or more prevalent than LGBQAO respondents. Further research is needed to identify what those factors may be.

## LIMITATIONS

In addition to limitations previously described, there are other limitations that should be understood when considering these findings. First, the National Transgender Discrimination Survey asked respondents about one dimension of sexual orientation: identity. As outlined in a Sexual Minority Assessment Research Team (SMART) 2009 report describing best practices for collecting data on sexual orientation, there are other dimensions of sexual orientation that the NTDS did not include in the questionnaire, such as sexual behavior and sexual attraction (SMART 2009). Write-in responses to Question 69 in the NTDS, such as those presented earlier, suggest that these identity terms do not have a static meaning and have individualized meanings for some trans and gender-nonconforming people. For instance, one NTDS respondent asked, "Trans woman attracted to men. Is that gay or straight?" Had the NTDS questionnaire included a question about respondents' sexual attraction, not only would it have provided respondents more options to describe their sexual orientation but it also would have allowed more insight into the respondents who selected the identity categories analyzed in this study, offering additional information about what those categories meant to respondents.

Second, this study presents mainly descriptive analyses of sexual orientation in the NTDS. It is possible that some of the differences found in experiences of discrimination and other outcomes could be explained at least in part by demographic and other group differences. For instance, the relatively higher income and rates of homeownership among heterosexual respondents could be driven in part by the fact that this group was slightly older than the LGBQAO respondents. Analyses conducted for this study did not control for these demographic differences or other group differences. Therefore, the findings of this study require further investigation to control for group differences in demographics and other factors.

Finally, respondents who selected "other" reported diverse identities that require further investigation. Potential differences among those selecting "other" were masked in this study by keeping those respondents in one group for purposes of analysis. For instance, those who identified as "pansexual" may be quite different demographically and in their experiences from those who identified their sexual orientation as "transgender." These potential differences require additional investigation.

## CONCLUSION

Understanding how sexual orientation and gender identity intersect in people's lives and impact their experiences is helpful in determining how public policy and public administration can be responsive to the needs of the trans community and the LGBT community at large, particularly when developing and implementing laws and regulations to protect against discrimination. For instance, three states currently have in place laws prohibiting discrimination based on sexual orientation but no prohibitions on discrimination based on gender identity or expression.[6] Yet, Allegra R. Gordon and Ilan H. Meyer (2007) found in a study of non-trans lesbian, gay, and bisexual adults that 19 percent of participants experienced discrimination based on their gender expression. Therefore, laws protecting individuals from discrimination only on the basis of sexual orientation do not provide adequate protection for lesbian, gay, and bisexual people who do not identify as trans.

Similar to the findings from Gordon and Meyer's study (2007), findings from this study suggest that laws protecting individuals from discrimination need to include sexual orientation, gender identity, and gender expression in order to provide adequate protection for trans and gender-nonconforming people. Sexual orientation seems to matter among NTDS respondents in how they experienced discrimination, particularly in the area of public accommodations and in health. A few respondents to the NTDS also described how the discrimination they experienced could have been rooted in anti-gay bias as well as in anti-trans bias. One trans woman explained, "I identify as feminine and prefer female company. . . . Even when in an androgynous 'male' mode I've been called a faggot. Some people are ignorant no matter what." Another respondent stated, "It's hard to tell what treatment resulted from being perceived as gay with my partner versus being perceived as gender nonconforming." These statements underscore the need for protection in the three key areas of sexual orientation, gender identity, and gender expression in antidiscrimination protections, such as the Employment Non-Discrimination Act (commonly called ENDA). Working toward these comprehensive protections is something in which the LGBT community can be—and should be—united.

## NOTES

The author would like to thank Yolanda Martínez-San Miguel, Ilan Meyer, Brad Sears, and Sarah Tobias for their thoughtful reviews of this chapter. The author also thanks the National LGBTQ Task Force and the National Center for Transgender Equality for the use of the NTDS dataset.

1. Findings from the Pearson's chi-square test of independence tell us whether two variables have a statistically significant relationship. For instance, this test can tell us if sexual orientation is related to having experienced a particular form of discrimination. Findings from a t-test for difference in means tell us if the difference between two group means is statistically significant. For instance, a t-test can tell us if there is a significant difference in reported experiences of discrimination between respondents of different sexual orientations. A couple of notes of caution in interpreting these results: First, the NTDS respondents were not randomly selected to participate in the survey. Therefore, the tests for statistical significance are only able to assess differences among groups within this sample and the ability to generalize based on these findings is limited. Second, the NTDS sample is large, which can inflate the statistical significance of both the chi-square test and the t-test. This means that even small group differences can be found to be statistically significant and/or indicate a statistically significant relationship. So while the differences and relationships explored in this study may be found to be statistically significant, some of these may not be particularly meaningful when the differences are small.

2. In this study, respondents reporting they identify as lesbian, gay, bisexual, queer, asexual, and "other" (LGBQAO) were combined for purposes of conducting t-tests. T-tests were conducted to test the mean difference between LGBQAO and heterosexual respondents in

selected demographic and outcome variables. T-tests were performed with the combined LGBQAO recode only and only on dichotomous or ordinal categorical variables where the mean and its relative direction are meaningful. In addition to t-tests, chi-square tests of independence were performed with the combined LGBQAO variable and the demographic or outcome variable of interest. Further analysis showed that when the groups comprising the LGBQAO category were analyzed individually, differences emerged between the various groups. Therefore, chi-square tests of independence were also performed with the disaggregated sexual orientation variable (recoded Question 69) and the demographic or outcome variable of interest.

3. U.S. population figure calculated using the 2008 Current Population Survey, Annual Social and Economic Supplement, U.S. Census Bureau, and U.S. Bureau of Labor Statistics.

4. U.S. population figure from World Health Organization, Global Health Observatory Data Repository n.d.

5. $\chi = 789.5254$, d.f. 4, $p < 0.01$.

6. These states include New York, New Hampshire, and Wisconsin. For more information, see National LGBTQ Task Force 2014.

## REFERENCES

Gordon, Allegra R., and Ilan H. Meyer. 2007. "Gender Nonconformity as a Target of Prejudice, Discrimination, and Violence against LGB Individuals." *Journal of LGBT Health Research* 3.3: 55–71.

Grant, Jaime M., Lisa A. Mottet, Justin Tanis, Jack Harrison, Jody L. Herman, and Mara Keisling. 2011. *Injustice at Every Turn: A Report of the National Transgender Discrimination Survey.* Washington, DC: National Center for Transgender Equality and National Gay and Lesbian Task Force. Accessed February 17, 2015. http://www.thetaskforce.org/injustice -every-turn-report-national-transgender-discrimination-survey.

Kessler, Ronald C., Guilherme Borges, and Ellen E. Walters. 1999. "Prevalence of and Risk Factors for Lifetime Suicide Attempts in the National Comorbidity Survey." *Archives of General Psychiatry* 56: 617–626.

National LGBTQ Task Force. 2014. *State Nondiscrimination Laws in the U.S.* Washington, DC: National LGBTQ Task Force. Accessed February 17, 2015. http://www.thetaskforce.org/ static_html/downloads/reports/issue_maps/non_discrimination_5_14_color_new .pdf.

Nock, Matthew K., and Ronald C. Kessler. 2006. "Prevalence of and Risk Factors for Suicide Attempts versus Suicide Gestures: Analysis of the National Comorbidity Survey." *Journal of Abnormal Psychology* 115.3: 616–623.

Paul, Jay P., Joseph Cantania, Lance Pollack, Judith Moskowitz, Jesse Canchola, Thomas Mills, Diane Binson, and Ron Stall. 2002. "Suicide Attempts among Gay and Bisexual Men: Lifetime Prevalence and Antecedents." *American Journal of Public Health* 92.8: 1338–1345.

Sexual Minority Assessment Research Team (SMART). 2009. *Best Practices for Asking Questions about Sexual Orientation on Surveys.* Los Angeles: Williams Institute. Accessed February 17, 2015. http://williamsinstitute.law.ucla.edu/wp-content/uploads/SMART -FINAL-Nov-2009.pdf.

World Health Organization, Global Health Observatory Data Repository. N.d. Region of the Americas: United States of America statistics summary (2002–present). Accessed February 17, 2015. http://apps.who.int/gho/data/view.country.20800.

## PART V

TRANSFORMING DISCIPLINES AND PEDAGOGY

# 12 · ADVENTURES IN TRANS BIOPOLITICS

## A Comparison between Public Health and Critical Academic Research Praxes

SEL J. HWAHNG

When I was asked to present at the Trans Politics Conference that took place at Rutgers University in New Brunswick, New Jersey, on April 18–19, 2013, I was faced with an interesting challenge. I had correctly assumed that the audience for this conference would probably be informed by critical humanities and social scientific fields, and that they may have known very little about public health research and praxis. Although I have a bachelor's degree in biology and had been involved in some biomedical and clinical research during and right after my undergraduate education, much of my graduate school training involved interdisciplinary critical humanities and social scientific academic texts, analyses, methodologies, and theories. During my graduate school training I became frustrated by the glaring absence in the research of the most socioeconomically marginalized (including sexual and gender minority) people and communities of color. Soon after finishing graduate school I first became involved in public health research through a postdoctoral fellowship and realized that the much larger resources available in this field also allowed for greater access to the most highly socioeconomically marginalized people/communities of color, including those who were sexual and gender minorities.[1]

Currently, the bulk of my trans/gender-variant research and publishing is within public health and empirical social scientific contexts. I have also been involved for the last several years in scientific programming for the LGBT Caucus of the American Public Health Association and have been exposed to a considerable amount of the newest research trends and findings in trans/gender-variant public health research. Thus, I think it is important to examine the gaps between public health (as a *praxis* of research, inquiry, and methodology) and critical academia (as a *praxis* of research, inquiry, and methodology).

This chapter is exploratory, and I suggest that the goals of public health research—to investigate social, psychological, and biomedical processes of health outcomes and to cure, mitigate, or eradicate negative health outcomes—cannot be separated from public health's location/entrenchment within the medical/health industrial complex. Similarly, the goals of critical academic research/inquiry, especially those goals in the humanities and social sciences focused on progressive social transformation and emancipation, cannot be separated from critical academia's own location/entrenchment within the higher education/academic industrial complex.

For the sake of this chapter, critical academic inquiry is defined very broadly as the aforementioned aspects of humanities and social science research and scholarship that may engage with certain narratives of Foucauldian biopower, poststructuralism, queer theory, Trans Studies and, in the case of social scientific research, may also include empirical (almost always qualitative) research. By categorizing all of the above as "critical academic research/inquiry," I do not mean carelessly to collapse these various approaches, analyses, and disciplines together. However, I am suggesting in this "category," a cross-dialogue among critical academic humanities and social scientific fields in which many of the same concepts or theories are oftentimes referenced. Similarly, applied research fields such as public health, social work, criminology, and public policy may sometimes reference research and findings across the various *applied* fields, but I have hardly ever seen cross-referencing (and especially, meaningful cross-referencing) *between* the critical academic and applied fields.

I also want to suggest that it is perhaps the *gaps* between applied fields and critical academic fields, as well as the *maintenance of these gaps*, that reinforce the status quo. I thus invite the reader to consider how these gaps could start to close. I also invite the reader to consider how historically separate praxes could truly cross-pollinate, collaborate, and inform one another.

## THE GAPS BETWEEN PUBLIC HEALTH
## AND CRITICAL ACADEMIC RESEARCH

Table 12.1 presents an exploration of the gaps between (trans) public health research praxis/discourse and (trans) critical academic research praxis/discourse. One aspect I have been most struck by is the gap between methodology and theory used in each case (table 12.1, comparison 1). When I started in public health research as a postdoctoral fellow, my lack of training in methodology

TABLE 12.1 Gaps between Public Health and Critical
Academic Research Praxes and Discourses

| Public health research praxis/discourse | Critical academic research praxis/discourse |
|---|---|
| 1. Methodological precision and sophistication | Theoretical precision and sophistication |
| 2. Because of funding opportunities, often has access to highly marginalized populations such as poverty-class trans/gender-variant women of color and other highly marginalized sexual and gender minorities | Because of funding constraints, often has access to more privileged populations only and must often utilize non-empirical and secondary sources on marginalized sectors |
| 3. Emphasis on scientific empiricism as "primary sources" | Emphasis on other types of primary sources (such as journalist accounts) as well as secondary sources and analyses |
| 4. Empirical studies of large or larger samples | Empirical studies are small samples or secondary sources |
| 5. Often vast amounts of data are collected/generated that are not thoroughly processed or theorized | Data may be well processed and theorized, but samples are so small that applicability/relevancy are questionable and/or the study of poverty-class people of color is often excluded from analyses and theorizations |
| 6. "Applied" fields—knowledge production for the sake of informing interventions among social service organizations/health care providers and health care policy | "Academic" fields—intellectual knowledge production for students in higher education and perhaps for "general" public (often privileged) |
| 7. Because of larger funding streams, specialized conferences are more ubiquitous and publishing occurs more rapidly and has a short shelf-life (often only five-year relevancy) | Because of smaller funding streams, less specialized conferences foster more interdisciplinary knowledge exchange, and publishing occurs more slowly and is sustained longer (classics, canon, etc.) |
| 8. Peer-reviewed journals (hierarchically ranked; impact factor); books considered secondary, useful for teaching students | Books (publishers hierarchically ranked) and some peer-reviewed journal publishing |
| 9. Quantitative research as primary; qualitative research as exploratory, secondary, or in tandem with quantitative research | Qualitative (including ethnographic) research as legible; quantitative research as illegible |
| 10. Multiple generations of poverty/low-income/poverty-class | Working-class |

(*continued*)

TABLE 12.1    Gaps between Public Health and Critical
Academic Research Praxes and Discourses (continued)

| Public health research praxis/discourse | Critical academic research praxis/discourse |
|---|---|
| 11.  Resiliency | Agency |
| 12.  Social determinants of health | Structural oppression |
| 13.  Heath disparities | Social injustice/social inequalities |
| 14.  Social ecology | Cultural landscape/ethnoscape/habitus |
| 15.  MSM/W; WSW/M; LGBT | Queer; Trans; LGBT |
| 16.  Effective and improved health care— "scientific objectivity" privileged over "political views" (except in the case of some Native American public health research that refers to sociopolitical concepts such as decolonization) | Intellectual knowledge production for academic interest and/or sociopolitical transformation (often referring to or connecting with concepts such as decolonization) |

became quite apparent. My postdoctoral fellowship included funding for course-work, so I was trained fairly quickly in both quantitative and (more advanced) qualitative methodologies, including the use of computer programs such as SPSS, Stata, and ATLAS.ti. In my postdoctoral fellowship program, I also gained recognition as being adept at theorizing, that is, suggesting and creating concepts, models, and paradigms from empirical data findings. In the course of this work I learned that many of the theories in public health research were less developed and sophisticated than those in critical academic fields and that my theoretical dexterity was in part informed by my critical humanities training.

Yet I greatly respect the methodological precision and sophistication of public health research. I especially appreciate how many research scientists have been able to access and conduct methodologically rigorous research on populations of highly marginalized low-income people of color. For instance, the amount of research in public health on low-income trans/gender-variant women of color exponentially exceeds the amount of research I have come across in critical academic fields on this important demographic. Due to limited funding streams, critical academic researchers have not been able to garner the necessary resources to conduct rigorous research on highly marginalized low-income people of color. This limitation is especially acute in the critical academic scholarship on queer/trans/sexual and gender minority populations, which is greatly skewed toward the examination of white and/or socioeconomically privileged individuals and communities and in which discussions of low-income individuals and communities of color are descriptive, based on historical evidence, and/or reference small samples (see Halberstam 1998, 2005; Prosser 1998; Stryker and Aizura 2013; also my critiques in Hwahng 2013; see also table 12.1, comparison 2).

This brings us to the question of the divide between speculation and theory in table 12.1, comparison 1 and comparison 2. Must theory always follow upon a proposed hypothesis that was built upon previous literature and research utilizing "incremental logic," in which the hypothesis is then proved or not proved in standard scientific methodology? Or can theory be elaborated from other means, other types of logics or meaning-makings, as espoused in much critical academic discourse? But the question then remains, how to make this type of theory-making understandable to researchers ensconced within public health and other applied and scientific fields who reify specific forms of scientific logic and empiricism?

A long-standing critique from critical humanities and social scientific academicians is the overarching emphasis on empirical research as the primary and perhaps only valid source of information considered in public health research. Critical academic fields have often emphasized other types of non-empirical "primary sources," such as journalism, as well as secondary analyses (table 12.1, comparison 3). Granted, there are certain assumptions that are not interrogated but that are implicit in public health research on the sanctity of "scientific logic" or the "hypothesis-proof-theory" trajectory, in addition to the masculinist underpinnings of much of scientific rationalism and an emphasis on a linear "scientific progression" of research.[2] Nonetheless, empirical research can be a welcome contribution to a critical academic research praxis that often references either no empirical research whatsoever or empirical research with very small samples that are sometimes also methodologically weak or questionable (table 12.1, comparison 4).

It is unclear whether the emphases in critical academia on primary sources, such as journalism, and on secondary sources have developed independently or as a result of financial constraints. Indeed it seems ideal for researchers from any field or praxis to have a full range of options to pursue research according to whatever methodological architectures would best fit their goals and agendas. Because of widely divergent funding streams, this type of "true interdisciplinarity" may only be possible in collaborations across what would be considered highly disparate praxes.

The developments of these two distinct and larger praxes (with their respective "industrial complexes") limit their respective potential efficacy toward true social transformation, justice, and equity. In public health research, because of larger funding streams, vast amounts of data are collected and generated (table 12.1, comparison 5). Most public health research scientists find themselves entrenched in a "grant-funding" mill/cycle, forcing them to fund most of their salary through grants, or "soft money." Thus, public health research scientists often do not have time to process their data thoroughly before they must move on to writing more grant proposals to fund their salaries. Because this data is not thoroughly processed, the ability to construct more elaborate theories is frequently limited.

What results is much redundancy in public health research—for instance, research scientists from various regions of the United States will often utilize the same or similar recruitment methods and disseminate the same or similar findings *ad nauseam* on HIV risk among low-income trans/gender-variant women of color. A relevant question is, then, does all this research actually improve the health and well-being of trans/gender-variant women of color? Although there seems to be some progress, in which data collected on certain groups of trans/gender-variant women of color indicate higher frequency of safer sex practices and regular HIV testing, often these "improvements" in behavior are temporary, and intervention studies often only test during, and for a limited amount of time after, the delivery of interventions for behavioral change. The pathway from intervention testing to full-scale implementation of an intervention is long and arduous, and often funding may not be available to provide *sustainable and long-term* evidence-based interventions. Public health research scientists also shy away from addressing social transformation itself, for fear of appearing unscientific, since by utilizing strictly scientific methodology, how could social transformation actually be measured?

In critical academic fields, on the other hand, there appears to be much written on social transformation. Yet how would social transformation be implemented in realms *beyond* middle-class, socioeconomically privileged communities and populations? When critical academic researchers are able to access more socially and economically marginalized populations, their samples are often small (as in critical anthropology). Consequently, much of the applicability of critical academic research praxis is limited to highly socioeconomically privileged populations. Or the sample size is so small that its relevance to other realms of biopower—such as public policy or wide-scale interventions that directly provide programming, public education, and services to socioeconomically marginalized populations—is considered either inconsequential or unrecognizable by applied researchers and policymakers.

For example, the critical anthropology monograph *Travesti: Sex, Gender, and Culture among Brazilian Transgendered Prostitutes* (Kulick 1998) seems to have had a wide impact within critical academic fields such as Anthropology, Sociology, Literature, and Cultural Studies. However, this pivotal text is glaringly absent from public health literature, even among the multitude of public health studies and publications focused on diasporic African poverty-class trans/gender-variant female sex workers (Herbst et al. 2008; Nemoto et al. 2004; Sausa et al. 2007), which is similar to the population that was the focus of Kulick's study.

Because of my cross-training I was able to determine that the insights from Kulick's study could be very useful to understanding public health concerns such as HIV risk transmission. Kulick devotes considerable attention to understanding the interpersonal and sexual dynamics between *travestis* and their primary male partners, and public health research scientists have identified primary male partners as the main source of HIV/STI infection among trans/gender-variant women of color (Hwahng and Nuttbrock 2007; Hwahng and Nuttbrock 2014; Melendez and Pinto 2007; Nemoto et al. 2004; Operario et al. 2011).[3] Since Kulick's study is not referenced or utilized in the general public health literature, an opportunity to understand these interpersonal and sexual dynamics more deeply is lost (as revealed in Kulick's findings).

Another gap that limits the potential for effective collaborations and social transformation is the production and circulation of knowledge and power in "applied" versus "academic" fields (table 12.1, comparison 6). In public health research praxis, knowledge production is undertaken for the sake of both informing interventions among social service and health care providers and informing health care and social welfare policy. In contrast, critical academic research praxis is often limited to knowledge production for students in higher education, other critical academicians, and other small and highly privileged readerships within the general population.

One of my first realizations of the extent of the different patterns of knowledge distribution between applied and academic fields came when I first embarked on my public health research career. I was assisting a research scientist recruiting low-income drug-using anatomically female/female-assigned-at-birth women of color who have sex with women in the Bushwick neighborhood of New York City (NYC) in 2004 when it was less gentrified than it is now. I was speaking with a research participant who appeared to me as someone who was sexual minority and gender-variant, and they asked me where they could find support around being "gay." I told them there were support groups at the NYC LGBT Center. They had never heard of the center, nor did they know where it was located. At that moment I was struck by the socioeconomic divide in the United States that severely limits access to information and resources for the most disenfranchised gay/queer/trans people, while privileged gay/queer/trans people often have access to a relative multitude of information and resources.

A more recent research observation came from interviewing low-income trans/gender-variant people of color in NYC who stated that they would rather access medical services at a clinic in the Bronx *even when* a well-known LGBT clinic in the West Village was geographically closer to them and logistically more accessible (Hwahng et al. 2013). The participants stated they felt more comfortable in the Bronx clinic because they had known the providers through their personal social networks before they started to access services. During this latter study I had been working as a public health research scientist for several years, and by this time I was well aware of the vast race/class/privilege divides in NYC and was not surprised by these responses. The participants' preference for the geographically less accessible Bronx clinic really enunciated the vast gaps and disconnections of communities, social networks, privilege, and resources that I have discovered during the last decade of my career.

There are also other gaps in knowledge distribution between public health and critical academic research praxes (table 12.1, comparison 7). Because of larger funding streams in public health, specialized professional conferences seem more ubiquitous, and publishing occurs more rapidly and has a short shelf-life—often, articles and books are considered relevant for only up to five years after publication. The ubiquity of specialization can lead to less knowledge exchange between fields and disciplines, even among those within public health, which can result in increasingly reductionist thinking. At the American Public Health Association annual meetings I have often heard critiques of the various "silos" of sections, caucuses, special primary interest groups, committees, forums, and assemblies that seem to have little communication, cross-referencing, or information-sharing with each other.

As to the shelf-life of publishing, the short road to irrelevancy may lead to frequent publishing but, alongside the rapid pace of the grant-funding mill, can also lead to poorly and partially analyzed data and superficially constructed or clichéd theoretical and conceptual frameworks and conclusions. For instance, how many times have I read that the social contexts of HIV among low-income people of color, including trans/gender-variant people of color, were attributed to "racism and poverty," with no further analysis or discussion of racism or poverty nor of how these social vectors/conditions are scientifically linked to HIV risk and vulnerability?

Within critical academia, there appear to be fewer specialized conferences and more interdisciplinary conferences and forums. But does the *praxis* of critical academic interdisciplinarity, often trapped within examining the always already privileged, have the political reach to effect social justice and transformation? In critical academia, publishing seems to occur more slowly and its relevance is sustained for longer periods of time. While this can be useful in creating a thoroughfare of intellectual continuity, if critical academic texts are initially premised on research and conclusions based on race, class, and gender privilege, these texts may actually not be applicable to the entire variation of lived experience, especially of those most socioeconomically marginalized. Thus critical academic texts, especially those far removed temporally from their initial research and publication date, may actually *reinforce* delimitations instead of contributing to more inclusive and expansive articulations necessary for actual social justice.

In tandem with the gaps between the two praxes in regards to lengths of time of publishing relevancy are the differences between publishing outlets (table 12.1, comparison 8). In public health research praxis, publishing in top-ranked scientific peer-reviewed journals is considered preferable. These journals are methodically ranked by what is known as the impact factor, which is the number of times the articles in a given journal have been cited by other indexed scientific journals. Books are considered secondary to journal publishing and are viewed as useful for "educational" purposes for students. Public health research scientists often publish literature reviews or large-scale overviews of dated research in books; their most current research findings are often reserved for peer-reviewed journals, which include a more rapid turnaround time from article submission to publication.

There also appears to be a conceit among public health research scientists, especially those who are highly successful in obtaining grant funding. Elaborating upon George Bernard Shaw's phrase "those who can, do; those who can't, teach," journal publishing is considered within the realm of "doing" and understood as an essential aspect of the craft of a scientist, similarly to how an artist must often exhibit in order to be considered viable. Book publishing, on the other hand, is often considered within the realm of "education" rather than "scientific research."

Since most successfully funded research scientists are able to devote the majority if not all their time to research, educators are often viewed as those who have been unable to secure large-scale funding on a consistent basis. The role of educator is thus considered of secondary importance to that of the scientific research scientist and (following the masculinist logic in public health research) is seen as fulfilling a (feminized) maternal role of helpmate to students. In contrast, the successful first-tier public health research scientist par excellence is viewed as fulfilling the (masculine) paternal mission of leading the way into ever greater scientific discovery with the promise of transforming health (which may not quite deliver).

In critical academia books are of primary importance, and publishers are often ranked hierarchically. Because of the more limited number of outlets, the hierarchical ranking of publishers does not seem to be as methodical or as painstaking and meticulous as in public health research. However, since publication of one or two books for tenure is often *de rigueur* in Research I universities as well as in other academic institutions, there is much more of a focus on monograph publication in comparison to journal publishing. Because of the relatively slow turnaround time with book publishing, an overemphasis on monographs can foster the development of intellectual thought that favors overviews and generalizations. In some cases, these generalizations can also be balanced with more quick and nimble thought processes developed from journal publication.

Since the teaching load for academicians even at top Research I universities is much greater than for consistently funded research scientists, many critical academicians consider themselves as much educators as researchers and may struggle to publish even the minimum required for tenure. Securing tenure from an educational institution is often viewed as the only viable option to ensure longevity as a critical academician. By contrast, because of the valorization of science in society, public health research scientists have the "luxury" of prioritizing their research, yet they must participate in the continual securing of grant-funding to pay their salaries.

## LANGUAGING THE GAPS

Language and terminology "code" the respective praxes, and gaps in the use of language and terminology also contribute to the lack of understanding and collaboration between public health and critical academic research praxes. Perhaps the most glaring gap is the primary importance of quantitative research, data, and analysis in public health research and the near ubiquitous illiteracy in regards to quantitative research within most critical academic fields (table 12.1, comparison 9). That most critical academicians cannot read, understand, cite, critique, or respond to quantitative research and analysis is an almost tragic example of non-translation, especially since quantitative research and data are what often drives and informs public policy, including health policy, and the dissemination of public and private funding to programs and interventions. Understanding quantitative analysis is also fundamental to understanding how public health and applied researchers engage in "meaning making" and, by extension, theory making.

Because of this illiteracy, most critical academic scholars and researchers cannot "read" most public health literature, which also points to the inherent contradictions of critical academicians' focusing on trans/gender-variant populations and communities. These critical academicians may purport to advocate for social transformation and justice, including improved services for the most socioeconomically marginalized (both within and beyond the current health and social service industrial complexes). However, these same critical academicians may be unable to base their scholarship on the sometimes vast amount of quantitative data and analysis driving the policies, programs, and interventions that affect and often target highly socioeconomically marginalized trans/gender-variant people and communities.

While some critical academic researchers and scholars may cite and utilize qualitative research, including ethnographic studies, it is important to understand the role of qualitative research in many of the applied fields, including public health. In public health research praxis, qualitative methodologies are sometimes utilized as exploratory initial investigations and at times may be a component of larger, more fully developed "mixed-methods" studies that also include quantitative research. Rarely are qualitative studies ever viewed as "stand-alone" fully developed studies, and they are hardly ever funded as the sole methodology of a full-fledged study. What this means is that public health research that is solely qualitative, while potentially "translatable" to critical academicians, will often be viewed as exploratory pilot data—and inconclusive—by public health research scientists. On the other hand, studies that are considered fully developed by public health research scientists, either utilizing solely quantitative methodologies or mixed-methods studies in which both the qualitative and quantitative findings are presented together, will not be "legible" to most critical academicians.

Thus, if critical academicians do venture into citing public health research articles and can only decipher those that are qualitative, these scholars will be reading and understanding only a fraction of the public health research findings, concepts, and theories on a given population, such as trans/gender-variant people. Only by being able to read and make sense of both qualitative and quantitative research will critical academicians be able to understand fully the breadth of public health research on a given population. It is perhaps because the training in understanding *quantitative* research appears daunting that many critical academicians shy away from tackling the public health research behemoth while still advocating for social transformation that includes a recirculation and reorganization of (medical and health) biopower.

Critical academicians may thus discuss and critique medical/health biopower as a response to many trans/gender-variant people and communities, from a wide variety of socioeconomic positionalities, vocalizing the primary importance of health care in their lives. Many trans/gender-variant people and communities must intimately interface with the medical and public health industrial complexes in order to access services related to their psychological well-being and other mental health issues, hormone and silicone administration, surgical procedures, other body modifications, along with basic and other health care needs. The inability of many critical academics to thoroughly examine the arrangements and circulation of biopower in medicine and public health is thus a conspicuous limitation, especially for those committed to the social justice and well-being of trans/gender-variant populations.

Another language gap involves terminologies and discourses within the respective praxes of critical academia and public health research. In the latter, various terms are utilized to describe the socioeconomically disenfranchised, including *low-income* and more recently individuals coming from *multiple generations of poverty*, which more precisely refers to individuals and communities ensconced in cycles of poverty (Reilly et al. 2013; see also table 12.1, comparison 10). In HIV and substance use public health research, the use of this last term points not only to the devastating effects of multigenerational poverty but also multigenerational socioeconomic marginalization and multigenerational social injustice (Sharkey 2013). In my own scholarship, I refer to those who have experienced multigenerational poverty as "poverty-class," which indicates the historical sedimentations of poverty that have accumulated through the generations and that situate and anchor individuals and communities within contemporary cycles of poverty (Hwahng 2013).

Individuals and communities within this "poverty-class" status are different from those who may experience "conditional" poverty but who, in fact, do not come from multiple generations of poverty. These include many Asian immigrants (including those from East Asia, Southeast Asia, and South Asia) who may experience poverty due to recent immigration into the United States but on further examination often come from middle-class backgrounds, may be well educated, may come from families who own property in Asia, and so on (Hwahng 2013; Hwahng and Lin 2009; Kang et al. 2003; Mehta 2014). This class privilege then, although not necessarily apparent during initial immigration, does become apparent in the often rapid rise of many Asian immigrants up the socioeconomic hierarchy to middle-class status (Mehta 2014; Ny and Nakasako 1995). This phenomenon contributes to the "model minority" myth in regards to Asian Americans, and yet this phenomenon is classed as much as it is raced.

Another example concerns mostly young white transpeople who are often highly educated, have attended elite colleges and universities, and yet are underemployed. These individuals may experience psychological depression and are often collecting disability benefits (Feldman 2009). On paper they may be living in low-income brackets, yet their backgrounds reveal they cannot be considered poverty-class. This is also revealed in the differential health disparities between the young, white, trans/gender-variant population and poverty-class trans/gender-variant populations of color, which I will elaborate later in this chapter.

In contrast, within U.S. critical academic research praxis, I have come across *all* low-income people referred to as *working-class* (Giffney and O'Rourke 2009; Halberstam 2005) without differentiating between those working in legal "blue-collar" or even legal unskilled professions and those who must subsist within the "underground" economy (Bourgois 2002) engaging in off-market activities that are often considered illegal or criminal, sometimes in conjunction with welfare or disability benefits. Perhaps due to the influence of Marxist scholarship, the use of *working class* as a catch-all term for people positioned below the middle class on the socioeconomic hierarchy is particularly dismissive of the intricacies of the lived experiences of those who are most socioeconomically marginalized. Steve Martinot's (2003) historical examination of the post-Reconstruction de-skilling of African Americans and their exclusion from white-dominated blue-collar trade unions is particularly telling of the widely divergent class and socioeconomic historical trajectories between differently racialized groups. Needless to say, this historical de-skilling and exclusion also contributed to the post-Reconstruction rise and establishment of poverty-class African Americans and other people of color. Poverty-class trans/gender-variant people of color often experience very different lived cosmologies as well as health disparities compared to white working-class trans/gender-variant people.

Other terms that reveal the distance between the two praxes are *resiliency* and *agency* (table 12.1, comparison 11). Within public health research *resiliency* connotes the particular strengths of individuals, communities, or populations. A current trend involves researching resiliencies in relation to health outcomes, particularly among populations that have historically been marginalized. A focus on resiliency serves to counterbalance the frequently overwhelming focus on health risks and vulnerabilities that, coupled with quantitative statistics, can appear to reduce socioeconomically marginalized populations and communities to merely dehumanized numbers, as "vectors" of disease transmission or "receptors" of contagion. In contrast, in critical academic research praxis, the term *agency* is often used, especially with reference to individuals or communities that have been historically marginalized and oppressed, to describe how they exert power and choice even in the face of overwhelming structural and interpersonal constraints (Cheng 2010; Pfeffer 2012). Oftentimes the examination of agency may be relegated to one individual or a handful of individuals. The individual may be delineated as an *auteur* of sorts, as someone who can still carve out at least some of their own destiny in the face of great hardship.

In public health research, on the other hand, *resiliency* almost always references a group, at either the community or the population level. Even when particular attention is focused on an individual, any observed attributes of strength, endurance, and creative problem solving are seen as reflective of the resiliency of their community or population. I personally favor contextualizing individual resiliency within group-level resiliency because this can potentially provide insights into mechanisms of social transformation that individualized "heroic" accounts cannot.

Furthermore, in public health, researchers are expected to maintain their scientific objectivity by avoiding overt political conclusions from their findings, since these are often considered "unscientific" and "polemical" and may undermine their credibility in the greater scientific community.[4] Research scientists are encouraged to work "within the system" of the various medical/health/social service/criminal-justice industrial complexes and governmental bureaucracies to bring about incremental change (Marmot 2004). The term *structural oppression* in critical academic discourse translates into *social determinants of health* in public health praxis, with the understanding that the more socioeconomically marginalized an individual or community is the more negative health outcomes they may experience (table 12.1, comparison 12). This latter term thus emphasizes the primacy of "health" while distancing itself from actively engaging with political forces that give rise to health outcomes.

Elaborating upon this premise of "scientific objectivity," the term *health disparities* becomes the proxy for *social injustice* or even *social inequalities* within critical academic discourse (table 12.1, comparison 13). The measurement of health disparities can be very precise. For instance, the disaggregation of health data among Latinos/as in the United States into ethnic-specific groups reveals that HIV vulnerabilities and illicit/injection drug use are far greater among certain Latino/a groups such as Mexicans or Puerto Ricans, reflecting the greater socioeconomic marginalization of these groups compared to other Latino/a groups in the United States such as (non African) Cubans or Argentinians (Bonilla-Silva and Glover 2004; Deren et al. 2011; Kang et al. 2005; Organista et al. 2004; Sanchez et al. 2004).[5]

Another example concerns trans/gender-variant women of color who have been measured to have exorbitantly high rates of HIV seroprevalence (49–50% in NYC; Nuttbrock et al. 2009), while the HIV rate among young white transpeople is dramatically lower, yet rates of depression are high for both groups (Feldman 2009; Hwahng and Nuttbrock 2014; Nuttbrock et al. 2010; Nuttbrock et al., 2014). A large portion of the high HIV seroprevalence among trans/gender-variant women of color seems to be attributed to factors including racial and class structural oppression as well as gender and sexual minority discrimination. In addition, their high rates of depression, at least during specific periods in the life course, may be linked to *familial* gender and sexual minority rejection and ostracism (in that the family, which had been a protective buffer against racial hostility, is no longer able to offer protection) rather than *structural* gender and sexual minority discrimination (Hwahng and Nuttbrock 2014; Koken et al. 2009). By contrast, the low-income status of young white transpeople may be attributed, at least in part, to depression, which may in turn be linked solely to the discrimination they experience as gender minorities. In sum, health disparities are a powerful barometer for the particular ways social injustices circulate, manifest, and in the case of trans/gender-variant women of color, are compounded by gender, race, and class.

*Social ecology* (table 12.1, comparison 14) is perhaps the public health praxis term that is most accessible to critical academicians. It often refers to both structural and interpersonal factors in a lived cosmology. Often the term *social ecology* and sometimes *social context* are utilized in public health discourse. However, in a praxis that places such great emphasis on measurable results, the associations between social ecological factors and health outcomes often remain unmeasured and thus cannot be "proven" scientifically. What occurs, then, is that behavior is measured scientifically and social context is not. Thus, social context remains in the realm of "description" or "speculation" and cannot effectively inform programs, interventions, or policy. Such an approach cannot effect social transformation or create long-term, sustainable, positive health outcomes. The preparation and presentation of scientific evidence that lacks adequate social contextualization may thus feed the public health industrial-complex machinery more than actually improving the health and lives of populations and communities.

In contrast, critical academic research praxis appears to place much greater emphasis on sociostructural contexts, such that various terms have developed to elucidate their intricacies. For instance, "cultural landscape" (Hirsch 1995; Sauer 1925) may refer to the interaction between people and their ecological environment, while "ethnoscape" (Appadurai 1990) may refer to the shifting flux of people within a given environment, and "habitus" (Bourdieu 1984) refers to lifestyles, values, dispositions, and expectations of particular social groups. The diversity of social contextual terms reflects the greater awareness on the part of critical academicians of the primacy of the sociostructural and its centrality to social transformation.

Finally, critical academic and public health researchers often utilize different terms for those who are considered sexual and gender minorities (table 12.1, comparison 15). In public health, terms such as WSW (women who have sex with women) and MSM (men who have sex with men) have developed that focus on "behavior" but are devoid of any other social contextualization. The term MSM is especially relevant to studies on HIV, and this term developed because research indicated that there were a large number of men who were having sex with men yet did not identify as "gay" or "bisexual" and may have even identified as "heterosexual," particularly among low-income men of color (Mutchler et al. 2008; Siegel et al. 2008).

Since one of the intentions of public health is to identify particular groups who may be vectors of disease transmission or reception, public health praxis reductively isolates behavior to the "mechanics" that most directly lead to disease transmission. Individuals who may identify as gay, bisexual, or heterosexual are grouped together under the category MSM or WSW and often their anatomy designates what category they are placed in. For instance, transmen are almost never included in the MSM category (because they are not anatomically male) and there is a long-standing pattern in public health of including trans/gender-variant women within the MSM category, even though the vast majority of trans/gender-variant women do not identify as men. This categorization is rationalized because the vast majority of trans/gender-variant women of color partner with cis-gendered men[6] (Hwahng and Nuttbrock 2007; Melendez and Pinto 2007; Nemoto et al. 2004; Nuttbrock et al. 2011; Operario et al. 2011).

Public health, through its primarily behavioral emphasis, views the mechanics of HIV transmission risk (i.e., primarily receptive anal and oral intercourse) between trans/gender-variant women and cis-gendered men as the same or similar to the mechanics of transmission risk between cis-gendered men.

Given the association of HIV with socioeconomic marginalization, it is not surprising that trans/gender-variant women of color and MSM of color have much higher HIV seroprevalence than white trans/gender-variant women and white MSM. However, even comparing trans/gender-variant women of color and MSM of color reveals that the HIV seroprevalence *rate* tends to be higher among trans/gender-variant women of color (Centers for Disease Control and Prevention 2015b). Nonetheless, there are overall larger *numbers* of MSM of color who are infected with HIV (Centers for Disease Control and Prevention 2015a) because the general population of MSM of color is larger than the general population of trans/gender-variant women of color.

The MSM/WSW category is in contrast to the queer or trans discourses in critical academic research praxis, which emphasize the importance of queer or trans identity as a social vector of both marginalization and agency. However, the emphasis on queer or trans identity also elides those individuals who may identify as heterosexual or who refuse to identify in terms of sexual orientation and yet engage in at least some same-sex behavior. Also, in specific critical academic frameworks that favor intersectional analysis, other identity vectors such as race and class might be taken into consideration to determine overall privilege. For, obviously, a poverty-class, African American, cis-gendered, heterosexual-identified man and a middle-class, white, cis-gendered, homosexual-identified man would experience different forms of oppression and privilege even if both engaged in *same-sex* behavior. And although both public health praxis and critical academic praxis will also utilize the acronym *LGBT* at times, there are particular tensions in the use of this term between the two praxes. Public health emphasizes *LGBT* behavior often vastly devoid of sociopolitical movement contexts while critical academia often emphasizes identity politics and the association of the term *LGBT* with sociopolitical movements.

In my own empirical research on low-income heroin-, crack-, and cocaine-using African American and Latina (anatomically female/female-assigned at birth) women, I refer to the category "women who have sex with women and men" (WSWM). I found that although a majority had female primary relationship partners, and many engaged in sex with men for drugs and/or money, none identified as queer or lesbian (Hwahng and Ompad 2012). A couple of participants identified as "aggressives" and a few utilized the term *bisexual* to describe their behavior but not their identity. Several women also stated that they had been paid by men to have sex with other women in conjunction with trading sex with men, such as the men observing and/or participating in the female same-sex activity. I was also struck that many of the women with female primary relationship partners also expressed or exhibited gender-variant identities and/ or behaviors and they thanked me after the interview because this was the only or one of the few times they had ever had the opportunity to discuss or reflect on their sexual orientation or gender identity in their lifetimes. It is disconcerting that the women of color at the time of their interviews ranged from thirty-nine to fifty-seven years old and had few to no prior opportunities for reflection on their sexuality or gender expression. This is in stark contrast to the multitude of opportunities often available to anatomically female/female-assigned-at-birth students in higher education settings. It was also unclear to me if these research participants identified as women by choice or because they had no time or space for dialogue or reflection about their gender identity and therefore iden- tified as "women" as a default category. This points to the heterosexualization and normativization that occurs among poverty-class anatomically female/ female-assigned-at-birth people of color when research scientists only consider heterosexual behavior noteworthy for HIV/STI risk (because of the focus on the mechanics of disease transmission). It may also be the case that poverty-class anatomically female/female-assigned-at-birth people (and even those who are transmasculine/masculine-of-center) are conditioned to identify as "women" in order to receive health and social services. Clearly, within the highly patriarchal context of the low-income illicit drug–using social economy, the term *WSW* can signify many different types of people, practices, and constraints. Yet nuanced investigation of the WSW category has *not* been a focus or priority of public health research praxis, possibly because *WSW* is not a research population that has proven itself to be highly fundable.

## CONCLUSION

While public health praxis concerns itself with effective and improved health care, it does so by establishing "scientific rigor, objectivity, and rationalism" as opposed to a politics that cannot be scientifically proven (table 12.1, com- parison 16).[7] However, public health praxis is not set up to effectively measure socio-structural-political causes or effects on health, and the deployment of scientific rationalism often interferes with other types of logic that could lead to more productive collaborations. While critical academic research praxis is clearer on the generation of intellectual knowledge for both intellectual interest and sociopolitical transformation, it is limited by the available resources to con- duct comprehensive and methodical research among the most severely socio- economically marginalized populations. In addition, many critical academicians are unable to read and integrate data generated by applied fields such as public health that have conducted comprehensive research among socioeconomically marginalized populations. Thus, they cannot integrate this knowledge into their scholarship. Public health research scientists, on the other hand, could greatly benefit from exposure to critical academic research and theories to guide their study design and inform their conclusions. However, it is difficult for me at this present moment to imagine public health research scientists taking time out of the grant-funding, finding-dissemination, and publication-generating mill to learn and understand a considerable body of important critical academic texts/concepts.[8]

Although I cannot give definitive suggestions at this point in time on how to impact the knowledge production of biopower within public health and critical academic research praxes, as an initial step I have provided an examination of the gaps between the two praxes that, if cross-fertilized, could lead to powerful collaborations toward social transformation. Since it appears that many critical academics are more clearly invested in social transformation, with the understanding that only through social transformation can optimal health be achieved for all, it is perhaps up to them to initiate closures of and bridges between the gaps I have elucidated in this chapter as avenues to reorganize and recirculate biopower in public health. The critical academic fields of biopolitics and bioethics may prove to be highly productive in this regard.

I also would like to suggest that the field of women of color feminism may be highly generative by providing frameworks to examine how the intersectionalities of structural and other oppressions operate in order to construct a trans activist and sociopolitical movement that truly serves all trans/gender-variant people, including those who are the most socioeconomically marginalized. In Beth Richie's excellent synopsis of the institutionalization and bureaucratization of the anti-violence-against-women movement, she remarks that this trajectory has most benefited privileged cis-gendered women, whereas poverty-class African American cis-gendered women are still underserved. In essence, the "movement" was lost in order for the privileged to win benefits from the "mainstream" (Richie 2012, 65–98). Given that this institutionalization was also funded by U.S. tax dollars, I am critical of a similar trajectory in which the institutionalization of a trans/gender-variant health (and by extension a trans/gender-variant sociopolitical) movement would focus only on "easy wins" that benefit the socioeconomically privileged.[9] Going "beyond hetero/homo normativities" is a central focus of this edited volume, and I support neither a "beyond" that reifies a *transnormativity* focused on socioeconomically privileged trans/gender-variant people nor a *transgender nationalism* that imagines a new space of "possibility" and "freedom" for "upstanding" trans/gender-variant citizens based on shared privilege and mainstream acceptance.

Public health research praxis points out that the majority of trans/gender-variant people in the United States may actually be low-income trans/gender-variant women of color (Herbst et al. 2008; Hwahng et al. 2012; Hwahng and Nuttbrock 2014). In many metropolitan areas in the United States, immigrant trans Latinas not only comprise a large portion of the trans/gender-variant women population (Bazargan and Galvan 2012; Cerezo et al. 2014; Hwahng et al. 2012; Pinto et al. 2008; Rhodes et al. 2013) but a sizable portion of these immigrant trans Latinas are also undocumented (Bazargan and Galvan 2012; Cerezo et al. 2014; Hwahng et al. 2012).[10] Thus, in adapting the critiques from the INCITE! Women of Color against Violence collective (2006), what would it look like to build a trans/gender-variant sociopolitical/health movement that *centers* the most vulnerable trans/gender-variant people? This would be a trans/gender-variant sociopolitical/health movement worth fighting for, one that would merit the bridging of gaps and the recirculation and reorganization of biopower.

## NOTES

I acknowledge Yolanda Martínez-San Miguel, Sarah Tobias, Mel Michelle Lewis, and the anonymous peer reviewers for feedback and support on this book chapter.

1. For instance, during my postdoctoral fellowship I participated in a research study totaling over three million dollars examining a variety of health outcomes and risk factors among trans/gender-variant women in NYC. These financial resources allowed our research team to comprehensively map NYC and employ multifaceted participant recruitment strategies, including building relationships with various trans/gender-variant women communities and hiring key informants from these various communities along with research team members also participating in active recruitment. The financial resources also allowed for successful data collection—including renting interview sites in geographic locations that were accessible to many participants and funding multiple team members to conduct interviews during times in which participants were available (including daytimes, evenings, as well as weekends).

2. In this chapter, *masculinist logic* is defined as approaching social phenomena through a highly linear and reductionist focus that greatly privileges "behavior," fails to intersect behavior thoroughly with social and political contexts, unreflexively accepts scientific objectivity and rationalism as "truth" without question, and naturalizes hierarchization, corporatization, and industrial-complexification as structures necessary for the promotion of health.

3. Because of my cross-training I was able to adapt the "developmental homosexuality" concept in Kulick's study to Public Health Studies—creating a "developmental androphilia" model informed by high rates of adolescent gender-related abuse that was found among trans/gender-variant women of color (Hwahng and Nuttbrock 2014). However, this type of adaptation across the praxes is extremely rare. There is thus a vast divide, which may appear insurmountable, between public health and critical academic research praxes.

4. Indeed, the notion of "health" is almost viewed as a commodity separate from other components in a lived experiential cosmology although, granted, there is some public health research that examines the intersection of, say, housing and health, or the environment and health. Yet the "solutions" concluded from such findings that reveal associations or even causal pathways are still often steeped within the various already established industrial complexes and invariably stop short of calling for or contributing to actual social transformation.

5. Interestingly enough, health data does not disaggregate in similar patterns among Asians in the United States, and there are no Asian groups that are measured as particularly vulnerable to HIV or specific forms of illicit drug use. This is most likely due to the often much higher socioeconomic status of many Asian communities, due to patterns of U.S. immigration that greatly favor more privileged Asians entering into the United States, even those who are undocumented (Mehta 2014). For instance, Kang and colleagues (2003) indicate that individuals from China would have to pay $35,000 to $50,000 (and adjusting for inflation these numerical sums may be markedly higher at this present moment) to enter the United States without documents and would have the capacity to garner these funds among their social networks. In contrast, access to this amount of funding is vastly different from the funding access of many undocumented Mexicans in the United States.

6. The term *cis-gendered men* refers to men who are anatomically-male and were assigned male at birth.

7. For examples of Native American public health research that refer to sociopolitical concepts such as decolonization, see Balsam et al. 2004; Duran and Walters 2004; Simoni et al. 2004; Simoni et al. 2006; Walters 1997; Walters et al. 2011.

8. It is noteworthy that while, in critical academia, there is a field of "Science and Technology Studies" that has developed to examine specific phenomena within the medical and health fields, there is no counterpart in which a public health field is devoted to studying critical academia or even critical academicians. There have been studies from time to time that examine experiences of faculty (even LGBT faculty), and currently, a study is being conducted by researchers at the University of Georgia examining mental health outcomes and experiences among LGBT faculty of color (Singh 2014). Nonetheless, a handful of these studies does not constitute a field or subfield of research. Since public health research praxis is more concerned with empirical reductionism and fails to incorporate other aspects of critical thought such as reflexivity, this praxis is often only focused on researching socioeconomically marginalized communities through an empirical research agenda. Thus, this praxis has been unable to make comparisons or linkages between, say, the health of marginalized communities of color and the health of professionalized people of color, and what linking similar or dissimilar patterns of health outcomes could reveal for social transformation.

9. A similar tendency occurs in the provision of services for trans/gender-variant children, since the so-called improvement of services for children tends to benefit the privileged (Green 2012). While more services are being provided for mostly white, privileged trans/gender-variant children, there appears to be no specific services available for poverty-class trans/gender-variant children of color, especially those mired within government bureaucratic child welfare systems, such as the NYC Administration for Children's Services.

10. In New York City immigrant trans Latinas not only appear to be the *largest* group of trans/gender-variant women of color, but the vast *majority* of them are also undocumented (Hwahng et al. 2012).

## REFERENCES

Appadurai, Arjun. 1990. "Disjuncture and Difference in the Global Cultural Economy." *Theory, Culture & Society* 7: 295–310.

Balsam, Kimberly F., Bu Huang, Karen C. Fieland, Jane M. Simoni, and Karina L. Walters. 2004. "Culture, Trauma, and Wellness: A Comparison of Heterosexual and Lesbian, Gay, Bisexual, and Two-Spirit Native Americans." *Cultural Diversity and Ethnic Minority Psychology* 10.3: 287–301.

Bazargan, Moshen, and Frank Galvan. 2012. "Perceived Discrimination and Depression among Low-Income Latina Male-to-Female Transgender Women." *BioMed Central Public Health* 12.663: 1–8.

Bonilla-Silva, Eduardo, and Karen S. Glover. 2004. "'We Are All Americans': The Latin Americanization of Race Relations in the United States." In *The Changing Terrain of Race and Ethnicity*, edited by Maria Krysan and Amanda E. Lewis. 149–183. New York: Russell Sage Foundation.

Bourdieu, Pierre. 1984. *Distinction: A Social Critique of the Judgement of Taste.* Cambridge, MA: Harvard University Press.

Bourgois, Philippe. 2002. *In Search of Respect: Selling Crack in El Barrio.* 2nd ed. New York: Cambridge University Press.

Centers for Disease Control and Prevention. 2015a. *HIV among Gay and Bisexual Men.* Accessed July 17 2015. http://www.cdc.gov/hiv/group/msm/index.html.

———. 2015b. *HIV among Transgender People.* Accessed July 17, 2015. http://www.cdc.gov/hiv/group/gender/transgender/index.html.

Cerezo, Alison, Alejandro Morales, Danielle Quintero, and Stephanie Rothman. 2014. "Trans Migrations: Exploring Life at the Intersection of Transgender Identity and Immigration." *Psychology of Sexual Orientation and Gender Diversity* 1.2:170–180.

Cheng, Sealing. 2010. *On the Move for Love: Migrant Entertainers and the U.S. Military in South Korea.* Philadelphia: University of Pennsylvania Press.

Deren, Sherry, Michele Shedlin, Sung-Yeon Kang, and Dharma E. Cortes. 2011. "HIV Risk and Prevention among Hispanic Immigrants in New York: The Salience of Diversity." *Substance Use & Misuse* 46: 254–263.

Duran, Bonnie, and Karina L. Walters. 2004. "HIV/AIDS Prevention in 'Indian Country': Current Practice, Indigenist Etiology Models, and Postcolonial Approaches to Change." *AIDS Education and Prevention* 16.3: 187–201.

Feldman, Jamie. 2009. "Sex and Gender (Don't) Matter: Understanding Sex between Nontransgender Men and Trans Women and Trans Men." Paper presented at the Conference "Medical Anthropology at the Intersections: Celebrating 50 Years of Interdisciplinarity," Yale University, New Haven, Connecticut.

Giffney, Noreen, and Michael O'Rourke. 2009. *The Ashgate Research Companion to Queer Theory.* Burlington, VT: Ashgate.

Green, Jesse. 2012. "S/He: Parents of Transgender Children Are Faced with a Difficult Decision, and It's One They Have to Make Sooner than They Ever Imagined." *New York* 1–10.

Halberstam, Judith. 1998. *Female Masculinity.* Durham, NC: Duke University Press.

———. 2005. *In a Queer Time and Place: Transgender Bodies, Subcultural Lives.* New York: New York University Press.

Herbst, Jeffrey H., Elizabeth D. Jacobs, Teresa J. Finlayson, Vel S. McKleroy, Mary Spink Neumann, and Nicole Crepaz. 2008. "Estimating HIV Prevalence and Risk Behaviors of Transgender Persons in the United States: A Systematic Review." *AIDS and Behavior* 12.1: 1–17.

Hirsch, Eric. 1995. "Landscape: Between Place and Space." In *The Anthropology of Landscape: Perspectives on Place and Space*, edited by Eric Hirsch and Michael O'Hanlon. 1–30. New York: Oxford University Press.

Hwahng, Sel J. 2013. "Research/Advocacy/Community: Reflections on Asian American Trauma, Heteropatriarchal Betrayal, and Trans/Gender-Variant Health Disparities Research." *Health, Culture and Society* 5.1: 199–229.

Hwahng, Sel J., Bennett Allen, Cathy Zadoretzky, Hannah Barber, Courtney McKnight, and Don Des Jarlais. 2012. "Resiliencies, Vulnerabilities, and Health Disparities among

Low-Income Transgender People of Color at New York City Harm Reduction Programs."
New York: Baron Edmond de Rothschild Chemical Dependency Institute, Mount Sinai
Beth Israel (formerly Beth Israel Medical Center).

Hwahng, Sel J., and Alison J. Lin. 2009. "The Health of Lesbian, Gay, Bisexual, Transgender,
Queer, and Questioning People." In *Asian American Communities and Health: Context,
Research, Policy, and Action,* edited by Chau Trinh-Shevrin, Nadia Islam, and Mariano Rey,
226–282. San Francisco: Jossey-Bass Publishers.

Hwahng, Sel J., Maria Messina, and Antonio Rivera. 2013. "Hangin' in Harlem: Low-Income
Transfeminine and Transmasculine People of Color in New York City." Paper presented at
the Fifth Annual Health Disparities Conference, Teachers College, Columbia University,
New York, March 15–16.

Hwahng, Sel J., and Larry Nuttbrock. 2007. "Sex Workers, Fem Queens, and Cross-Dressers:
Differential Marginalizations and HIV Vulnerabilities among Three Ethnocultural
Male-to-Female Transgender Communities in New York City." *Sexuality Research & Social
Policy* 4.4: 36–59.

———. 2014. "Adolescent Gender-Related Abuse, Androphilia, and HIV Risk among Trans-
feminine People of Color." *Journal of Homosexuality* 61.5: 691–713.

Hwahng, Sel J., and Danielle C. Ompad. 2012. "Gender of Primary Relationship Partners,
Social Contexts, and HIV Risk among Low-Income Drug-Using Women of Color Who
Have Sex with Women and Men in New York City." Paper presented at the Nineteenth
International AIDS Conference, Washington, DC, July 22–27.

INCITE! Women of Color Against Violence. 2006. *Color of Violence: The Incite! Anthology.*
Boston: South End Press.

Kang, Ezer, Bruce D. Rapkin, Carolyn Springer, and Jen Haejin Kim. 2003. "The 'Demon
Plague' and Access to Care among Asian Undocumented Immigrants Living with HIV
Disease in New York City." *Journal of Immigrant and Minority Health* 5.2: 49–58.

Kang, Sung-Yeon, Sherry Deren, Jonny Andia, Hector M. Colon, and Rafaela Robles. 2005.
"Egocentric HIV Risk Networks among Puerto Rican Crack Users in New York and in
Puerto Rico: Impact on Sex Risk Behaviors over Time." *AIDS Education and Prevention*
17.1: 53–67.

Koken, Juline A., David S. Bimbi, and Jeffrey T. Parsons. 2009. "Experiences of Familial
Acceptance-Rejection among Transwomen of Color." *Journal of Family Psychology* 23.6:
853–860.

Kulick, Don. 1998. *Travesti: Sex, Gender, and Culture among Brazilian Transgendered Prostitutes.* Chicago: University of Chicago Press.

Lightman, Alan. 2014. *The Role of the Public Intellectual.* MIT Communications Forum [cited January 15, 2014]. Available from http://web.mit.edu/comm-forum/papers/lightman.html.

Marmot, Michael. 2004. *The Status Syndrome: How Social Standing Affects Our Health and
Longevity.* New York: Owl Books.

Martinot, Steve. 2003. *The Rule of Racialization: Class, Identity, Governance.* Philadelphia:
Temple University Press.

Mehta, Suketa. 2014. "The Superiority Complex: A New Book from the 'Tiger Mom' Seeks to
Explain Why Some Groups Succeed in America and Some Fail. But When Does Cultural
Pride Cross Over into Racism?" *TIME,* February 3, 35–39.

Melendez, Rita M., and Rogério Pinto. 2007. "'It's Really a Hard Life': Love, Gender, and HIV
Risk among Male to Female Transgender Persons." *Culture, Health & Sexuality* 9.3: 233–245.

Mutchler, Matt G., Laura M. Bogart, Marc N. Elliott, Tara McKay, Marika J. Suttorp, and
Mark A. Schuster. 2008. "Psychosocial Correlates of Unprotected Sex without Disclosure

of HIV-Positivity among African-American, Latino, and White Men Who Have Sex with Men and Women." *Archives of Sexual Behavior* 37: 736–747.

Nemoto, Tooru, Don Operario, JoAnne Keatley, Lei Han, and Toho Soma. 2004. "HIV Risk Behaviors among Male-to-Female Transgender Persons of Color in San Francisco." *American Journal of Public Health* 94.7: 1193–1199.

Nuttbrock, Larry, Walter Bockting, Mona Mason, Sel Hwahng, Andrew Rosenblum, Monica Macri, and Jeffrey Becker. 2011. "A Further Assessment of Blanchard's Typology of Homosexual versus Non-Homosexual or Autogynephilic Gender Dysphoria." *Archives of Sexual Behavior* 40: 247–57.

Nuttbrock, Larry, Walter Bockting, Andrew Rosenblum, Sel Hwahng, Mona Mason, Monica Macri, and Jeffrey Becker. 2014. "Gender Abuse and Major Depression among Male-to-Female Transgender Persons: A Prospective Study of Resilience and Vulnerability." *American Journal of Public Health* 104.11:2191–2198.

Nuttbrock, Larry, Sel Hwahng, Walter Bockting, Andrew Rosenblum, Mona Mason, Monica Macri, and Jeffrey Becker. 2009. "Lifetime Risk Factors for HIV/STI Infections among Male-to-Female Transgender Persons." *Journal of Acquired Immune Deficiency Syndromes* 52.3: 417–421.

Nuttbrock, Larry, Sel Hwahng, W. Bockting, A. Rosenblum, M. Mason, M. Macri, and J. Becker. 2010. "Psychiatric Impact of Gender-Related Abuse across the Life Course of Male-to-Female Transgender Persons." *Journal of Sex Research* 47.1:12–23.

Ny, Sokly, and Spencer Nakasako. 1995. *a.k.a. Don Bonus: A Film by Spencer Nakasako & Sokly Ny.* U.S.A.: Center for Asian American Media.

Operario, Don, Tooru Nemoto, Mariko Iwamoto, and Toni Moore. 2011. "Unprotected Sexual Behavior and HIV Risk in the Context of Primary Partnerships for Transgender Women." *AIDS and Behavior* 15.3:674–682.

Organista, Kurt C., Hector Carrillo, and George Ayala. 2004. "HIV Prevention with Mexican Migrants." *Journal of Acquired Immune Deficiency Syndromes* 37 (Supplement 4): 227–239.

Pinto, Rogério M., Rita M. Melendez, and Anya Y. Spector. 2008. "Male-to-Female Transgender Individuals Building Social Support and Capital from within a Gender-Focused Network." *Journal of Gay and Lesbian Social Services* 20.3:203–220.

Pfeffer, Carla. 2012. "Normative Resistance and Inventive Pragmatism: Negotiating Structure and Agency in Transgender Families." *Gender & Society* 26: 574–602.

Prosser, Jay. 1998. *Second Skins: The Body Narratives of Transsexuality.* New York: Columbia University Press.

Reilly, Kathleen H., Alan Neaigus, Samuel M. Jenness, Holly Hagan, Travis Wendel, and Camila Gelpi-Acosta. 2013. "High HIV Prevalence among Low-Income, Black Women in New York City with Self-Reported HIV Negative and Unknown Status." *Journal of Women's Health* 22.9: 745–754.

Rhodes, Scott D., Omar Martinez, Eun-Young Song, Jason Daniel, Jorge Alonzo, Eugenia Eng, Stacy Duck, Mario Downs, Fred R. Bloom, Alex Boeving Allen, Cindy Miller, and Beth Reboussin. 2013. "Depressive Symptoms among Immigrant Latino Sexual Minorities." *American Journal of Health Behavior* 37 (3):404–413.

Richie, Beth E. 2012. *Arrested Justice: Black Women, Violence, and America's Prison Nation.* New York: New York University Press.

Sanchez, Melissa A., George F. Lemp, Carlos Magis-Rodriguez, Enrique Bravo-Garcia, Susan Carter, and Juan D. Ruiz. 2004. "The Epidemiology of HIV among Mexican Migrants and Recent Immigrants in California and Mexico." *Journal of Acquired Immune Deficiency Syndromes* 37 (Supplement 4): 204–214.

Sauer, Carl Ortwin. 1925. "The Morphology of Landscape." *University of California Publications in Geography* 2.2: 19–53.

Sausa, L. A., J. Keatley, and D. Operario. 2007. "Perceived Risks and Benefits of Sex Work among Transgender Women of Color in San Francisco." *Archives of Sexual Behavior* 36.6: 768–777. http://link.springer.com/article/10.1007%2Fs10508–007–9210–3.

Sharkey, Patrick. 2013. *Stuck in Place: Urban Neighborhoods and the End of Progress toward Racial Equality*. Chicago: University of Chicago Press.

Siegel, Karolynn, Eric W. Schrimshaw, Helen-Maria Lekas, and Jeffrey T. Parson. 2008. "Sexual Behaviors of Non-gay Identified Non-disclosing Men Who Have Sex with Men and Women." *Archives of Sexual Behavior* 37: 720–735.

Simoni, Jane M., Shalini Sehgal, and Karina L. Walters. 2004. "Triangle of Risk: Urban American Indian Women's Sexual Trauma, Injection Drug Use, and HIV Sexual Risk Behaviors." *AIDS and Behavior* 8.1: 33–45.

Simoni, Jane M., Karina L. Walters, Kimberly F. Balsam, and Seth B. Meyers. 2006. "Victimization, Substance Use, and HIV Risk Behaviors among Gay/Bisexual/Two-Spirit and Heterosexual American Indian Men in New York City." *American Journal of Public Health* 96.12: 2240–2245.

Singh, Anneliese. 2014. Personal communication. In possession of the author.

Stryker, Susan, and Aren Z. Aizura, ed. 2013. *The Transgender Studies Reader 2*. New York: Routledge.

Walters, Karina L. 1997. "Urban Lesbian and Gay American Indian Identity: Implications for Mental Health Service Delivery." *Journal of Gay and Lesbian Social Services* 6.2: 43–65.

Walters, Karina L., Ramona Beltran, Tessa Evans-Campbell, and Jane M. Simoni. 2011. "Keeping Our Hearts from Touching the Ground: HIV/AIDS in American Indian and Alaska Native Women." *Women's Health Issues* 21.6S: S261–S265.

Wheeler, Darrell P., Jennifer L. Lauby, Kai-lih Liu, Laurens G. Van Sluytman, and Christopher Murrill. 2008. "A Comparative Analysis of Sexual Risk Characteristics of Black Men Who Have Sex with Men or with Men and Women." *Archives of Sexual Behavior* 37: 697–707.

# 13 · STICK FIGURES AND LITTLE BITS

## Toward a Nonbinary Pedagogy

A. FINN ENKE

"The first thing we learn in Gender and Women's Studies 101 is to question the gender binary: critique the binary. We learn that anyone can exist anywhere along the spectrum. And then we walk out of our GWS classrooms and face these bathroom signs that say 'men' and 'women' with these binary stick figures. Why can't we learn how to change the signs, if we're so good at critiquing the binary?"

—College student, *The Quest for Gender Neutral Bathrooms: Trailer* (Film produced by Etonde Awaah)

In 2009 Etonde Awaah, a student in my LGBT Studies Capstone seminar, made a video exploring the relationship between the feminist theory that students learn in class and the "on the ground" commitment to challenging the structures in our built environment that reinforce binary gender normativity and sexist oppressions. Based on interviews with students, faculty, and staff, the film examined the specific terrain of gender-segregated bathrooms and the lack of facilities available for people who may not be comfortable or welcome in gender-designated bathrooms. Awaah's project included screening the video trailer at a department meeting so that the identified problem of bathrooms with stick figure signs could become a pedagogical community matter rather than an issue believed to affect just a few people. In turn, faculty acknowledgment of the need for at least one gender-neutral bathroom constituted a kind of "buy in" that those of us most vested in the issue could utilize to actively challenge the administrative barriers to creating accessible non-gendered bathrooms.

Collaboratively, we designed a solution that provides people across gender expression, ability, and religious identity with safe and accessible bathroom options in the halls of the Gender and Women's Studies department. We successfully created a more equitable environment, but the question remains—as Awaah pointed out—does a "third" bathroom really challenge the binary, or is it just an exception that will always stand apart from the unchanged status quo?

This very question finds its roots in pervasive linguistic practices that bear on bodies as surely as do our built environments. I return to the quote offered in the epigraph and ask what it would mean to "change the signs" if we take language itself as the quintessential sign system. I want to build a transfeminist perspective that can engage linguistic signifiers as a basis for exploring alternatives to normativizing language in the classroom. For example, how might we challenge the work that the ubiquitous use of binary-gendered third-person singular pronouns (*he* or *she*) does to produce binary gender at the expense of gender variation? Though gender-neutral pronouns such as *they, ze,* and *em* have gained increasing circulation, they may not do enough, and it is pedagogically as well as ethically valuable to push this further.

In this chapter, I reflect on what pronouns are doing in the classroom and offer a trans pedagogical approach to linguistic engagement. Many educators currently find themselves responding to increasing demands to verbally acknowledge a broader spectrum of gender identities and at the very least to use the pronouns that people request. The structures of language and often the structures of our classes inhibit our ability to comfortably acknowledge all kinds of human variation. Pronouns and gender come to the fore not because they are more important than, say, race or age but because every time reference is made to someone else, that reference imposes a gender category onto that person. Virtually every conversation, regardless of the topic, will assign gender to others multiple times. Simultaneously, conversations and references—by gendering or misgendering—have the power to affirm or refuse the ability of some persons to participate as speaking subjects and even to exist in language at all. For some people, pronoun use can make a class stressful and even impossible—and yet, sometimes, engaging the question directly equally threatens to shut people down. A transpedagogical approach seeks to invite everyone into the process of linguistic creativity and agency while minimizing the stresses that accompany privileged trans and feminist knowledge as well as widespread ignorance of trans and gender variation.

Over a decade of addressing this issue both as an educator and as a trans person has convinced me that there is no single or universal "right," "best," or problem-free solution to the pronoun challenge in the classroom. But as educators in contexts that allow extended engagement with challenging issues, we also have the opportunity to invite playful ways of entering language in order to learn more about the power of everyday communications. The classroom context itself, with the help and feedback of students and other educators, has led me to explore the possibility and implications of *nonbinary* pronouns. For example, pronouns could be randomized single syllables, or colors, or come from any field of objects or letters that don't instantiate or inscribe binary perception. If one limitation of gender-neutral pronouns is that they don't do enough to undermine the assumptions of universal binary gender, how might we further invite people's imagination into the sign system that is language? Doing so has the potential to complicate the binary often posed between trans* people and people who do not appear to be transgender, and to simultaneously create more room for people to have complicated gender histories and/or futures and/or present embodiments. More broadly, this can facilitate greater flexibility with language, teach about the relationship between language, agency, and identity, and increase creative confidence and openness to learning while decreasing the intimidation that accompanies the social and political inequities present in every context. In this chapter, I first offer some transfeminist perspective on language and gender, pointing out how this becomes relevant in our classrooms. I then turn to classroom practices and reflect on a decade of trial, error, and transformation in the ways we use little language bits and addresses in learning environments.

## STICK FIGURES AND LITTLE BITS

Before considering classroom practices, I want to put pronouns into perspective by drawing on two related theoretical premises that have enjoyed lasting authority across academic disciplines. First, humans have for millennia granted that language itself is a sign system; like visual symbols, words are symbols that function as referents.[1] A visual symbol such as a stick figure on a bathroom door is meant to reference beings who are far more complex than the symbol itself. Theorists have also recognized that stick figures on bathroom doors have this power because they simultaneously call on or reference an entire social system called binary gender. From a post-structural perspective, the sign and the signified are not separate and autonomous but are mutually imbricated with and constitute each other.[2] In the bathroom sign example, the stick figure is not a static representational entity that simply points to "real" entities outside of itself (males, females; binary gender system), but rather, the signs themselves produce binary gender; the stick figures and the beings they invoke mutually produce one another. Thus, we might well ask how deeply we intend to critique binary gender if we can't change the sign system as well.

Bringing this first premise into consideration with technologies of gender (to use Theresa de Lauretis's term [1987]), scholars and activists have also long granted that language is one of the most powerful mechanisms through which normative gender is produced and reinforced while also stigmatizing gender variation and nonconformity. Feminist efforts to change language enjoyed widespread interest in the 1960s and 1970s when people learned to talk of humankind and people rather than mankind and men. In the midst of multiple social justice movements, many critiqued the way some honorifics (such as *Sir, Dr., Mrs.*) are explicitly designed to inscribe social, occupational, or marital status; some eschewed the honorifics to which they were by race and class "entitled," while others newly acquired the right to use them. Some successfully established alternatives such as *Ms.*

Also around forty years ago, some intentional communities in the United States created alternatives to common pronouns in order to resist the erasures produced by the universalizing use of *he* and *man.* They adopted new third-person singular and plural pronouns; one of the most widespread was the pronoun *co*, taken from the prefix meaning "with." The practice of using *co* expanded recognition that binary gender pronouns themselves are troubling carriers of information that prejudice the reader or hearer of the pronoun; that is, because people—alongside identity categories and codes—have been socialized in structures of sexist, racist, and classist hierarchies, identity-laden pronouns (*he, she*, etc.) make it impossible for people to perceive the third person openly and also interferes with people's ability to represent themselves in their own terms.[3]

Despite these interventions, the relationship between language, knowledge production, gender production, and mastery over third persons goes relatively unquestioned. With little conscious attention to its necessity, many expect third-person singular pronouns to carry one particular kind of information. The smallest bits of language—the parts of speech that are felt to uphold every spoken and written sentence, the parts that are supposed to come "automatically"—may be the most pernicious and powerful of all. To put it bluntly: in English, conventional singular third-person pronouns (*he, she*) act as a technology that produces a whole social order that relentlessly perceives and thinks in binary gender.

If we understand pronouns as signifiers, we might say that binary gender pronouns don't just reflect binary gender, they create, teach, and enforce binary gender. Is there any linguistic necessity for pronouns to confer gender? English speakers don't expect first- or second-person pronouns to ascribe gender. While in some languages (for example, Japanese, Hindi, Bamana) first- and second-person pronouns do ascribe gender, English-speaking cultures communicate fine without this function. English speakers also don't expect the gender of every person in a third-person plural group to be provided; *they* is completely adequate. But most English first-language users are quite attached to the way the third-person singular assigns gender. If gender is so critical in this context of speech, why isn't other information equally critical? Why don't English pronouns impose other kinds of information such as age, rank, race, occupation, nationality, class, ability, or disability status? All these possibilities highlight the way that language and cultural expectations produce each other, and it seems fairly clear that the sole purpose of gendering pronouns is to produce binary gender as a systemic and cultural mechanism of social order.

Recalling the epigraph with which I started, I want to suggest that binary gender pronouns are the stick figures of language, and they are painted onto the subjects and objects of nearly every communication. They are the signs that carelessly tell us who and what someone is, and because they reinforce normative hierarchies, they have the power to permit or deny the third person to enter the conversation as a self-representing first person. What's more, the structure of English appears to require speakers to make and articulate a binary gender assessment of every person spoken about. This virtually always takes place without the explicit consent of the person being spoken about. Even when individuals request a pronoun that is appropriate to their gender identities, all the power to affirm or refuse those identities in speech lies solely with the speaker.

All of this is critically relevant in the classroom, particularly if we believe that all people belong in the room as speaking subjects in the first, second, and third person. Educational equity demands that we pay attention to the ways that misgendering (referring to people with pronouns that undermine their gender identities) creates significant educational barriers. Gendering practices (and therefore misgendering practices) take place constantly in our institutions. Every day trans and gender-nonconforming students of color and white students struggle to stay in school as professors fail to address them by name and with their preferred pronouns; as some professors also make transphobic comments in class and during office hours; and as administrators often fail to acknowledge these matters as violences that put students at high risk of attrition and that increase the likelihood of further violences (Beemyn 2005; Beemyn and Rankin 2011; Kosciw et al 2010). These stresses can make it impossible for students to stay in school, and much less excel. As an educator I have a certain responsibility to create an equitable environment, but it is not pedagogically sound to simply hand out directives as though I can wield my power to make students comply with my version of justice.

While classrooms are rarely if ever "safer spaces" for everyone, I seek practices that allow each student to feel invited into language rather than feeling erased by language. In the space of the classroom that we create together, who can speak in the first person, or be addressed in the second person, or exist in the third person? As a transqueersbian with my own share of gender trouble, I know intimately that we need to change language in order to exist in language. Along with disability and performance studies scholar Petra Kuppers, I am motivated to find ways "to challenge representation and the processes through which we make meaning out of what we see" (2000, 129). If pronouns typically impose normative assumptions about others, how might we subvert the "representational certainties" of gendering language in the classroom? Beyond critique and subversion, how can we restore hope in self-representation and connection, particularly for and with those most in need of substantiating our queer or trans-ing (and disabled, aged, raced, and classed) embodiments?

## GENDER NEUTRAL BITS

Language is changing, and the concept of gender-neutral pronouns in English is gaining some traction in some circles. Examples include *they, them, their; ze, hir, hir,* or *zir; em, em, em's; per, per, per's; xe, xem, xir;* or using a person's name instead of pronouns. And yet, as trans and genderqueer people are all too well aware, not all pronoun choices are equally usable by others. Learning to use the third-person singular *they* fluently, for example, takes most people a lot of practice, and many people are unwilling to make the effort. It is irrelevant that English usage guides for hundreds of years have allowed the "singular *they*" because the barriers to gender-neutral pronouns go far beyond ideas of "correct grammar." As long as trans and genderqueer embodiments are stigmatized or unimaginable, and as long as gender-neutral pronouns are unappreciated in the vast majority of contexts, using them may feel like aggressively speaking a foreign (queer) language in otherwise polite company. To practice *they* or other neutral pronouns requires a political and artistic commitment to change language so that all pronoun choices are equally present and usable.

While grammar implicates everyone in making or changing gender, the challenge is not simply one of grammar, because grammar is imbricated in the way people perceive. As Jack Halberstam and others have pointed out, a binary gender lens veils gender variation and multiplicity not simply by being rigid (there is only male and female) but also by being flexible enough to incorporate those who appear to exceed the boundaries (Butler 1996; Halberstam 1998). No matter how queer a person may appear, it is always possible to interpret their embodiment through a binary lens and assign one of two sex/genders upon them; and whether someone is accommodated or punished, they are punished or accommodated as ultimately male or female.

This relentlessly binary lens limits the effectiveness of neutral pronouns in two ways. First, there is a tendency to reserve neutral pronouns such as *they* only for known trans and genderqueer people, as if all non-trans genders are properly named by *she* or *he*. Using *they* only to reference trans* embodiments secures binary normativity and the not-ever-trans stability of *she* and *he* (Towle and Morgan 2006). Second, people who are not comfortable using neutral pronouns to refer to those of us who request them consistently revert back to the pronoun associated with the birth-assigned sex they assume they see; it's as though neutral pronouns signal an absence that must be filled in with a "real" gender, that is, a gender fixed by binary notions of anatomy and identity. Under the circumstances, gender-neutral pronouns cannot always substantiate trans and gender-queer embodiments and, much less, complicate the binaries posed between male and female and between trans and not-trans.

Perhaps our pronoun choices should get to be more complicated. People's gender identities are social and situational as well as personal, and thus anything but static. As Leslie Feinberg has often explained:

> Referring to me as "she/her" is appropriate, particularly in a non-trans setting in which referring to me as "he" would appear to resolve the social contradiction between my birth sex and gender expression and render my transgender expression invisible. I like the gender neutral pronoun "ze/hir" because it makes it impossible to hold on to gender/sex/sexuality assumptions about a person you're about to meet or you've just met. And in an all trans setting, referring to me as "he/him" honors my gender expression in the same way that referring to my sister drag queens as "she/her" does. (qtd. in Tyroler 2006)

Feinberg's response reflects the context-specific process of creating gender, and it acknowledges that different communities "see" and interpret the meaning of gendered embodiments differently. Gendering is a collective process. That doesn't mean it's up to other people. Feinberg is very clear that for Feinberg, the right pronoun is the one that makes hir *transness* most tangible *in the given context*. In fact, Feinberg wants pronouns to do this instructional work most of all in non-trans settings where people are likely to forget or not to know that Feinberg is not simply male but trans. Other trans and gender-nonconforming people have other identities and needs, including for pronouns to reflect a male or female identity.

At the same time, using non-gendering pronouns should not have to negate people's complex gender identities. If all people used *ze*, for example, it would still be possible to acknowledge everyone's unique gender identity, and those identities would not be reduced to the binary stick figure pronouns currently expected. Critically, whether or not people's personal pronouns are consistent across time and space, they involve social as well as personal valences. That is to say, as long as pronouns are going to ascribe gender, most people need those pronouns to do the work of affirming the right gender. I mean to emphasize that we cannot pronounce our gender identities by ourselves; it is always others who have the power to speak or refuse to speak our correct pronouns. In short, the relational and situational dimension of gender belies the possibility of a single or static social gender identity, and thus our pronoun vernacular may need to be equally complex.

## FROM NEUTRAL TO NONBINARY BITS IN THE CLASSROOM

In the discussion-based classroom, a precondition of people's participation is to address each other by name, with correct pronouns, and at least an effort to use correct pronunciation. To do this simple thing requires a lot of undoing. Most people in the classroom are likely to make assumptions about other people's gender and therefore pronouns. Class rosters notoriously get names wrong and relying on them leads to mis-naming and mis-gendering that can make it impossible for students to stay present. Responding to the infinite variety of ways people navigate gendered desires, expressions, and norms, current wisdom suggests that we should *never* assume we can perceive a person's gender identity, personal pronouns, or particular and contextual needs regarding name and pronouns. This along with a desire to acknowledge gender variation and trans existence has led to one method of trying to make classes more welcoming to trans, gender-nonconforming, and genderqueer students, and that is to begin each course by asking people to introduce themselves with their pronoun preferences as well as their names. As someone who regularly experiences misgendering, I often imagine a world in which everyone regularly asks everyone else their pronoun preferences (and often, not just once).

And yet, we may be placing an inappropriate burden on students when we require introductions using names and "personal gender pronouns" (pgp). We must consider that most people still initially find the question threatening, confusing, insulting, perhaps offensive for personal, social, or religious reasons. Pronouns are stressful because trans, gender-creative, gender-nonconforming, and queer identities and expressions remain highly stigmatized. Pronouns are stressful because, in many contexts, ignorance about trans and genderqueer existence is also highly stigmatized. As long as gender nonconformity remains stigmatized, the personal pronoun go-around can be alienating for everyone, and the stakes are high for those who are most vulnerable: trans and gender-nonconforming students of color and white students, those who may not be out or who are wrestling with or in crisis about their gender identity, and those who do not have strong or any support networks. At the same time, as long as ignorance about trans is met with disdain rather than dialogue, the exercise can be silencing rather than illuminating for those who might otherwise appreciate learning about gender. How then can we lay the groundwork that allows all students (regardless of their prior experience with or beliefs about diversity) to be fully present?

We should carefully consider the implications of activities that require students to align themselves with any kind of social category or identity; we can't create the conditions for self-representation simply by asking people for certain kinds of identifying information. The personal pronoun question is not a neutral question with a range of equally valid answers. There is a disparity in perceptions of the quality of information provided by trans and non-trans people. When trans and gender-nonconforming people declare our pronouns and this outs us, we are often criticized for too much self-disclosure; in fact it is not unusual for people to think we are talking about sexual information and even our genitals when we declare our pronouns. Most important, inside and outside the classroom, students are the ones navigating the social repercussions of their responses, and we can't guarantee their personal and institutional safety and well-being.

For all these reasons, before we take it as a given that we must ask, we could develop alternative ways of using language that do not require people to use pronouns in such sensitive ways. Let me again reiterate that countless conversations and pedagogy forums with trans and gender-nonconforming students and educators have taught me that there is no single "preferred" or "best" way to deal with pronouns in the classroom; there are drawbacks and advantages to just about every strategy, and each student and teacher brings a unique set of needs, skills, and perspectives to the issue. Nevertheless, I believe it is possible simultaneously to reduce the stress that many people feel around pronouns and potential mis-gendering and to invite people to engage language and self-expression creatively in ways that honor each person's belonging in the learning community. This could also be an invitation to enter nonbinary imagination.

## PLAY

I have tried a number of different techniques over the years to invite new insights about pronouns and subjectivities, as well as to help make educational environments more welcoming to trans and gender-nonconforming people.[4] In 2007 and 2009 in my Transgender in Historical Perspective class (a large lecture with a TA and discussion sections), I asked students to try for the first five weeks to universally use *they, ze,* or other forms of gender-neutral pronouns—for each other, for our authors, and whenever referring to another in the third person. I called it an experiment and asked them simply to observe whatever happened.

Many found it worthwhile because it helped them become aware of how constantly language imposes binary gender on to people and in our cognition, and they experienced how challenging it can be to create a new linguistic practice. This led many to feel that it is critical to change language. Students talked about learning new languages; some ESL speakers talked about stressful experiences trying to master gendering in English pronouns. Some also explained that they realized how attached they were to "their own" pronoun, and also to a socially secure gender identity; some admitted to feeling a range of discomforts around people thinking they might be transgender.

Both years, however, a significant number of people protested the entire exercise. They identified as non-trans women, they felt that their own hardwon pride in being women was being denied, and they insisted on the right to be called *she*. For them, feminine pronouns were statements of their identities; one commented, "as a feminist, I am not a 'they.' I'm proud to be a 'she.'" Perhaps the experience helped them understand the violence of misgendering, though none expressed interest in trying to solve that broader problem. Some trans students also spoke about their desire to have others use their personally appropriate pronouns; as one transitioning student said, "This class is actually my only chance of getting to have people use my correct pronoun." Several weeks in, students decided collectively to try to honor people's self-statements about pronouns. This had mixed results. Some students made self-statements in protest of neutrals; many students assumed that only trans students would need to state their personal pronouns. Some students continued to practice the neutrals *they* or *ze* for students who did not specify their pronouns, and others made gendered pronoun assumptions. Although many students were making an effort to respect each other, the perceived use and misuse of pronouns sometimes became fuel for polarization and mistrust.

The lesson I learned from the process—not news to those who practice feminist and radical pedagogy—is that it is very difficult to create an open and respectful learning environment when *anyone* feels that their identity or beliefs or worldview are refused or stigmatized. Because the exercise felt to some simply like "turning the tables" and creating a new unfair hierarchy, we lost an opportunity to learn together and build a diversity that was truly inclusive of each individual.

A few months into 2009, I learned about a grade school in Sweden that used the Swedish word for "friend" as everyone's pronoun—in fact as the only pronoun people could use for each other. (This was three years before Sweden officially created a new gender-neutral pronoun, *hen*.) I shared this with my students, and I saw their faces light up as if I had been talking about puppies. Thinking about *friend* as a pronoun opened up their imagination in a pleasing way.

The following semester, I offered the pronoun *friend* to my students in all my classes, and they took to it readily. On the first day, when I explained the pronoun *friend* and suggested they try it for each other and all authors, they smiled gamely. Over weeks, I witnessed many develop ease using *friend*; challenges with written grammar conventions (*friend* is also a noun and doesn't automatically conjugate) were not insurmountable. Most discussion sections picked it up quickly, and although not every student fully got the hang of it, neither did anyone raise concerns about erasures, political correctness, or misgendering. Some students felt that the word itself—and using it with each other—helped foster a friendlier environment in which they could work things out together. *Friend* thus came to function in an entirely new way as a part of speech that was still connected to its more common connotations. Students liked being referred to as *friend*, and they did not miss the gendering that standard pronouns accomplish. Since then, I have suggested using this in all my large classes and lectures regardless of the topic, and students take to it rather well.

This experience showed me the benefits of circumventing the charged and intimidating "political correctness" factor, as well as the well-founded fear of misgendering, and replacing it with a more truly respectful and egalitarian pedagogical practice. The exercise was limited, however, in that it did not compel students to experiment more actively with parts of speech or to reflect much on their own desires to exceed conventional language in order to communicate better. In short, using *friend* was my idea, not theirs, and it was so simple that it did not draw enough attention to the arbitrary and consequential aspects of structures of speech.

I wanted an exercise that reinforced the fact that, grammatically speaking, a pronoun is simply a placeholder, and thus, pronouns can theoretically be derived in any way at all and can carry any kind of information or no information. Simultaneously, I wanted people to exercise personal input in the pronouns used. Additionally, a true trans-pedagogy would invite people to become comfortable with change. These goals led me to develop a pronoun exercise that allows each person more creative latitude in pronoun selection and offers a range of nonbinary modalities. I call it "what's our category?" and have used it in every small class (up to twenty-five students) regardless of topic.

It goes like this: I ask students to write their names on large name tags placed on their desks and to use these every class period. On the first day of the semester, I request that we don't make assumptions about anyone else's gender identity or history and briefly explain some of the pedagogical, social, and personal issues involved with pronoun use. I give a little grammar lesson about the linguistic functions (placeholders) and social functions (gender assignment) of common pronouns. I suggest that for our authors and people outside the room we can try to use *friend* or *they* or other non-gendering pronouns and later we'll reflect on how that feels. For us in the classroom, however, I suggest that we each choose our own personal pronoun each week from a category that students create. Each person writes their chosen pronoun in large letters on their name tag.

At the beginning of each week, I invite students to choose a category from a wide-open field. "Animals" is often one of the first categories that classes think of on the first day. Individuals can then choose anything within animals, and if they need to, they can mess with the category itself. "Open" or "no category" is also a possible choice, but every class has always preferred to choose a specific and new category each class period. They clearly take pleasure in it: they've thought of categories as diverse as colors, flowers, trees, geological formations, weather, modes of transportation, condiments, tools, expletives, mythical creatures, cartoon characters, herbs and spices, genres of music, tools, punctuation, ono-matopoeia, "things that scare you," and "things that make you happy," to name some examples.

Students tend to be egalitarian about everyone getting a chance to make up the category, and they are highly creative when thinking of things within the cat-egories as well. We then take a minute or two for everyone to introduce our-selves by name and personal pronoun. As we speak in class, we may also preface our comments with "I'm (name) and my pronoun today is (pronoun)." Liber-ated from the pressure for the pronoun to reflect some deep abiding and true aspect of their identity, their pronoun choices are often related to their moods and needs of the moment or to a pleasure or memory or simply the sound of the pronoun itself. While most classes have enjoyed it when multiple people hap-pen to choose the same pronoun, in one course students made sure their own choices were unique. They explained to me, "Since this is the first time we have ever been allowed to actually choose our own, it's an opportunity to make it per-sonally relevant." Students occasionally subvert the exercise, for example some have chosen things that don't obviously "fit," and a few have chosen gestures rather than or in addition to sounds. In these ways, their pronouns successfully circumvent the binary and dichotomizing habits of sighted language.

It works, and here's why: above all, it is fun. It can be fun in part because it is not politically overdetermined and does not invite language policing or inse-curity. Everyone has a truly open choice about how personal they might or might not make it, but it is never as loaded or dangerous as gender. It also seems that people tend to think of things that make them feel good in some way, and most categories turn out to contain an infinite number of such things.

Perhaps for those reasons, the exercise also facilitates students' engagement with each other. Students enjoy uttering each other's individualized pronouns so much that they create opportunities to reference each other. It seems to fos-ter an inclusive impulse as well. One seminar was uncharacteristically stymied to choose a category on the last day of the semester; ultimately they decided to make one shared pronoun that everyone would use, and they did it by writing down the first letter of each person's name and then figuring out how to arrange the letters into a pronounceable eight-syllable word.

"What's our category?" also works because it undoes the will for diagnostic mastery. No one is expecting themselves or others to "look like" their chosen pronouns, and students offer and take each other's pronoun explanations at face value and as expressions of the moment. There is evidence that they understand

and value the release from the pressures of the diagnostic gaze. In each class, although I don't emphasize it, students take greater care (in writing as well as speech) to refer to our authors and people outside the classroom with *friend* or *they*. One student explained to me, "Well, we get to choose our pronouns every day, but our authors don't, so it feels like just calling them 'friend' gives them a little more respect. I feel that's important even if I totally don't agree with the author and don't like what they wrote." It seems that students come to experience the habits of binary pronouns as potentially violent; through an exercise that releases them from this violence by providing a nonviolent alternative, they make friends with not-knowing.

Recently, I've also been offering this first-letter practice: a person's pronoun is created by taking the first letter or sound of their name followed by the vowel sound *ee*. The pronoun declension used for me, for example, would be *fe, fe, fe's*. Frank might love *fre's* pronoun because it's pronounced free. Harold and Harriet would both get the pronoun *he, he, he's*. Jonah, Jane, and Jonathan all get *je, je, je's*. This has potential because it makes pronouns do what they are supposed to do, and do it even *better*, in both writing and speech: the pronoun unmistakably refers back to and signals the person earlier named. Moreover, such pronouns carry no social information other than harking back to a person's name. Promising as this is, it invariably begs the question: why not just always use people's names instead of third-person singular pronouns? For my pedagogical purposes, it lacks the opportunity to engage language and sign systems creatively, but it is worth a try now and then.

None of these classroom practices are a substitute for learning and teaching the arts of gender-neutral and nonbinary pronouns. Students in fact have identified that their greatest immediate need is to have opportunities to *practice* using varied pronouns. Recently a student in an advanced undergraduate seminar intervened in our expansive category exercise saying, "I love everyone choosing these creative pronouns, but I really need practice to be totally fluent with the pronouns that my friends and others are actually asking for. Why don't we practice using a different pronoun each week from ones people use?" After all these years of trying to teach alternate pronouns, I was bowled over by the simplicity of the suggestion: if we're going to learn a new language, let's treat this like a language class. Each week we choose a single pronoun from a long list, we make up a practice sentence showing every declension, and then we use only that pronoun in every sentence, for every author and person in the class. We are all growing more fluent and therefore more able to honor everyone's gender identities.

Addressing pronouns at all is a single step in changing the many institutional violences that make it hard for trans, queer, and gender-nonconforming students of color and white students to be in school. Nevertheless, the lessons I have learned from watching students and others create and learn pronouns are worth taking to heart, because they can even guide us in other challenging contexts. Here are a few:

- we can use language creatively and—if we are not afraid—we can still understand each other;
- it feels really good to respect each other's choices;
- it feels really good to have our own choices recognized and respected;
- we can make up new words and people understand their meaning very well;
- pronouns can change and it is not a crisis;
- it is deeply important that every person be recognized in and through language;
- when people are addressed they can become full participants in the conversation.

Creating and learning a new language does not happen automatically or simply because one believes it should happen. It takes work, it takes practice, and it takes a certain kind of courage. The process will inevitably transform one's own views and one's prior attachments. There are those who say it isn't worth it, or that it's someone else's job, or that it's not that important. All the more reason then, for feminist and queer theorists, scholars, and practitioners who have long critiqued gender norms and binaries to model a more flexible and respectful language. We discover in the process that it is easy to critique stick figure representations of humans, but it is quite another thing to "change the signs" in practice. Changing the sign is challenging precisely because it is never about just a few people who can stand out as exceptions to the status quo. Changing the signs, and changing our language, ultimately involves everyone.

## NOTES

1. Saussure (1916), one of the founders of structural semiotics in the late nineteenth and early twentieth century, is generally credited with theorizing the "signifier" and "signified" in which the sign directly refers to that which it signifies.
2. Jacques Derrida launched the post-structuralist critique that neither signifier nor signified is a static or autonomous entity and thus a direct relationship between them is impossible. This poststructuralism also has at its core a project of deconstructing binary oppositions. See particularly *Of Grammatology* and *Writing and Difference*, both first published in 1967 (Derrida 1980, 1998).
3. The Fellowship of Intentional Communities publication, *Communities*, has recently made an editorial decision to replace *co* in print with *they*, based on the wider use and awareness of *they*.
4. What takes place in the classroom is, of course, not extricable from the larger culture, and this has shifted markedly since 2005 toward an increased awareness of trans existence and an

increase in the percentage of people who are already fluent in and open to gender-neutral and non-gendering grammars.

## REFERENCES

Beemyn, Genny. 2005. "Making Campuses More Inclusive of Transgender Students." *Journal of Gay and Lesbian Issues in Education* 3.1: 77–89.

Beemyn, Genny, and Susan Rankin. 2011. *The Lives of Transgender People.* New York: Columbia University Press.

Butler, Judith. 1996. *Gender Trouble: Feminism and the Subversion of Identity.* New York: Routledge.

de Lauretis, Theresa. 1987. *Technologies of Gender: Essays on Theory, Film and Fiction.* Bloomington: Indiana University Press.

Derrida, Jacques. 1980. *Of Grammatology.* Baltimore: Johns Hopkins University Press.

———. 1998. *Writing and Difference.* Chicago: University of Chicago Press.

Halberstam, Judith. 1998. *Female Masculinity.* Durham, NC: Duke University Press.

Kosciw, Joseph G., Emily A. Greytak, Elizabeth M. Diaz, and Mark J. Bartkiewicz. 2010. *The 2009 National School Climate Survey: The Experiences of Lesbian, Gay, Bisexual, and Transgender Youth in Our Nation's Schools.* New York: Gay, Lesbian and Straight Education Network.

Kuppers, Petra. 2000. "Toward the Unknown Body: Stillness, Silence, and Space in Mental Health Settings." *Theater Topics* 10.2: 129–143.

Saussure, Ferdinand de. 1983. *Course in General Linguistics.* 1916. London: Fontana/Collins.

Towle, Evan, and Lynn Morgan. 2006. "Romancing the Transgender Native: Rethinking the Use of the 'Third Gender' Concept." In *The Transgender Studies Reader,* edited by Susan Stryker and Stephen Whittle, 1:666–684. New York: Routledge.

Tyroler, Jamie. 2006. "Transmissions: Interview with Leslie Feinberg." In *Camp:* Kansas City Anti Violence Project Newsletter, July 28. Accessed October 27, 2013. http://www.campkc.com/campkc-content.php?Page_ID=225.

# CONCLUSION
# TRANS FANTASIZING
## From Social Media to Collective Imagination

YOLANDA MARTÍNEZ-SAN MIGUEL
AND SARAH TOBIAS

Our introduction to this anthology opened with an enumeration of some significant events that relate or resignify how Trans Studies and identities are conceived in U.S. popular culture. A more recent development allows us to explore the links between gender and sexuality. On December 4, 2014, Neda Ulaby wrote a short article for National Public Radio's program *All Tech Considered* entitled "Sapiosexual Seeks Same: A New Lexicon Enters Online Dating Mainstream." In this article Ulaby announces that the online dating site OkCupid has added a new lexicon to enable users to provide more fluid descriptions of their sexual and gender identities. OkCupid's action follows a similar move by social media giant Facebook (mentioned in the introduction to this volume), indicating that mainstream dating sites have now begun to broaden the horizons of identity to better serve the needs of their clientele. Ulaby's article cites Cornell psychology professor Ritch Savin-Williams. "Young people like the idea of fluidity," he says, commenting that this age cohort is much more inclined to transcend gender binaries and recognize the existence of a spectrum of sexual orientations. A particular point of fluidity involves the way in which gender and sexuality tend to be conflated in the case of the dating scene, especially since gender has become central to the definition of sexual orientation.

We would like to take this apparent conflation to reconsider how the essays included in this anthology relate to Queer and Sexuality Studies. We would also like to accept the invitation of our colleague Heather Love to reflect on how some of the essays in this anthology engage in a sustained interrogation of normativity, while others propose a different kind of relationship with notions such as normalcy or the norm. In a recent article, Love (2015) also meditates about the differential meanings of "deviance" and "normativity" in the context of early scholarship in Gay, Lesbian, and Queer Studies in the humanities and in the social sciences. Her work invites scholars interested in Gender and Sexuality Studies to complicate the ways in which normativity and deviance are conceived as theoretical frameworks. These two issues—intellectual genealogy and the concept of normativity—are deeply connected to the work that we are proposing in this anthology.

When we began to imagine this project, we realized that scholars active in the field of Trans Studies were discussing the intersection of identity, gender, and sexual orientation in ways that went far beyond the notions of normativity that were prevalent in Queer and Sexuality Studies during the early 2000s. Their work challenged and transcended typical conceptualizations of heteronormativity and homonormativity, rendering these categories limited in their analytical scope. Yet, unwittingly, in our own desire to break with normativity as a central script, we reiterated a conflation of gender and sexuality that does not take full advantage of the more capacious interrogation of gender end embodiment frequently proposed in Trans Studies. Guided by the innovative work characterizing much of Trans Studies, our introduction to this anthology ends precisely by invoking a space beyond the normative to broaden the ways of being in the world that we can encompass.

Some of the essays included in this volume explore the productive intersections between sexuality, sexual orientation, and gender (Chen, Crawford, Park, and Valens). Other essays focus on the analysis of the possible and impossible alliances between LBGQ and trans movements (Enriquez) or subjectivities (Herman) and the implications for social justice and public policy. But most of the essays engage with trans subjectivities in reflections concerning citizenship, education, and interdisciplinary research without engaging sexuality as a central category of analysis. This is hardly a problematic issue, since trans identities, bodies, subject positions, perspectives, and voices exist both inside and outside of the notion of sexuality. What Queer and Trans Studies actually share is the consistent interrogation of normative definitions of sexuality, gender, and/or social and political identities that make it difficult for people to live their lives and perform their identities to the fullest.

On the one hand, Trans Studies invites us to reflect more specifically on gender and the possible parallels that can be established with sexuality, sexual orientation, and sexual desire. For example, sexuality and desire can be polymorphous, fluid, and perverse (to remember Freud's formulation here [2000]), and the body can be an instrument, vessel, or mediating instance upon which these human expressions are inflected, experienced, and/or even conceptualized. This is one of the many reasons why Audre Lorde's (1984) theorization of the erotic as another form of knowledge that should be recognized and celebrated is such a useful formulation for the conceptualization of identities reflecting the intersection of gender, sexuality, and race. In Lorde's formulation, desire is defined by the object of choice for pleasure and enjoyment, and one's gender seems to be central to the definition of a particular form of sexual identification. Thus sexuality and embodiment seem to be intimately linked. When scholars working in the field of Trans Studies redefine gender identity as a fluid category that is experienced on a continuum, this creates an interesting parallel with some of our current conceptualizations of non-normative sexualities. Placing gender in conversation with normativity has generated very productive insights for many scholars in Women's and Gender Studies, Queer Studies, and Trans Studies.

On the other hand, the relationship between gender, sexuality, and the body can be more complicated than this apparent continuity between embodiment and identity. Here the work on fantasy and identification (Rodríguez 2014), or the centrality of symbolic productions in the articulation of collective identities (Anderson 1991; Bourdieu 1984) clearly suggest that identification happens through many dimensions of the self that coexist in a complex relationship with embodiment. In psychoanalysis more concretely, the exploration of dreams or the unconscious (Freud 1999), or even the analysis of nightmares among colonized subjects (Fanon 2008), are predicated on the problematic boundaries between the body and the identification processes.

One of the most interesting consequences of how gender is theorized in Trans Studies is a proposed decoupling of embodiment and identities that still resists the universalizing and abstracted myth of Western rationalism. This is a theoretical and experiential move that needs to be made carefully, since embodiment is and has been a central issue in Feminist, Race, and Ethnic Studies, Critical Epistemological Studies, as well as in colonial and decolonial theories. The interrogation of any linear or transparent relationship between embodiment and identification is complicated, given that embodied ways of knowledge are at the root of some of the more complex (and early) debates between women of color and the gay and lesbian movements. Perhaps part of the problem we are trying to analyze here stems from the conflation between embodied ways of knowing and forms of identity that reside in the body. However, we need to remain cognizant of the many implications of letting our epistemologies and ontologies exist outside a direct correlation with embodiment. As many of us know, the possibility of passing becomes one of the most painful differentiating instances between some articulations of gay and/or queer identities and the constitution of ethnic and racial identities. At this particular juncture, it is interesting to note that questioning the relationship between embodiment and gender identity suddenly locates gender in a similarly intractable space to the one usually assigned to race and ethnicity. Our embodied readability as gendered and racialized subjects therefore presents a very specific limit to ways of knowing and being in the world that are inscribed upon or signified by the body, or framed as culturally intelligible (Butler 1999). This is another moment when the comparison with the normative—both heteronormative and homonormative—can be (and has been) a creative space for critical reflection.

Interrogating the relationship between embodiment and gender identity adds another rich layer to the conceptualization of identity that resides in the body. Yet it is not exhausted by the particular ways in which we experience the world according to our individual location within the binary of gender. The productive potential of truly imagining a world that is post-gender and post-racial is one of the provocations shared by many of our contributors. So in light of this, we would like to explore the potentiality of a space beyond the normative that is not necessarily oppositional but, perhaps, interrogates the univocal function that normativity plays in the context of all forms of identification. By examining the terrain beyond hetero- and homo-normativities, we seek to open the field to other conversations that do not necessarily respond to the hegemonic logic behind the notion of the norm. We would like to engage briefly with this kind of theoretical imaginary in the remaining sections of this chapter.

## IMAGINING WITH AND WITHIN NORMATIVITY

> "Así que lo que le contaba su amigo le parecía totalmente descabellado y trató de consolarlo diciéndole que no se preocupara, que esa noche iban a la barra y de seguro la homofobia estaría intacta allí."[1]
>
> [So what his friend told him seemed totally preposterous and he tried to comfort him, telling him not to worry, that that night they were going to the bar and that surely homophobia would be
> intact there.]    —Luis Negrón

This passage in this epigraph belongs to a short story entitled "Mundo cruel" (Cruel World), and it narrates a stressful day in the life of a group of Puerto Rican gay men who need to find a way to keep existing when homophobia no longer prevails. Following a similar structure to other narratives and films that explore human existence without racism, sexism, classism, and other forms of social inequality, Negrón's story explores the internal contradictions that become constitutive of many identity formations. For this group of gay men, the end of discrimination and oppression is synonymous with the end of an identity, particularly because their gay identity has been predicated on the articulation of a mode of being that is defined in opposition to the normative. Negrón criticizes ways of being gay that are founded on simplistic articulations of normativity as always subversive; these men illustrate the sexist, classist, and racist premises that often inform articulations of white, middle-class, male gayness. Yet what is most shocking in this particular story is that, for the protagonist, the achievement of a utopian egalitarian world unravels a personal crisis that culminates in the death of imagination.

Following Negrón's provocation, we would like to explore another alternative that complicates this representation of the many ways in which marginality reiterates the same modes of oppression it is supposedly questioning. We would like to focus more specifically on modes of political and social intervention that take place within what can be defined as the normative. If the anti-normative is not necessarily subversive, what defines a politically transformative act? And what happens when we move beyond the anti-normative as the prevalent mode for the theoretical intervention?

Robyn Wiegman has devoted an important section of her book *Object Lessons* to explore precisely this question. In her reflection on Queer Studies, Wiegman establishes a distinction between "normal," "normalization," and "normativity," and invites scholars and critics to avoid some of the common conflations of these three notions. In her lecture entitled "Eve's Triangles: Queer Theory without Anti-Homonormativity," Wiegman reminds us that Queer Studies' original objective was the study and critical analysis of the normative (2012a). This in itself was not problematic. However, Wiegman argues that the focus of the institutional version of queer theory has subsequently shifted to the articulation of anti-normative practices, behaviors, and identities. In this context, the anti-normative ends up functioning as a structure of belonging that becomes a mode of identification instead of serving as an epistemic category. This modality of queer theory conflates academic inquiry and political motives, creating an epistemic crisis in the field. This conflation, according to Wiegman, also has consequences for our contemporary theories on gender:

> I had taken queer critical interest in heteronormativity as a means for rendering legible—as identity, embodiment, politics, and practice of living—all the ways in which queer refused to live according to heteronormativity's intransitive gender rules, which meant that heteronormativity was the reference and text against which queer gender did its most inventive, antinormative, and decidedly transitive work. But just how coherent, comprehensive, and generative was heteronormativity as a theory of gender? (2012b, 317)

Wiegman's meditation inspires our own set of questions regarding Trans Studies. Is the interrogation of the normative Trans Studies' most significant contribution to our contemporary notions of gender? Is it time to ask questions that go beyond conformity (or nonconformity) to norms, in order to formulate answers that are more complex than explicit resistance? Are subversion, resistance, and rupture the best or only ways to explore alternatives to the norm?

## FROM IDENTITY TO POLITICS AND BACK AGAIN

Our argument thus far has addressed normativity and its oppositional discourses primarily in terms of issues related to identity, gender, and sexuality. Wiegman's own definition of heteronormativity as "the central political term for a distinctly queer approach to the study of sexuality" as well as "the animating agency of its own ongoing academic institutionalization" certainly reflect this imperative (2012b, 303). Yet it is important to note that the concept of heteronormativity has not always been defined in such terms. In fact, for some, it has focused not on identity, gender, or sexuality per se but on "a field of sexual meanings, discourses and practices that are interlaced with social institutions and movements" (Seidman 1994, 169). In other words, heteronormativity has referenced the study of sexuality through an extensive range of mediating social and institutional structures.

Such an approach to normativity can be seen in the early writings of Michael Warner, who is often credited with originating the term *heteronormativity*. Remarking upon the deficiencies of traditional social theory, Warner argues that struggles around gender and sexuality are tied to norms embodied in social institutions, including "the family, notions of individual freedom, the state, public speech, consumption and desire, nature and culture, maturation, reproductive politics, racial and national fantasy, class identity, truth and trust, censorship, intimate life and social display, terror and violence, [and] health care" (1993, xiii). It is the all-encompassing, hegemonic privilege (and power) of heterosexuality within these institutions that constitutes heteronormativity. In a 1998 article, Warner and his co-author Lauren Berlant stress that "to be against heteronormativity is not to be against norms" but, rather, against "maintaining a normal metaculture. . . . Heterosexuality involves so many practices that are not sex that a world in which this hegemonic cluster would not be dominant is, at this point, unimaginable" (1998, 557). By contesting the "normal metaculture," queer theory and practice are counterpoints to heteronormativity. Although they lack a stable point of reference, take many forms, and are "radically anticipatory" in character, they nevertheless aspire toward a different, less constricting set of possibilities (Berlant and Warner, 1995, 344).

It follows from this perspective that queer politics may be understood to surmount issues of identity, intimacy, and subjectivity and to embrace the transformation of sociocultural institutions and structures. Our desire to think about how Trans Studies might challenge or move beyond heteronomativity is not just a wish to provide an account of how the field elicits distinctive approaches to the fluidity of identity, gender, and sexual orientation. It is also an aspiration to address the special ways in which Trans Studies seek to transform heteronormative hegemony. To the extent that Trans Studies disrupts existing power relations, enables the recognition of gender diversity, and contests the constrictive tenets of normalcy embedded in social institutions, it simultaneously transcends heteronormativity and constitutes a resoundingly queer, political response.

As generously noted by Love, the essays included in this anthology engage in a vision of Trans Studies that imagine many different relationships with normativity. While some deliver a call for inclusion of difference in existing social, political, and institutional spaces, all seek to disrupt "heteronormativity as usual." This is the case, for example, in Enke's invitation to create pedagogical and communal spaces in which subjects can redefine personal pronouns beyond the dichotomy of male/female or the existing confines of gender-neutral language. This is also the case in the efforts toward institution building explored by Park, Beemyn and Rankin, Rodríguez de Ruíz and Ochoa, and Hwahng, and the discussion of policy and coalitional possibilities by Enriquez and Herman. The political choices in many of these cases are complex and nuanced, and none can be simply categorized (or dismissed) as singularly anti-normative. Like Warner and Wiegman, these writings suggest that there are many ways to go beyond heteronormativity within a social, political, and institutional context, eschewing an essentialized understanding of the anti-normative that is effectively as normalized as the normative.

Thus far, our argument has paid scant attention to the concept of homonormativity, which we also suggest stands in contradistinction to Trans Studies. Most scholars now understand homonormativity through Lisa Duggan's paradigmatic definition as "a politics that does not contest dominant heteronormative assumptions and institutions but upholds and sustains them while promising the possibility of a demobilized gay culture anchored in domesticity and consumption" (2003, 179). Duggan describes homonormativity as the defining feature of a new, third-way, centrist, gay movement that emerged in the United States in the late 1990s. This movement was heavily influenced by the prevailing neoliberal focus on economic privatization, and the corollary moderate to conservative positions on cultural issues advocated by centrists. Shaped by writers including Jonathan Rauch and Andrew Sullivan, homonormativity was pitted firmly against a more liberationist, deliberatively public-seeking strain of gay activism that had prevailed from the era of gay liberation in the 1970s through the politics of ACT UP in the 1980s. It sought to "shrink gay public spheres and redefine gay equality . . . as access to the institutions of domestic privacy, the 'free' market, and patriotism" (Duggan 2003, 179). Same-sex marriage and access to the military are the two key policies that emerged from this movement.

Homonormativity, in Duggan's account, encompasses a relentless aspiration to normalization that is decidedly unqueer. For Duggan, homonormativity consolidates rather than disrupts political power relations, assimilates sexual and gender minorities under existing heteronormative standards, and creates no space to recognize or celebrate difference. As such, it represents a recipe for political disengagement and amounts to a "kind of political sedative—we get marriage and the military then we go home and cook dinner, forever" (Duggan 2003, 189). There is no place within this vision for policy change that seeks to secure economic justice, ameliorate homelessness, or reshape the criminal justice system. Moreover, as many LGBT critics have argued, a focus on marriage restricts access to benefits for many who are unwilling or unable to partake in this institution, including significant numbers of trans and gender-nonconforming individuals. This approach therefore reinforces a dichotomy between those people in the LGBT community who desire normalcy and assimilation and those who do not, rendering individuals within the latter group stigmatized and deviant.

Yet at this juncture it is important to note that although Duggan's conceptualization of homonormativity is dominant in scholarly and activist circles, this is not the only definition. Trans activists have proposed a different meaning of this term. For instance, according to Susan Stryker:

> Homonormativity, as I first heard and used the term in the early 1990s, was an attempt to articulate the double sense of marginalization and displacement experienced within transgender political and cultural activism. Like other queer militants, transgender activists sought to make common cause with any groups—including nontransgender gays, lesbians, and bisexuals—who contested heterosexual privilege. However, we also needed to name the ways that homosexuality, as a sexual orientation category based on constructions of gender it shared with the dominant culture, sometimes had more in common with the straight world than it did with us. (2008, 145–146)

Stryker's analysis of the way in which the concept of homonormativity has been used by trans activists to address simultaneously issues related to politics, institutions, and structure, on the one hand, and issues related to gender, sexuality, and identification, on the other, provides a rejoinder that is key to our own argument.

Noting the pejorative connotations of homonormativity, Stryker argues that trans activists typically associated this concept with three different groups. First, the accusation of homonormativity was leveled against gay men and lesbians who rejected any affinity with trans issues and politics and, instead, pursued an exclusionary vision of social change. Homonormativity therefore represented resistance to broadly based political alliances designed to end systemic oppression, coupled with a desire on the part of certain gay men and lesbians to acquire access to socially sanctioned privileges such as those enunciated by Duggan above. Second, the term was used to criticize (some) lesbians for refusing to support male-to-female trans people while tentatively acknowledging female-to-male trans people, claiming, on essentialist biological grounds, that the former were actually men and the latter women. Thus homonormativity embodied a resistance to feminist claims that the categories of "women" and "lesbian" are political in character rather than ontological. Third, the accusation was made against "those who conceptualized 'T' as an identity category analogous to 'GLB' and who advocated for a GLBT community on that basis" (2008, 147).

It is the third understanding of homonormativity that is most relevant to our own argument, representing a link between politics and identity. Stryker maintains that adherents of this approach inappropriately misconstrue trans as either a distinct form of gender *or* a particular type of sexual orientation. In the former instance, "trans people are simply considered another type of human than either men or women, which leads to such homonormative attempts at 'transgender inclusion' as questionnaires and survey instruments within GLBT contexts" (2008, 148). In the latter instance, trans people are "constructed as a properly distinct group of people with a different orientation than gays, lesbians and bisexuals (or, for that matter, straights)" (2008, 148). In both these instances, Stryker maintains that the conceptualization of *trans* does nothing to trouble the construction of gay, lesbian, or bisexual identity formations and, instead, represents merely an add-on category, extending the acronym LGB by a single letter.

By contrast, Stryker insists that both trans activism and the theory associated with it consider trans to be akin to a modality such as race or class rather than a discrete category. Accordingly, Stryker observes that: "Transgender theory and activism call attention to the operations of normativity within and between gender/sexual identity categories, raise questions about the structuration of power along axes other than homo/hetero and man/woman binaries, and identify productive points of attachment for linking sexual orientation and gender identity activism to other social justice struggles" (2008, 149). Trans activism therefore reveals that understandings of "homo, hetero, and bi" are all predicated on congruent conceptions of what it means to be a woman or a man. By problematizing these conceptions, trans activists challenge the necessity for trans people to define themselves against hetero/homo norms. In so doing, they also profoundly queer "the dominant relationship of sexed body and gendered subject" (2008,

146–147) and open spaces for a series of political alliances to confront constrictive norms and structures of many sorts. Politics, in this context, becomes tantamount to Jacques Rancière's (2010) understanding of "dissensus," disruptively vocalizing wrongs in order to challenge hegemonic logics.

## BEYOND QUEER AND TRANS STUDIES

In many ways, the predicament presented by anti-normativity in Queer Studies is not unique to this particular field, nor is it the only formulation of this question within Queer and Sexuality Studies. A similar set of questions has been raised in Cultural and Area Studies. For example, Alberto Moreiras questions the notion of "difference" in Latin American Studies in his book *The Exhaustion of Difference* (2001). Similarly, José Muñoz (1999) complicates the debates in Queer and Ethnic Studies when he proposes "disidentifications" as another alternative to "identification" and "counteridentification." For Moreiras and Muñoz, difference and identity have exhausted themselves as productive theoretical prisms because they have become normative scripts within institutionalized fields of study or schools of thought. In other words, difference and identity cease to function as epistemic interventions when they are no longer an object of analysis or when they become a specific intellectual positionality that occupies the role of the normative. Exhaustion invites a transformative process that generates new kinds of questions within the same disciplinary field (Moreiras 2001) or promotes the articulation of a new theoretical paradigm that assumes the undesirability of finding one particular notion, category, or conceptualization as adequate to account for the complex totality of our own personal modes of identification and disidentification (Muñoz 1999).

In this last context, the normative is both an exhausted category and an ever present reality. We must recognize that identity has not ceased to be a prevalent mode of being in the worlds that we inhabit. As we know perhaps too well, not only is identity at the core of many contemporary social experiences and mobilizations, it is also the motor behind very powerful social media and marketing campaigns. Big Brother is here, and we feed him with our daily statuses, pictures, locations, and data or through our own behaviors as consumers. We also know that not all of these practices are essentially subversive or conformist in all contexts and at all possible moments. It is at this particular juncture that we want to reconsider the openings made possible by imagining the transformative moves that take place *within* what can be conceived as the normative. Trans subjects and allies relate to normativity in many different ways throughout the multiple dimensions of our identities. Instead of prescribing or describing correct or incorrect modes of relationship with the normative, our task is to accept "the incommensurability between the idioms of social movements, their theoretical projections and the academic institutionalization of identity" (Wiegman 2012b, 311).

So we would like to close this final reflection by accepting the invitation to interrogate anti-normativity as the central or predominant discursive mode in the critical work we do as scholars or activists, as intellectual interlocutors in this world that is not close to being post-gender or post-normative. We would also like to accept Wiegman's invitation to explore a more complex network of identifications and disidentifications that take place through the kind of political and intellectual interventions in which we partake. Part of that work is evidenced in the publication of this anthology. Another part is still work in progress located in political activism to welcome real *diversality*[2] into our communal, social, and familiar spaces, or the institution building initiatives that attempt to bring Trans Studies and trans bodies to the institutions in which we work and learn. Perhaps the most significant part of our own identification with Trans Studies comes from our conviction that all spaces, as imperfect as they are, should be open and accessible to all the forms of being in the world that each one of us constantly inhabits.

At this particular juncture, we invoke fantasy and imagination as two powerful prisms that inform our scholarship and activism. First, we take as inspiration the foundational work done by Juana María Rodríguez (2014) with fantasy as a tool to transform the critical interventions we propose in Queer, Trans, and Sexuality Studies. Yet following the lead of Rosamond King (2014) we also redefine imagination as a powerful tool that allows us to acknowledge the many creative modes of survival and coexistence that have characterized individuals and communities who identify with transgressive genders, sexualities, and desire. Finally, we invoke Michael Warner, who has argued that "heteronormativity can be overcome only by actively imagining a necessarily and desirably queer world" (1993, xvi). As part of this utopian framework that values human creativity, we strive to envision disruption, coexistence, and resistance to normalcy as ways of being that should manifest a productive potentiality for all of us, so we are not trapped in that cruel world depicted by Negrón that is engendered by lack of imagination. We imagine a world that is queerly impermanent and aspirational, where we are not tethered by hegemonic notions of rectitude that have been solidified through our social institutions. This is a world in which political "dissensus" prevails. In this instantiation of a new world, not only could frogs become princesses and princesses become frogs (Stone 1996), but frogs and princesses could express their perpetually contingent selves, through many incarnations and possible inventions.

## NOTES

1. The epigraph is from Luis Negrón, "Mundo Cruel," 89–90, 88.
2. The term *diversality* is coined by Bernabé, Chamoiseau, and Confiant to refer to "the conscious harmonization of preserved diversities" (1990, 114) as opposed to notions of universality that end up reiterating the domination of First World, white definitions of identity.

## REFERENCES

Anderson, Benedict. 1991. *Imagined Communities: Reflections on the Origins and Spread of Nationalism*. New York: Verso.
Berlant, Lauren, and Michael Warner. 1995. "What Does Queer Theory Teach Us about X?" *PMLA* 110: 343–349.
———. 1998."Sex in Public." *Critical Inquiry* 2.2: 547–566.
Bernabé, Jean, Patrick Chamoiseau, and Raphaël Confiant. 1990. *Éloge de la créolité/In Praise of Creoleness*. Translated by Mohamed B. Taleb Khyar. Baltimore: Johns Hopkins University Press.
Bourdieu, Pierre. 1984. *Distinction: A Social Critique of the Judgement of Taste*. Cambridge, MA: Harvard University Press.
Butler, Judith. 1999. *Gender Trouble: Feminism and the Subversion of Identity*. New York: Routledge.
Duggan, Lisa. 2003. *The Twilight of Equality: Neoliberalism, Cultural Politics, and the Attack on Democracy*. Boston: Beacon Press.
Fanon, Frantz. 2008. *Black Skin, White Masks*. Translated by Richard Philcox. 1952. New York: Grove Press.
Freud, Sigmund. 1999. *The Interpretation of Dreams*. New York: Oxford University Press.
———. 2000. *Three Essays on Sexuality*. New York: Basic Books.
King, Rosamond. 2014. *Island Bodies: Transgressive Sexualities in the Caribbean Imagination*. Gainesville: University Press of Florida.
Lorde, Audre. 1984. "Uses of the Erotic: The Erotic as Power." In *Sister Outsider: Essays and Speeches*, 53–59. Freedom, CA: Crossing Press Freedom Series.
Love, Heather. 2015. "Doing Being Deviant: Deviance Studies, Description, and the Queer Ordinary." *Differences* 26.1: 74–95.
Moreiras, Alberto. 2001. *The Exhaustion of Difference: The Politics of Latin American Cultural Studies*. Durham, NC: Duke University Press.
Muñoz, José Esteban. 1999. *Disidentifications: Queers of Color and the Performance of Politics*. Minneapolis: University of Minnesota Press.
Negrón, Luis. 2010. "Mundo cruel." In *Mundo cruel*, 85–92. Río Piedras: La Secta de los Perros, Editorial.
———. 2013. "Mundo cruel." In *Mundo cruel*, translated by Suzane Jill Levine, 83–91. New York: Seven Stories Press.
Rancière, Jacques. 2010. *Dissensus: On Politics and Aesthetics*. Edited and translated by Steven Corcoran. New York: Continuum.
Rodríguez, Juana María. 2014. *Sexual Futures, Queer Gestures and Other Latina Longings*. New York: New York University Press.
Seidman, Steven. 1994. "Queering Sociology, Sociologizing Queer Theory: An Introduction." *Sociological Theory* 12.2: 166–77.
Stone, Sandy. 1996. "The 'Empire' Strikes Back: A Posttranssexual Manifesto." In *Body Guards: The Cultural Politics of Sexual Ambiguity*, edited by K. Straub and J. Epstein, 280–304. New York: Routledge.

Stryker, Susan. 2008. "Transgender History, Homonormativity, and Disciplinarity." *Radical History Review* 100: 145–157.

Ulaby, Neda. 2014. "Sapiosexual Seeks Same: A New Lexicon Enters Online Dating Mainstream." *All Tech Considered*. National Public Radio.org. Accessed on December 29, 2014. http://www.npr.org/blogs/alltechconsidered/2014/12/04/368441691/sapiosexual -seeks-same-a-new-lexicon-enters-online-dating-mainstream.

Warner, Michael. 1993. *Fear of a Queer Planet: Queer Politics and Social Theory*. Minneapolis: University of Minnesota Press.

Wiegman, Robyn. 2012a. "Eve's Triangles: Queer Theory without Anti-homonormativity." Lecture at Stony Brook University, October 24. Accessed January 1, 2015. https://www .youtube.com/watch?v=P9tREBlw_UQ.

———. 2012b. *Object Lessons*. Durham, NC: Duke University Press.

# NOTES ON CONTRIBUTORS

AREN Z. AIZURA is an assistant professor in Gender, Women, and Sexuality Studies at the University of Minnesota. Aizura's research looks at how queer and transgender bodies shape and are shaped by technologies of race, gender, transnationality, medicalization, and political economy. His current book project, "Mobile Subjects: Travel, Transnationality, and Transgender Lives," maps the figure of transsexual transition as a travel narrative. Aizura is the coeditor of the *Transgender Studies Reader 2*, which was published by Routledge in 2013 and was awarded the 2013 Ruth Benedict Book Prize by the Association of Queer Anthropology. His work has appeared in the journals *Inter-Asia Cultural Studies, Medical Anthropology, Asian Studies Review*, and the books *Transgender Migrations: Trans Feminist Perspectives in and across Transgender and Gender Studies*, and *Queer Bangkok*. He is a member of the editorial board of *TSQ: Transgender Studies Quarterly*.

GENNY BEEMYN is the director of the Stonewall Center at the University of Massachusetts–Amherst and the Trans Policy Clearinghouse coordinator for Campus Pride (www.campuspride.org/tpc). They have published and spoken extensively on the experiences and needs of trans people, particularly the lives of gender-nonconforming students. Beemyn has written or edited nine books/journal issues, including *The Lives of Transgender People* (with Sue Rankin; Columbia University Press, 2011) and special issues of the *Journal of LGBT Youth* on "Trans Youth" and "Supporting Transgender and Gender-Nonconforming Children and Youth" and a special issue of the *Journal of Homosexuality* on "LGBTQ Campus Experiences." Beemyn's most recent works are *A Queer Capital: A History of Gay Life in Washington, D.C.* (2014) and the "Transgender History" chapter for *Trans Bodies, Trans Selves* (2014). They are currently working on a book entitled *Campus Queer: The Experiences and Needs of Non-Binary College Students*, which focuses on the lives of students outside of gender and sexual binaries. Beemyn has a Ph.D. in African American Studies and master's degrees in African American Studies, American Studies, and higher education administration.

TOBY BEAUCHAMP is an assistant professor of Gender and Women's Studies at the University of Illinois, Urbana-Champaign, and holds a Ph.D. in Cultural Studies from the University of California, Davis. His essays have been published in *GLQ, Feminist Formations*, and *Surveillance and Society*. He is currently completing a book manuscript provisionally titled "Going Stealth: Transgender Politics and U.S. Surveillance Practices."

NORA BUTLER BURKE lives in Montréal where she is a graduate student at Concordia University. Her current research examines the impacts of immigration penality in the lives of migrant trans women in Montréal. She was previously the coordinator of Action Santé Travesti(e)s et Transsexuel(le)s du Québec (ASTT(e)Q), a project of CACTUS Montréal, working with low-income and sex-working trans women.

JIAN CHEN is an assistant professor of English at the Ohio State University. Chen's research focuses on Queer and Trans Studies; U.S. Asian American and comparative racial formations; film, digital media, and visual cultures; transnationalisms; and post-semiotic cultural and social theories. He is completing a book manuscript on trans U.S. Asian American performance, film, and digital media. Chen's scholarship has been shaped by his cultural activism in film and performance curation and community-based organizing and fund-raising to counter sweatshop immigrant exploitation and hate, intimate, and state-sponsored violence impacting LGBTQ communities.

LUCAS CRAWFORD is the 2013–2015 Ruth Wynn Woodward Endowment Lecturer in Gender, Sexuality, and Women's Studies at Simon Fraser University in British Columbia, Canada. Crawford is also the 2015 Critic-in-Residence of Canadian Women in the Literary Arts (CWILA). Prior to this, Crawford held a postdoctoral fellowship in Architecture and Gender Studies at McGill University in Montréal. Crawford is the author of three forthcoming books: *Transgender Architectonics: The Shape of Change in Modernist Space* (2015), *The High Line Park Scavenger Hunt* (2016), and *Sideshow Concessions* (2015). Other articles have appeared in or are forthcoming from *Women's Studies Quarterly, Transgender Studies Quarterly, Sexualities, Journal of Homosexuality, English Studies in Canada, Mosaic,* the *Routledge Queer Studies Reader,* the *Transgender Studies Reader* (volume 2), and in a number of magazines and newspapers. Transgender, ruralism, fat, food, architecture, and perfumery are often the subjects of Crawford's poetry, organizing, and research. Crawford grew up in rural Nova Scotia and now lives in Vancouver.

A. FINN ENKE is a professor of history, Gender and Women's Studies, and LGBTQ Studies at University of Wisconsin, Madison, where ey teaches at the confluence of transgender, queer, feminist, and disability histories. Enke's book publications include the edited collection *Transfeminist Perspectives in and beyond Transgender and Gender Studies* (2012), and *Finding the Movement: Sexuality, Contested Space, and Feminist Activism* (2007). Ey's current research and writing include a book on trans pedagogies; a history of the relationships between transgender and feminist activisms from the 1960s to the present; and a graphic novel titled *With Finn and Wing: Growing Up Amphibious in a Nuclear Age*. Enke has served as book review editor for *Transgender Studies Quarterly* since 2014.

MICKAEL CHACHA ENRIQUEZ is a radical queer activist based in Montréal (QC). He is co-founder of the P!NK BLOC and co-organized the first Trans March on Montréal in August 2014. His research focuses on LGBTQ communities. In 2013 he finished a master's of sociology and Feminist Studies degree from the University of Québec, Montréal. He won the Best Feminist Studies Thesis Prize (UQAM) and published his research on trans activism in Québec: *Le mouvement trans au Québec: Dynamiques d'émergence d'une militance*. For three years, he also coordinated an intervention-research project, which aimed to improve the access of trans elders to health and social services.

JODY L. HERMAN is the Williams Scholar of Public Policy at the Williams Institute at the UCLA School of Law. At the Williams Institute, her work has included research on the fiscal impacts of discrimination against transgender people, employer-provided health benefits coverage for gender transition, the development of trans-inclusive questions for population-based surveys, and suicidality among transgender people, among other topics. Before joining Williams, she served as a coauthor on the groundbreaking report *Injustice at Every Turn*, based on the National Transgender Discrimination Survey (NTDS) conducted by the National Gay and Lesbian Task Force and the National Center for Transgender Equality. She holds a Ph.D. in public policy and public administration from George Washington University, where she also earned her master's degree in public policy.

SEL J. HWAHNG, PhD, is a co-investigator at the Baron Edmond de Rothschild Chemical Dependency Institute, Mount Sinai Beth Israel, and an adjunct professor at the Center for the Study of Ethnicity and Race, Columbia University. Hwahng has received numerous grants, awards, and fellowships from such organizations as the National Institute on Drug Abuse (NIDA), the National Institutes of Health, the American Public Health Association, the International AIDS Society, and the Association for Women in Psychology. Hwahng has participated as a research investigator on studies funded by institutions such as NIDA, Substance Abuse and Mental Health Services Administration, New York State AIDS Institute, and the Keith Haring Foundation. Publications include twenty-five sole-, first-, and co-authored articles and book chapters in peer-reviewed journals and edited volumes. Hwahng has been first author on multiple public health reports and advisor for edited volumes, reports, and health resource guides. Hwahng is program chair of the Lesbian, Gay, Bisexual, and Transgender Caucus of the American Public Health Association.

YOLANDA MARTÍNEZ–SAN MIGUEL is a cultural critic and literary theorist. She works on issues of sexuality and gender in the production of knowledge and cultural representations in Latin American colonial and Caribbean postcolonial literature and discourse. Her other areas of research and teaching interest include colonial Latin American discourses and contemporary Caribbean and Latino narratives, migration, and Cultural Studies. She has an MA and PhD in Latin American Cultural Studies from the University of California at Berkeley and a BA in Hispanic Studies from the University of Puerto Rico. Martínez–San Miguel is the author of *Saberes americanos: Subalternidad y epistemología en los escritos de Sor Juana* (1999), *Caribe Two Ways: Cultura de la migración en el Caribe insular hispánico* (2003), *From Lack to Excess: "Minor" Readings of Colonial Latin American Literature* (2008), and *Coloniality of Diasporas: Rethinking Intracolonial Migrations in a Pan-Caribbean Context* (2014). She was the director of the Institute for Research on Women in 2010–2013 and holds a joint appointment in Latino and Caribbean Studies and Comparative Literature at Rutgers University.

MARCIA OCHOA is an associate professor and chair of Feminist Studies at the University of California, Santa Cruz. She is a co-founder and advisory board member of El/La Para Translatinas, and the author of *Queen for a Day: Transformistas, Beauty Queens, and the Performance of Femininity in Venezuela* (2014), a queer diasporic ethnography of beauty, modernity, and femininity in a place renowned for its success in global beauty pageants. As an ethnographer of media and a specialist in gender and sexuality in Latin America, she is committed to writing the possibilities of queer/trans survival and imagination in the Américas. Ochoa is also co-editor of *GLQ: A Journal of Lesbian and Gay Studies*.

PAULINE PARK is chair of the New York Association for Gender Rights Advocacy (NYAGRA), a statewide transgender advocacy organization that she co-founded in 1998. She is also president of the board of directors and acting executive director of Queens Pride House, which she co-founded in 1997. Park helped create the Transgender Health Initiative of New York and oversaw the development in July 2009 of the NYAGRA transgender health care provider directory, the first print directory of transgender-sensitive health care providers published in the United States. Park led the campaign to pass New York City Council's transgender rights law in 2002. Park also served on the steering committee of the coalition that secured enactment of New York City Council's Dignity in All Schools Act (2004) and negotiated inclusion of gender identity and expression in New York State Legislature's Dignity for All Students Act (2010). Park did her BA in philosophy at the University of Wisconsin, Madison, her MSc in European Studies at the London School of Economics, and her PhD in political science at the University of Illinois at Urbana. In 2005, Park became the first openly transgendered grand marshal of the New York City Pride March. She was the subject of *Envisioning Justice: The Journey of a Transgendered Woman,* a thirty-two-minute documentary about her life and work by documentarian Larry Tung that premiered at the New York LGBT Film Festival in 2008. In April 2013 Park was named to the inaugural "Trans 100" list of leading activists and community members.

SUSAN R. RANKIN retired from the Pennsylvania State University in 2013 where she most recently served as an associate professor of education and senior research associate in the Center for the Study of Higher Education. Rankin has presented and published widely on the intersections of identities and the impact of sexism, genderism, racism, and heterosexism in the academy and in inter-collegiate athletics. Rankin's most recent publications include the *2010 State of Higher Education for LGBT People: The Lives of Transgender People* (2011), and the *2011 NCAA Student-Athlete Climate Study.* Rankin is the recipient of the Ameri-can College Personnel Association (ACPA) 2008 Voice of Inclusion Medallion and was named a 2015 ACPA Diamond Honoree for her outstanding and sus-tained contributions to higher education and to student affairs. As the principal of Rankin & Associates Consulting (R&A), Rankin has collaborated with higher education institutions for the past twenty years in reviewing their climates for learning, working, and living.

ALEXANDRA RODRÍGUEZ DE RUÍZ is a native Mexican who migrated to the United States as a fifteen-year-old. Her intersectional identities helped her build her sense of what community is and encouraged her to be a fighter and a survi-vor. She is known for her ability to mobilize and organize community in defense of human rights and equality, especially for transgender people in various parts of the world. Rodríguez de Ruiz is a presenter, an organizer, and a public speaker. She coined the term *translatinas* and has been interviewed in print and on radio and television for her expertise in transgender issues. She is the recipient of the 2011 Claire Skiffington Vanguard Award from the Transgender Law Center in San Francisco and currently lives in Mexico City where she is a consultant on sexuality and gender, a homemaker, an entrepreneur, a student, and an avid activist who is always ready to participate in any action to defend and protect the human rights of all. She can be reached at alexandra@ellaparatranslatinas.org.

SARAH TOBIAS is a feminist theorist and LGBT activist whose work bridges academia and public policy. She is coauthor of *Policy Issues affecting Lesbian, Gay, Bisexual, and Transgender Families* (2007) and author of "Several Steps Behind: Lesbian and Gay Adoption" in *Adoption Matters: Philosophical and Feminist Essays,* edited by Sally Haslanger and Charlotte Witt (2005), as well as coau-thor and editor of numerous policy-related reports and articles. Tobias is the associate director of the Institute for Research on Women and affiliate faculty in the Women's and Gender Studies Department at Rutgers University. Prior to joining the institute in January 2010, she spent over eight years working in the nonprofit sector, holding staff positions and consultancies at organizations including Demos, the National Gay and Lesbian Taskforce Policy Institute, and the International Gay and Lesbian Human Rights Commission. She taught at Rutgers-Newark, the City University of New York (Baruch College and Queens College), and Columbia University. She has a PhD in political science from Columbia University and an undergraduate degree in history from Cambridge University, England.

KEJA VALENS is a professor of English at Salem State University where she teaches and researches literatures of the Americas and queer theory. She is particularly interested in the intersections of Caribbean and Queer Studies as they manifest in representations of gender, sexuality, family, and community. She is author of *Desire between Women in Caribbean Literature* (2013) and essays on gender and sexuality in Caribbean literature, Caribbean cookbooks, and with J. D. Scrimgeour, an essay on Aimé Césaire and Barak Obama. Valens is also coeditor of *The Barbara Johnson Reader* (2014), *Passing Lines: Sexuality and Immigration* (2006), and the forthcoming *Que(e)rying Consent*.

# INDEX

Page numbers in italics refer to tables and figures.

CPSIA information can be obtained at www.ICGtesting.com
Printed in the USA
BVOW06s0058100316

439780BV00009B/23/P